Learning to LEAD, Leading to LEARN

Lessons from Toyota Leader
ISAO YOSHINO
on a Lifetime of Continuous Learning

Cindy -
Keep leading
with
-Caring
-Curiosity &
-Courage!
- Katie Anderson

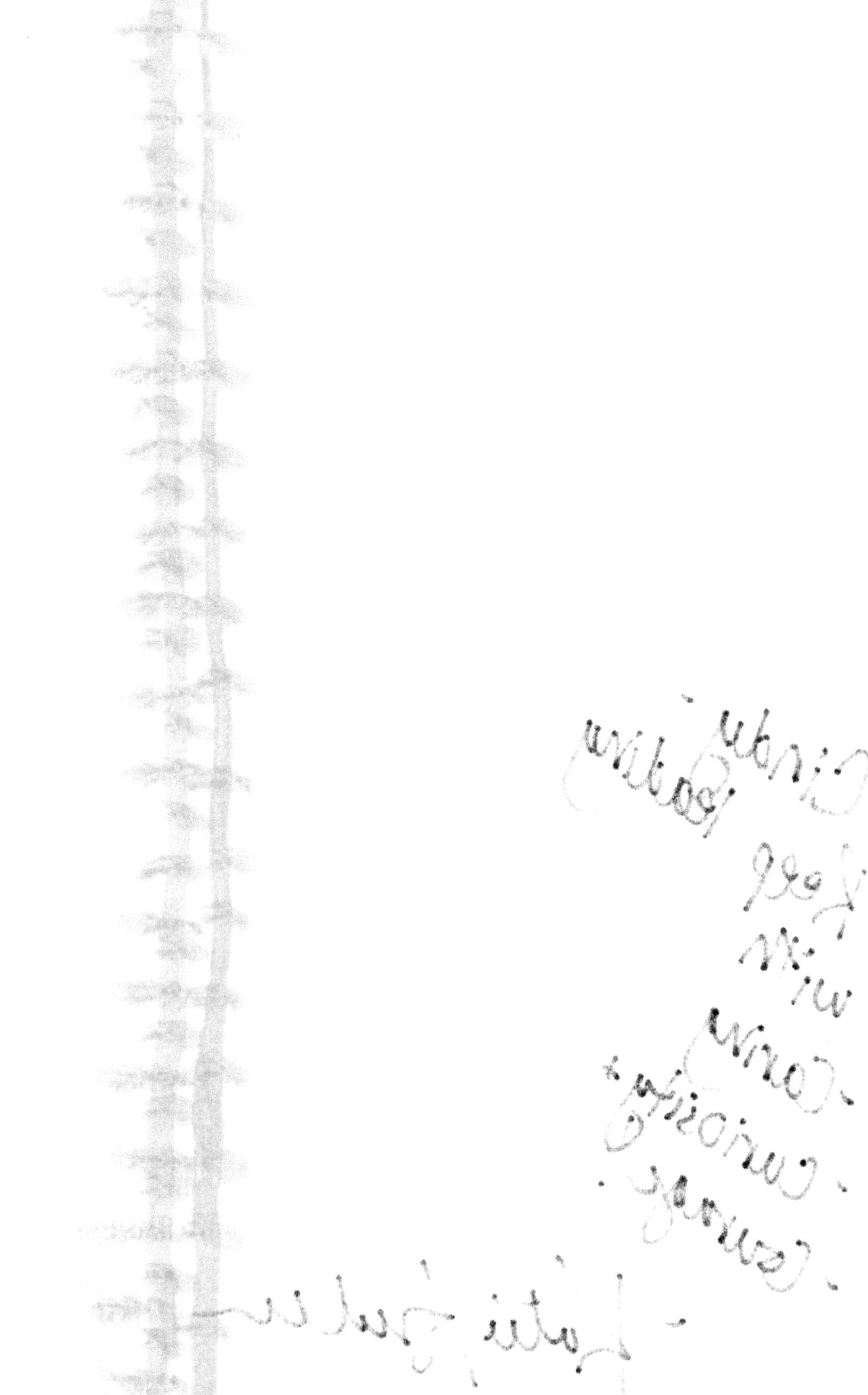

PRAISE FOR *LEARNING TO LEAD, LEADING TO LEARN*

"If leadership, lean, systems thinking, continuous improvement, company culture, learning, or storytelling bring you joy as they do me, you must BUY this book. If you are seeking the next step on your own journey of leadership transformation, then you must READ this book. If you want to become the leader you always knew you could be, then you must LIVE the lessons in this book. Thank you, Katie and Mr. Yoshino for your efforts and your results. The immortality gained from *Learning to Lead, Leading to Learn* will benefit generations to come."

Richard Sheridan
CEO and Chief Storyteller at Menlo Innovations and
Author of *Joy, Inc.* and *Chief Joy Officer*

"In *Learning to Lead, Leading to Learn,* Katie Anderson invites us into conversations with Mr. Isao Yoshino about his four decades of learnings at Toyota Motor Corporation. Together, book author and book subject extrapolate valuable lessons and insights from the fabric of the Toyota Way. The reader will walk along a distinctive journey of self-discoveries, experiments, failures, and successes in Toyota's and Mr. Yoshino's growth. These lessons can be translated to any level leader and in any industry. I encourage anyone who influences people in cultural change to embrace the shared wisdom in this book."

Tracey Richardson
Founder of Teaching Lean Inc. and Author of *The Toyota Engagement Equation*

"In her debut book, *Learning to Lead, Leading to Learn,* Katie Anderson has distilled countless hours of interviews, lecture transcripts, and conversation (and ample debate, too, I am sure) into a cohesive whole that's informative, inspiring, and entertaining. I am grateful to Katie for capturing Isao Yoshino's story ... and for going beyond just documenting history but weaving it all into a rich tapestry that readers of many interests will find compelling and useful. Explorers of lean thinking and practice will find a deep dive into the mind of a Toyota manager during the defining final third of the 20th century. Japanophiles will find access to the inner workings of Japan's largest industrial enterprise during the heyday of Japan Inc. And, perhaps most importantly, executive coaches — or anyone with an interest in the phenomenon of 'manager-as-coach' — will find in these pages a rich expression of the thinking and practices of a deeply thoughtful, extraordinarily reflective practitioner of the craft."

John Shook
Chairman of the Lean Global Network

"The real essence of the Toyota Way is learning your way to a dream — as individuals and organizations. Through the life and learning of Yoshino-san, Katie Anderson gives us a glimpse into this deep level of learning and teaching and sense of purpose. If you want to really understand continuous improvement, lean, and other derivatives, read this book."

Jeffrey Liker
Author of *The Toyota Way,* Second Edition

"One of the most valuable takeaways from my experience inside the Toyota organization — which in many ways coincides with that of Isao Yoshino's — is the simple but profound insight that learning and leadership go hand in hand, but learning comes first. This book plumbs the depths of this often-overlooked element of not only the success of Toyota, but also the successes of those who inhabit the company, often gleaned from hard-earned lessons and failure. The stories are rewarding, which is a testament to the obviously trustful relationship between the author and her subject. *Learning to Lead, Leading to Learn* may be the only book you'll ever need to read if you want to truly understand what makes Toyota tick."

Matthew E. May
Author of *The Elegant Solution* and *Winning the Brain Game*

"I highly recommend *Learning to Lead, Leading to Learn* for anyone who is interested in Japanese business, Toyota's unique corporate culture, and leadership. Full of fascinating stories and wisdom, the book is also a wonderful example of cross-cultural and cross-generational collaboration and friendship."

Rochelle Kopp
Managing Principal, Japan Intercultural Consulting

"People-centric systems are about learning to solve today's challenges. Leaders have to steer and structure this learning. Yoshino's invaluable reflections from Toyota will inspire leaders following this example."

Daniel Jones
Founder and Chairman, Lean Enterprise Academy, and Co-author of *The Machine that Changed the World* and *The Lean Strategy*

"*Learning to Lead, Leading to Learn* is a beautiful book! Katie Anderson has woven together Isao Yoshino's stories of learning and leading in a way that helps us all better understand the learning culture within Toyota. In this book, the reader gets to 'go to the gemba' at Toyota and observe how one individual learner became a teacher and leader (and continues to remain a learner). You will discover how all managers can be learners who are focused on the learning of his/her co-workers. And you will find valuable lessons on people-centric leaders — about the importance of seeing each worker as a human being with his or her own history, purpose, and dreams."

Dr. Jannes Slomp
Professor, World Class Performance, HAN University (Arnhem/Nijmegen), The Netherlands

"Isao Yoshino has a life's worth of wisdom to share and Katie Anderson does a fantastic job of bringing those lessons to us in *Learning to Lead, Leading to Learn*. Katie skillfully weaves together stories that share an insider's perspective on Toyota, and life, in a conversational tone that will be insightful to readers from any industry. This book will be helpful for those who are new to lean or the Toyota Production System, and it will fill in key details for those who have been practicing lean for a long time."

Mark Graban
Author of *Measures of Success* and *Lean Hospitals*

"Lean can be a very nuanced study. On the surface, you see the tools that people use but as you learn and grow, you begin to see the thinking that truly drives the improvement process. *Learning to Lead, Leading to Learn* is a book about that learning and growth, and about how we can all embrace the opportunities before us. Katie has done a great job of capturing the thinking and rich experiences of Isao Yoshino, who I had the privilege of meeting on one of our 'Lean Learning Trips' to Japan. For those who may never meet him, this book is your opportunity to learn directly from a truly remarkable man whose unique experiences can inspire your own leadership journey. Books like this are rare and you are bound to find the insights invaluable."

Steve Watts
Chief Operating Officer, Walters & Wolf Glass

"If you're interested in lean and learning, this is an absolute must-read! Katie Anderson's brilliant and original concept of warp (our deeper interests and goals) and weft (what we discover and learn in our journey) — illustrated through the real-life experience of Isao Yoshino, one of Toyota's great sensei — makes a unique, pleasant, and illuminating read. Don't miss it."

Michael Ballé
Co-author of *The Gold Mine* Trilogy and *The Lean Strategy*

"Wow! It's rare for a business book to pack a punch the way Katie Anderson's *Learning to Lead, Leading to Learn* does. Katie has produced a gem that illustrates — in the clearest way yet — what truly makes Toyota tick. She does so by weaving an inspiring biography (Mr. Yoshino's personal and leadership journey) with practical leadership principles, and through thought-provoking, humility-laced stories versus a formulaic '10 Steps to Magnificence'! And she does so in the most humanistic way I've seen in a business book.

An added benefit — and one I didn't see coming — is that U.S. readers may feel a bit more patriotic by reading this gem — at a time when we most need it. Want to be a better leader, a better improvement professional, a better human being? Read this book!"

Karen Martin
President and Founder, TKMG, Inc. and TKMG Academy, Inc.;
Author of *Clarity First* and *The Outstanding Organization*

"*Learning to Lead, Leading to Learn* is a fascinating story of the long career of Isao Yoshino, a consummate Toyota leader. Katie Anderson has woven Mr. Yoshino's own words into a fabric that reveals insights into the experience, reflection, and learning that help provide different and deeper views of the human underpinnings of Toyota. A terrific book on leadership and culture."

Peter Ward
Chairman of the Board, Lean Enterprise Institute; Richard M. Ross Emeritus Chair in Management and Founding Director, Master of Business Operational Excellence Program, Ohio State University

"This is a wise book that weaves a story of leadership between two core principles of purpose (i.e., what shapes us) and discovery (i.e., what defines us). It will be fascinating for students of lean; should be essential for students of leadership."

Michael Bungay Stanier
Author of *The Coaching Habit* and *The Advice Trap*

"Those who are lean practitioners always know that the best way to understand is to 'go and see!' In this wonderful book of stories and reflections about Mr. Yoshino's tenure at Toyota, Katie Anderson beautifully captures and helps us 'see' Mr. Yoshino's lessons on Leading to Learn and Learning to Lead. I know you will enjoy, learn and grow from this book as much as I have!"

Karyn Ross
Co-author of *The Toyota Way to Service Excellence* and Author of *How to Coach for Creativity and Service Excellence*

"*'At the beginning, we didn't realize how much we didn't know.'* This quote from Isao Yoshino applies to all of us on our lean journey. Well known Toyota-isms are woven together with the personal story of a Toyota manager, providing a humbling, rare insight into learning and leading using lean thinking. Anyone interested in improving themselves or their organization should read this and reflect."

David Brunt
CEO, Lean Enterprise Academy

"Katie Anderson has crafted a personal, lean learning journey from her conversations with Toyota leader Isao Yoshino that we all can savor. Out of their friendship comes a moving testament to the power of humanity, risk, failure, and reflection to positively impact the lives around us. It's a joy to soak up the reflections that culminated from Mr. Yoshino's decades of business leadership and Ms. Anderson's brilliant questions about what he learned during his career. Throughout the book, reflection questions invite the reader into the conversation. These serve as sparks to help us understand our own visions of who and what we can be, if we dare to weave our core purpose with our other passions. This captivating read will make you stop and consider your own untapped reservoirs of influence, generosity of spirit, and humble leadership."

Elisabeth Swan

Chief Learning Experience Officer at GoLeanSixSigma.com and Co-author of *The Problem-Solver's Toolkit: A Surprisingly Simple Guide to Your Lean Six Sigma Journey*

"*Learning to Lead, Leading to Learn* is an inspiring one-of-a-kind book for leaders at all levels, in any industry, and from any part of the world! This book describes the type of leader that every company would love to have and should strive to cultivate: humble, diligent, determined, and supportive of their team before their own interests. It is a book that teaches us how we can learn more deeply across our lifetime through purposeful reflection.

I first met Katie Anderson and Isao Yoshino during Katie's Japan Study Trip in 2018. I was amazed by Katie's spirit, energy, enthusiasm, and her love for Japan's culture and people-centered companies. I was also inspired by the life stories, knowledge, and wisdom that Mr. Yoshino shared with us throughout the week. Readers will love this book as now they, too, can learn from both Mr. Yoshino and Katie about the importance of *hansei*, leading with respect, caring for people, setting long-term goals, learning from success as well as failure, and how a person can accomplish a lifetime goal by helping others along the way. This is a must-read for anyone who wants to succeed in creating a working culture of respect, trust, and teamwork, based on people-centered leadership."

Javier Sala Mercado, MD, PhD

Founder of the Lean Institute Argentina; Vice CMO & COO, Instituto Modelo de Cardiologia Privado S.R.L., Cordoba, Argentina; Adjunct Assistant Professor, Wayne State University Physiology, Michigan USA.

"At the Lean Enterprise Institute, I had heard about the legend Isao Yoshino for years from John Shook and also from reading Shook's book, *Managing to Learn,* in which Yoshino inspired the character Sanderson. In 2017, I finally had the opportunity to meet Isao at an Educators Conference in the Netherlands. I was blown away with his humility and rich learnings about the decades he spent at Toyota. I was ecstatic that Katie and Isao had developed a relationship and a plan to share his wisdom, and I invited them to join us at the Catalysis European Summit in 2018 to share with European leaders. Now, I am equally excited to have this learning resource available to the world, so that we all can learn from Isao Yoshino's experience, learnings and wisdom. Of the thousands of books available about TPS, lean and continuous improvement, *Learning to Lead, Leading to Learn* is one worthy of your investment."

Helen Zak

Senior Advisor, Value Capture LLC/Value Capture Policy Institute

"*Learning to Lead, Leading to Learn* is a superb book! Its author, Katie Anderson, is one of the few Westerners (not living in Japan) who — in my view — grasps the essence of Toyota, partly thanks to her friendship and collaboration with one of its early leaders, Isao Yoshino.

From the author's blogs about her experiences in Japan and at Toyota and its subsidiaries, and from her conversations with her sensei, Mr. Yoshino, I can vouch that she brings to life some of the essential features of Toyota. In particular, she describes vividly through examples what has largely been missed by the Western 'lean' extended community — that the bottom line is not about lean and nimble techniques and tools (or the agile and responsive development of reliable cars), but it's ultimately about the empowerment and development of its total workforce, the people actually doing the work on the shop floor.

Many Western companies struggle to understand Toyota's secret of 'lean,' still not getting it even though it's no secret any more. But as Mr. Yoshino says, 'The only secret to Toyota is its attitude toward learning.' Many organizations could learn to learn if they have the right mindset; indeed, it's about *learning to lead* in order to be able to *lead to learn*."

François Knuchel

Paradigm-Shift Facilitator for Open 2 Flow

"The ability to learn — and then distill, leverage, and teach that knowledge — is a critical component of both individual and organizational success. In *Learning to Lead, Leading to Learn,* Katie Anderson memorializes her discussions with her sensei, Isao Yoshino, a manager at Toyota for nearly four decades. Mr. Yoshino describes how the company's culture of supporting learning at all levels, driven by people that *lead to learn,* is the underlying catalyst for their ongoing success. In addition to giving you suggestions on how to improve learning in your own organization, you will find the first-hand account of life inside Toyota to be intriguing, eye-opening, and highly engaging in its own right."

Kevin Meyer
Co-Founder of Gemba Academy

"Humans are hardwired to remember and learn from stories. Katie Anderson does the lean community a huge service by bringing storytelling to fundamental lean ideas through her interviews with Mr. Yoshino. Everyone will benefit from the depth and color that the book brings to otherwise dry disquisitions of the Toyota Way."

Dan Markovitz
Shingo Prize-Winning Author of *The Conclusion Trap* and *Building the Fit Organization*

"In 2014, I was seated with Katie Anderson at a conference when we heard Isao Yoshino and John Shook talk about their work together at Toyota Motor Company. Mr. Yoshino made a particularly insightful comment (which you will learn more about in *Learning to Lead, Leading to Learn*) and we immediately turned to each and silently exchanged a look of strong appreciation for what we'd just heard. Katie used that moment as the first of many stepping-stones to learn from and partner with Mr. Yoshino. In *Learning to Lead, Leading to Learn,* Katie uses the power of storytelling to share the decades-long path of daily intention Mr. Yoshino took to move his people, himself, and his company forward. She skillfully offers Mr. Yoshino's insights about how to humbly, respectfully, and deeply commit to creating the conditions for learning for those we lead — and for ourselves."

Margie Hagene
Leadership and Continuous Improvement Coach

"As usual, Katie Anderson shares a fresh and energizing lean perspective in her debut book. Readers of *Learning to Lean, Leading to Learn* will appreciate and enjoy exploring the contributions of a new breed of lean thought leaders. As Katie shares and builds upon the lifework of her mentor Isao Yoshino, together the two take lean forward for next-generation lean leaders and those who came before them."

Deborah Salimi
Co-founder, Lean Gulf Institute

"The stories in this book — like Mr. Yoshino's first-hand accounts of implementing process changes on the Toyota assembly line or of starting up NUMMI — are must-reads for anyone with an interest in TPS or the Toyota Way. And Katie Anderson brings her contagious enthusiasm, sincerity, and great writing skills to the task of shaping and organizing this information for English speakers."

Michel Baudin
Consultant, Trainer, and Author of *Lean Assembly*, *Lean Logistics*, and *Working with Machines*

"Because this book covers nearly four decades of Mr. Yoshino's life, *Learning to Lead, Leading to Learn* is a must-read for anyone at any level of leadership and especially those who *aspire* to be in leadership. Katie Anderson expertly coaxed out Mr. Yoshino's most priceless leadership lessons. The one that heads the top of my list is: *The job of a leader is to provide team members with a mission and support while they figure it out.* Not only does Katie get Mr. Yoshino to share his life stories, she gives you an opportunity to consider your own leadership journey through *hansei no shitsumon* or reflection questions. The answers to those questions will exponentially increase your leadership abilities."

Daniel D. Matthews
President/CEO, Continue 2 Improve, Author of *The Language of Leadership: Nicer Bark, No Bite* and *The A3 Workbook: Unlock Your Problem-Solving Mind*

"Whether you are an old pro at lean or someone new to the game, *Learning to Lead, Leading to Learn* is a worthy text. Learning at the feet of the master, you'll explore Katie Anderson's journey in working with Toyota's Isao Yoshino and mastering the principles of people-centered leadership. The narrative offers a rich tapestry of truths about continuous learning and leadership."

Cathy Fyock
Author of *The Speaker Author: Sell More Books and Book More Speeches*

"This is a must-read for anyone who is embarking on the journey of leadership, coaching, or building a learning organization. In contrast to all the 'how-to' books, *Learning to Lead, Leading to Learn* is constantly engaging: The reader is drawn into the story of an emerging leader, Isao Yoshino, who learned to lead, and then led to learn. In conversation and deep reflection with leadership coach Katie Anderson, Mr. Yoshino let us take part in his lessons of a lifetime."

Sabrina Malter
Strategy and Organizational Change Manager, Roche (Germany)

"As I reflect on my career as a leader, I wish I would have been more consistent and passionate at helping people develop their capability. I didn't have the benefit of insights like you will discover in *Learning to Lead, Leading to Learn.* In this important exploration of Mr. Yoshino's experience, Katie Anderson reveals the characteristics and behaviors of a leader who truly makes everyone around them better. Based on Mr. Yoshino's career insights and her own leadership coaching expertise, Katie outlines a vital leadership framework of "setting the direction," "providing support," and "developing yourself" — and challenges us to lead and learn differently and more meaningfully. This book is a very practical guide to understanding what unlocks the potential of collaborators in an organization to dream, and to achieve their dreams through alignment of intention; and it's a practical guide for anyone who wants to develop themselves into a better leader and a contributor to the greater good."

Jeff Hunter
Former Senior VP of Strategy and Marketing, ThedaCare, and Author of *Patient-Centered Strategy: A Learning System for Better Care*

"I had the absolute pleasure of meeting Isao Yoshino in May of 2019 during dinner, the night before he led workshops in Ottawa. I was profoundly impacted by his humility and his willingness to not only share his story, but to learn about mine as well. I held on to his every word of wisdom, and I am convinced that you will do the same while reading this book. I have also gotten to know Katie Anderson through her coaching communities and Japan Study Trips. Katie's approach of 'leading with intention to connect profoundly with your purpose' guided me in a powerful way. With an emphasis on listening and deep reflection, I continue to put these lessons into practice every day. My experiences with both Mr. Yoshino and Katie have deeply shaped my life, as a lean coach — and especially as a person. Having the two of them collaborating to bring these stories and lessons to life is something to be cherished. Enjoy this journey of reflection as you read, learn, and lead in a better way as a result!"

Stéfany Oliver
Lean Coach, Statistics Canada

"This book is the perfect blending of business-leader memoir and management 'how-to' for those of us wanting to embrace the opportunity to become heart-centered, thoughtful, people-centered leaders. Isao Yoshino's stories — presented to us and then expounded upon by leadership coach Katie Anderson — provide both a practical framework and a deeply personal source of inspiration for the reader's professional growth. *Learning to Lead, Leading to Learn* reminds us that 'organizational behavior' is first individual behavior — that culture and corporate success come down to the personal behaviors and attitudes of employees ... at every level. Just as Toyota believed it could not make cars without first making people, no organization can thrive without leaders who know how to lead and learn. With its fascinating sidebars on Japanese culture and Toyota philosophies, this book took me on a journey — across an ocean and back in time. The 'Practicing *Hansei*' questions throughout allowed me to pause, reflect and learn. Katie Anderson's *Learning to Lead, Leading to Learn* should be required reading in MBA programs and corporate leadership programs for high-potentials and executives alike."

Kate Colbert
Author of *Think Like a Marketer: How a Shift in Mindset Can Change Everything for Your Business*

"Anderson is masterful at finding the nuggets in Yoshino's experiences to help us become better leaders, and presenting those gems in ways that will inspire you as you strive to improve as a leader, and as you help your coworkers improve. Whether you are a newer or experienced manager, in a manufacturing environment or a business office, this book is for you. And if you have a passion for continuous improvement and leadership learning, the lessons in this book — from Yoshino and Anderson both — will, without a doubt, help you become a better leader."

Larry Ehl

Executive Chief of Staff and Senior Director of Strategic Initiatives, Port of Seattle

"This book is an in-depth and personal look into the principles and actions of one of Toyota's most admired leaders. All of us can learn from the many nuggets of wisdom Katie Anderson has distilled from interviews with Mr. Yoshino."

John S. Toussaint, MD

Chairman of Catalysis Inc.

"Into the global gloom of this strange moment in history, Katie Anderson brings a bright light — Isao Yoshino's story of becoming a manager at Toyota and learning while leading for 40 years. Katie explains how Yoshino found his North Star, overcame adversity, framed situations in a positive way, learned from failure, and, always, developed the people he worked with as well as himself.

So read this book. It will make you feel better. And, if you reflect on and heed its wisdom, you will become a better person and a better coach and manager as well. A gift to treasure in a dark time."

James P. Womack

Founder and Senior Advisor, Lean Enterprise Institute,
Co-author of *The Machine That Changed the World* and *Lean Thinking*

Learning to LEAD, Leading to LEARN

Lessons from Toyota Leader ISAO YOSHINO on a Lifetime of Continuous Learning

KATIE ANDERSON

Learning to Lead, Leading to Learn: Lessons from Toyota Leader Isao Yoshino on a Lifetime of Continuous Learning

By Katie Anderson

Published by Integrand Press (California).

This book is both a leadership book and an authorized biography of Isao Yoshino, who collaborated on this project with author Katie Anderson. Unless otherwise noted, sections of text that are both indented and italicized throughout the book are direct quotes from Mr. Yoshino.

All financial figures presented in this book are in U.S. dollars, unless otherwise specified.

Editing by:
Kate Colbert
Karyn Ross

Cover design by:
Ilana Dashe
Courtney Hudson

Typesetting by:
Courtney Hudson

First edition, July 2020

ISBN: 978-1-7348506-0-4

Library of Congress Control Number: 2020911480

Created in the United States of America

DEDICATION

This book is dedicated to my parents, Hardy Jones and Jane Bryan-Jones, who supported the weaving of my own life fabric. My parents were my first teachers, who always encouraged me to explore my dreams, helped me get up when I fell down, loved me unconditionally, and supported me always. Thank you, Mom and Dad, for modeling what it means to live a life of intention.

And to Isao Yoshino, whose friendship and wisdom has been a gift. Thank you for generously sharing your lessons of learning and leading, so that we can *all* learn.

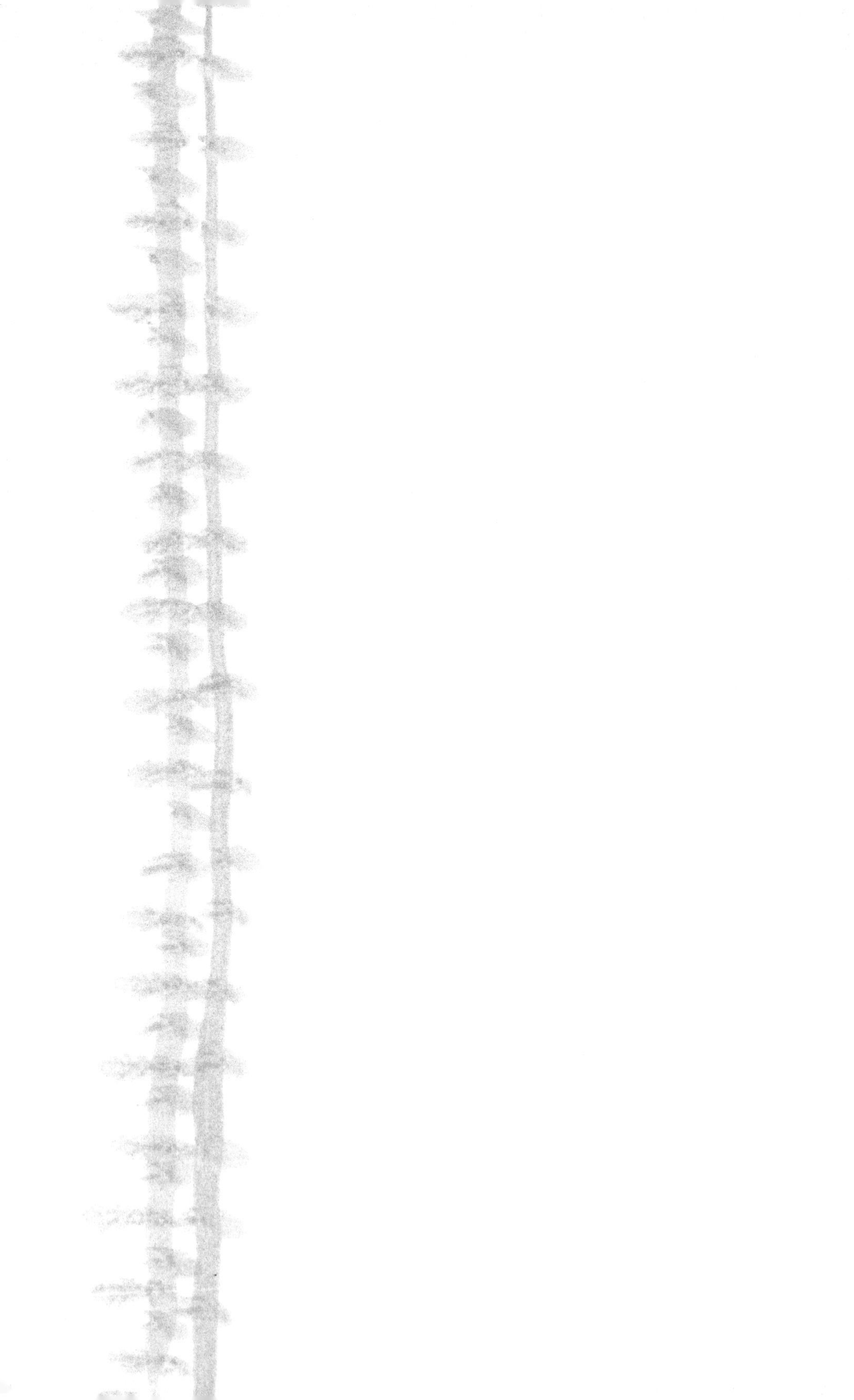

CONTENTS

PART II

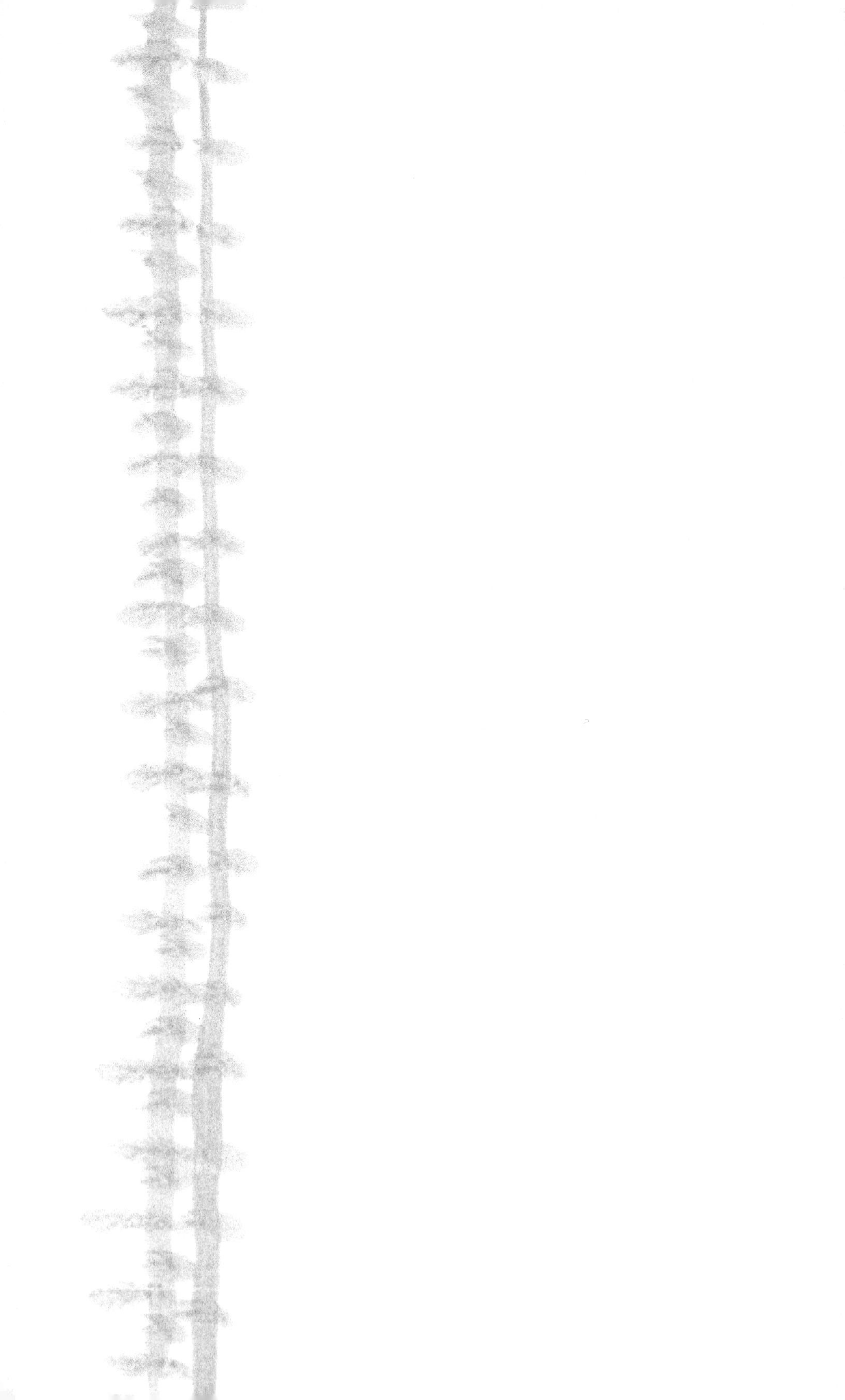

FOREWORD

By John Shook

What awaits you in the pages that follow is more than a biography or a collection of discrete interviews. In her debut book, *Learning to Lead, Leading to Learn,* Katie Anderson has distilled countless hours of interviews, lecture transcripts, and conversation (and ample debate, too, I am sure) into a cohesive whole that's informative, inspiring, and entertaining. Katie shares with the reader her joys in learning from Toyota leader Isao Yoshino about the art of learning, the privilege of leading, and the secret to crafting a life worth living.

Borrowing cleverly from Toyota's historical roots in the textile industry, Katie "weaves" Mr. Yoshino's stories of almost four decades inside Toyota into a complex but cohesive story of learning from experience (including hardship and failure).

Katie has focused her professional efforts on organizational and executive transformation, especially in healthcare, but also other industries, since 2006. She is also a student of lean thinking and the Toyota Way and is a nascent Japanophile. These varied interests collided for Katie in the person of Isao Yoshino. I won't repeat Katie's detailed introduction to Mr. Yoshino, which you will find in the coming pages. But I will share a bit of my own experience with him, a relationship of 25 years filled with professional and personal learning of the deepest kind.

Mr. Yoshino and I first met in the fall of 1983 as Toyota was preparing for a monumental task. The company had just signed an agreement with General Motors to form NUMMI — New United Motor Manufacturing, Inc., in Fremont, California. The joint venture was yet to be named, known internally simply as the "Fremont Project." The project was big news inside

Toyota — one of the biggest in the company's history. It was a time of great change in Toyota City and Mr. Yoshino was among those in the middle of it. Katie and Yoshino will tell you all about it.

Mr. Yoshino was in charge of not only training for Fremont employees but also of education for Toyota employees to prepare for the era of globalization that lay ahead.

The Fremont Project was a huge milestone for Toyota, a major piece of the company's *hoshin* objective of "internationalization." Even the seemingly minor task of recruiting me was itself a significant step for the company. The company's HR department was finalizing an initiative to hire non-Japanese as regular employees — a first for Toyota and still a rarity in Japan at that time — and hiring me was the first experiment for that undertaking. Following weeks of interviews with numerous Toyota executives, I met Mr. Yoshino during a marathon day of interviews and tests (there were other candidates) in Toyota City. I was fortunate to become one of the final pieces of the team Mr. Yoshino was forming to develop and deliver a training program for employees of the joint venture. The number of unknowns we faced was overwhelming.

For me, the job was a chance to realize my dream of working for a Japanese company. My explicit goal was to learn the secrets of Japan by working for the biggest, most Japanese company I could find. Toyota certainly qualified. I wanted to soak up everything. The opportunity to work as a member of Mr. Yoshino's new team was perfect — before I could help them teach their system to Americans, they had to teach me first. But could I learn quickly enough and deeply enough? Would I be able to handle the predictable culture shock of working in one of the most quintessential Japanese companies? I had been studying the Japanese language for several years before arriving in Japan, but my abilities were still insufficient to translate, interpret, or truly engage in business meetings using only Japanese. As enthusiastic as I was, I was equally anxious.

As it turned out, Mr. Yoshino, his team, and the entire head office campus could not have been more accepting of me as a true member of the family. I never felt even a tinge of the culture shock that was supposed to occur. Still, on many levels, I struggled. Speaking Japanese all day every day was exhausting. Learning the seemingly infinite number of cultural cues, some of which were general Japanese while many others were unique to Toyota, was daunting. And we were faced with such a huge task and its challenging timeline. Leaders from GM and NUMMI began arriving just a few months after I arrived.

In those early months, Mr. Yoshino kept a close eye on me. He would regularly take me aside in what was essentially a broom closet to have quiet one-on-one discussions, in English, about what was going on. Those discussions were a life saver for me. I could express myself freely on a wide range of topics. Anything was fair game. Eventually, after our NUMMI project work had settled into a comfortable routine and I had established myself in my new life as a "Toyota man," our broom-closet conversations evolved into country music jam sessions with me on guitar (not unusual, given I was from Tennessee) and Mr. Yoshino on banjo. To my delight, it turned out that Mr. Yoshino was far more of a fan of American country music than I ever was.

In one of those broom-closet conversations, we discussed someday writing a book together about the incredible experience we were going through. We didn't know at the time how our amazing journey would end, but we knew that something of historic magnitude going on. And we were smack dab in the middle of it. It was exhilarating. It remains the most impactful and rewarding experience of my career. We never wrote that book, but now Katie has done it for us.

So, I am grateful to Katie for capturing Isao Yoshino's story, including but going beyond just the NUMMI experience. Kudos to Katie, too, for going beyond just documenting history but weaving it all into a rich tapestry that readers of many interests will find compelling and useful. Explorers of lean thinking and practice will find a deep dive into the mind of a Toyota manager during the defining final third of the 20th century. Japanophiles will find access to the inner workings of Japan's largest industrial enterprise during the heyday of Japan Inc. And, perhaps most importantly, executive coaches — or anyone with an interest in the phenomenon of "manager-as-coach" — will find in these pages a rich expression of the thinking and practices of a deeply thoughtful, extraordinarily reflective practitioner of the craft.

John Shook
Chairman, Lean Global Network

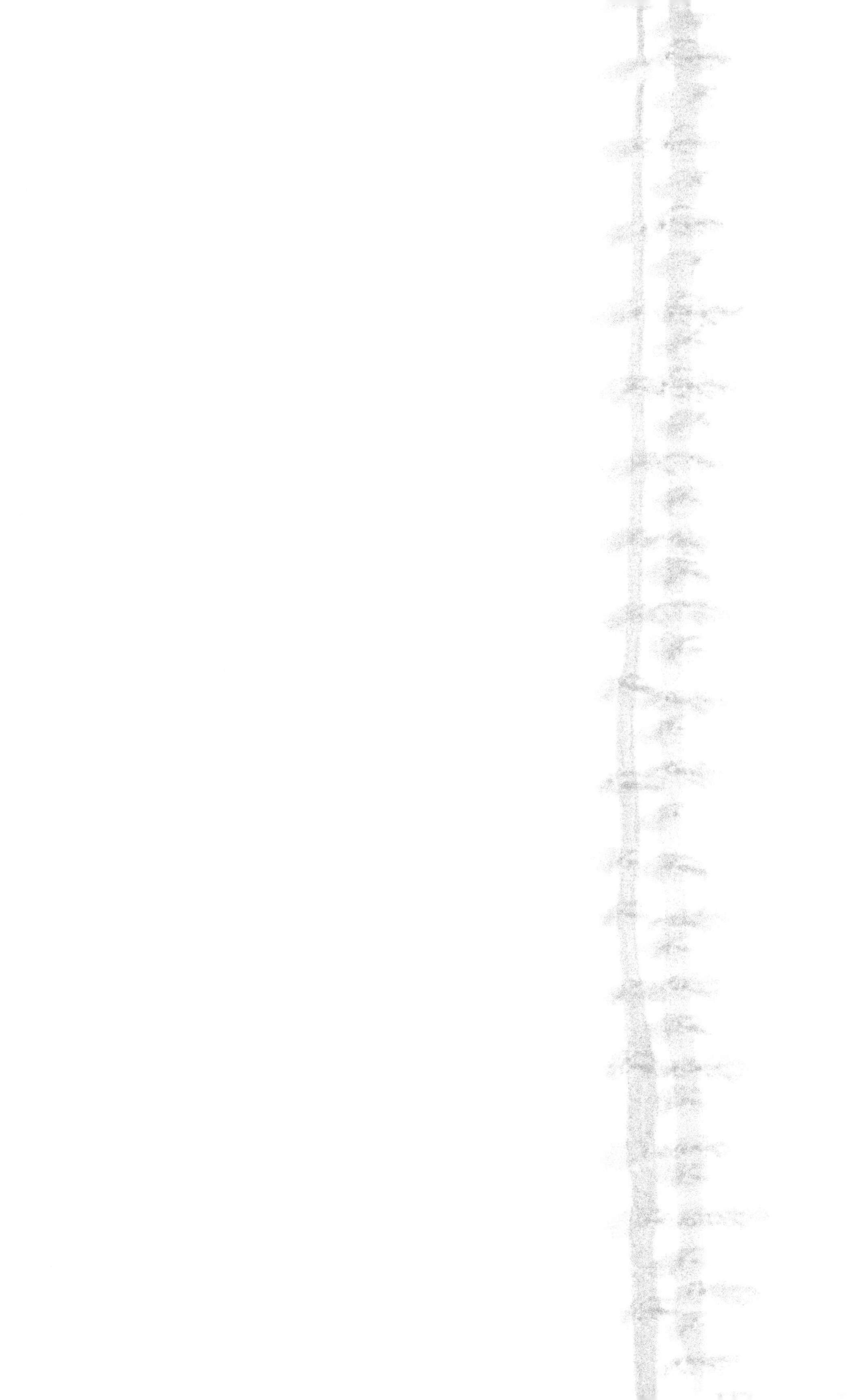

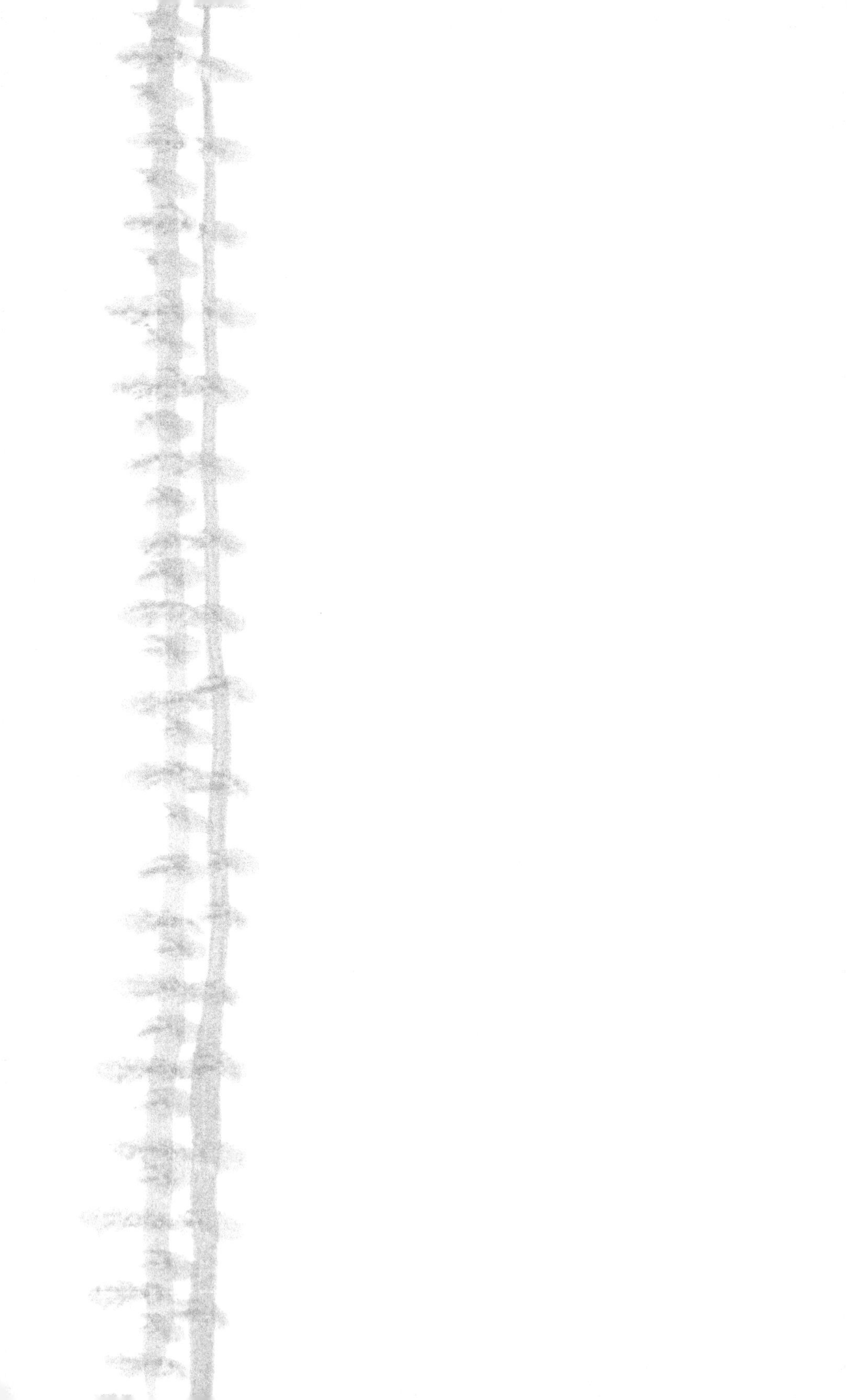

LETTER TO THE READER

By Isao Yoshino

I met Katie Anderson in 2014, a half-year before she moved to Japan. At our first meeting in Nagoya in April 2015, we immediately developed a relationship based on questions and reflecting on experiences. Since then, we have spent hundreds of hours talking together — in person in Japan, the U.S. and Europe, and on Skype in the times in between. Katie has asked what seems like millions of questions, helping me dig deep into my own past. Exploring questions has unleashed the power of us working together.

The process of being interviewed by Katie has revealed layers of learning. Just like in farming and gardening, if you don't dig down, you don't find what may be hidden there. Asking questions helps a person to dig deep into their own thinking to discover things they did not know before. The entire process of working on this book together has been very refreshing to me. Through Katie's questions in our many conversations and then reading the manuscript drafts, I felt I was getting a little smarter about myself by seeing my experiences from a different angle. Katie took my memories — helping me extract them through repeated conversations, by asking questions and more questions, and digging down further with patience and kindness — and framed them brilliantly as you will read in the pages of this book.

Katie will introduce you to the "fabric concept," which she came up with as a means of gleaning the deeper meaning of the stories presented here. The fabric concept entails identifying the vertical warp and horizontal weft threads that run throughout one's life. The vertical threads are those themes and dreams that run mostly unchanged throughout your life — the "known" elements that are deep inside. The horizontal threads are ones we discover along the way and choose to incorporate into our life, making our unique pattern in life. As we started using this metaphor, I came to realize how valuable it can be in understanding one's life. What is your vertical thread? Whatever it may be, the concept is there for your personal reflection. I believe it is so important for each of us have a purpose and a goal. And what are your horizontal threads? What have you learned about what is most important to you? Learning to see these threads of one's life, and how they relate together, helps us understand how the various episodes and periods of life make us who we are.

In the end, my conversations with Katie have helped me find many hidden gems in my life, things that I hadn't remembered in decades, and she has given me a way of looking at my experiences from different angles. That is the power of conversation and of *hansei* — of digging down, reflecting and re-learning.

For Katie, I think this book helped pull together her learnings about Toyota's way of thinking, practices, and culture, with new context provided by my personal experiences and memories. For me, this book represents a continuation of my life's "chain of learning" — a chain that started with my teachers at school, then leaders at Toyota, and now through the process of collaborating and working together on this book.

I want readers to recognize that I don't think of this book as my personal story. My own experience is not what is important — it is just the learning experience of one person. The many lessons about Toyota contained in this book come, after all, from just one man who spent 40 years there. I believe my conversations with Katie — and my memories — represent the general feeling of Toyota people in my days. Though my specific experiences are my own, this is not just Yoshino's personal history — it's like Katie asked all 70,000 people at Toyota about their experiences of learning to lead and leading to learn through me, and I directly answered. I am answering about our culture at Toyota and our way of thinking. These stories are the history of my involvement at Toyota, and the lessons I learned from my experiences. In many ways, it's not about me — it's about all of us.

My intention in creating this book with Katie was to share what I have learned. Toyota had so many people-minded leaders from whom I learned, and I am grateful for this opportunity to pay it forward. My intention is that my experiences might be helpful to people who wonder what they can do to learn and to lead. I want to pass down the tradition of what I have learned. The one thing that is solid in my life is that I've kept learning.

Passing on what I have learned is maybe my lifetime job.

Isao Yoshino
Okazaki, Japan

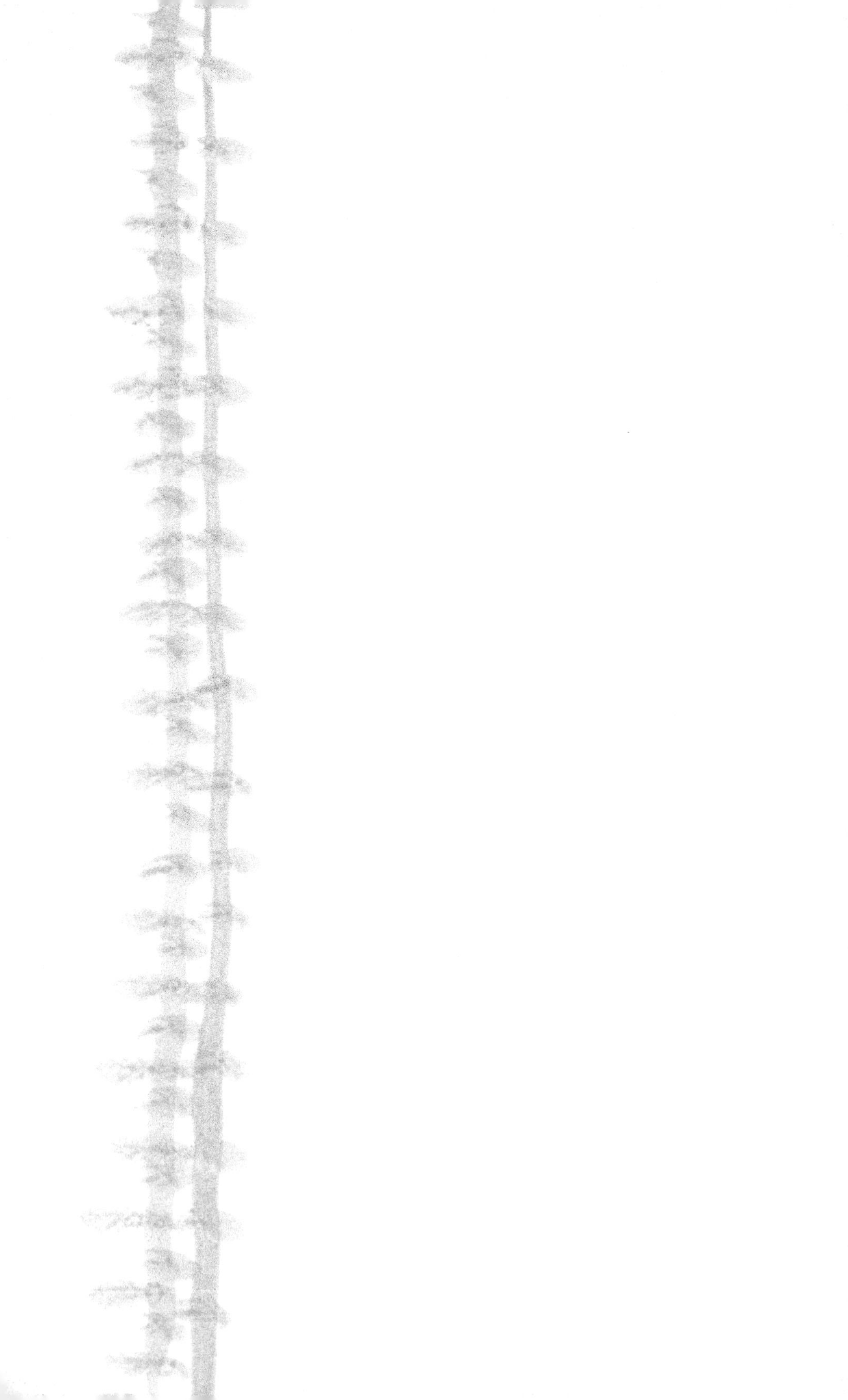

PREFACE

The moment that Isao Yoshino and I met for the first time was serendipitous and pivotal; it has deeply impacted the course of both of our lives. Little did we know what close friends we would become and how much we would learn from the hundreds of hours we have spent reflecting and growing together over the six years leading up to the publication of this book.

LOOKING BACK – MEETING FOR THE FIRST TIME

It was July 2014 and I was in Long Beach, California, for the Lean Coaching Summit and I had a lot on my mind. It was my first professional event since having my second child just a few months earlier, and my family needed to make an important decision.

Just a few weeks before, my husband had excitedly announced — via instant message in the middle of the day — that he'd been offered an opportunity for us to move to Japan for an 18-month assignment. For me, the idea was simultaneously exciting and a bit daunting. Neither of us was new to global travel and living, and we had often talked about our mutual interest in living abroad together. On one hand, I was no stranger to living internationally — having chosen to live for various periods of time in four other countries in the prior two decades. I was thrilled by the opportunity to immerse myself in Japanese culture and to learn as much as I could in the birthplace of the Toyota Production System (TPS) — the foundation of the process improvement and coaching work that I had made the focus of my career for nearly the past decade. On the other hand, we had a lot going on in our lives: our young family had just expanded, and I didn't know how an international assignment would impact my fledgling consulting business that was not yet a year old.

In the weeks leading up to the Lean Coaching Summit, I reached out to John Shook, the author of the foreword to this book and then the CEO of the Lean Enterprise Institute, to see if he would be willing to talk with me about life in Japan while we were both in Long Beach. He generously agreed, and as the weeks progressed, I couldn't help getting more and more excited about the possibility of moving to Japan — both personally and professionally.

When I arrived at the Summit — with my five-month-old and three-year-old sons in tow — I found out that Shook's own mentor and first boss at Toyota, Mr. Isao Yoshino, was going to make a surprise appearance as well. What luck!

I would have the opportunity to talk with Mr. Yoshino later that week, but I was first introduced to him when he and Shook stepped onto the conference mainstage together. They delighted the audience with impromptu stories about their relationship as manager and "subordinate"[1] during Shook's first years at Toyota in the early 1980s. They bantered back and forth about their time together at Toyota, with Shook referring to Mr. Yoshino as "*Kacho*," meaning Section Chief. Later, Mr. Yoshino told me via email:

> *I was so happy to hear him still call me "Kacho!" even though I am no longer his Kacho. It was John's own unique way of showing his gratitude to me for my support extended to him 30 years ago.*

As well as sharing quite a few amusing stories — some of which you will read here, some you will have to hear in person to get the full, inside story — Mr. Yoshino made many insightful comments that had me scribbling furiously in a notebook, trying to capture each word. These insights have expanded my own knowledge of leadership and are the foundation of the principles that you will be introduced to in this book. Mr. Yoshino's jovial presence and warm smile on stage shattered any preconceptions that I had about older Japanese "*sensei*" being stoic harsh taskmasters. This was

---

1 At Toyota during Yoshino's tenure, it was common to refer to direct reports as "subordinates." Yoshino does not use this term to be taken negatively; it is just the common term from his time at Toyota.

a leader who clearly led with his heart — as well as his mind — and I was eager to meet him!

On the final day of the Summit, I found myself sitting next to Mr. Yoshino in the hotel restaurant lobby. We struck up a conversation and I told him that I would likely be moving to Japan at the beginning of the year. Mr. Yoshino gave me his business card and said to contact him when we were settled in. He enthusiastically assured me that he would be happy to take me to Toyota City and would enjoy spending time together.

I couldn't believe my good fortune! Not only did I spend more than an hour talking with John Shook about Japan (and got his recommendations for people with whom to connect for professional learning opportunities), I now had a personal invitation from Shook's own mentor. I knew that moving our family to Tokyo was going to be a great adventure and learning experience!

I knew that moving our family to Tokyo was going to be a great adventure and learning experience!

A FRIENDSHIP BEGINS IN JAPAN

My family arrived in Tokyo the first week of January 2015. After settling into our new routine, I reached out to Mr. Yoshino to follow up on his generous offer and to make a date to get together. He invited me and my husband to Nagoya, where he would rent a car — a Toyota, of course — and drive us the 40 km (25 miles) to Toyota City for a tour of one of Toyota's factories. Afterward, we would visit his office at Nagoya Gakuin University to meet some of his students who were eager to practice their English with native speakers. We chose a day in April for our meeting without me realizing that it coincided with the start of a new academic calendar — and, as a university lecturer, this was his busiest time of the year. This generous invitation was just a hint of what I would soon discover was a deep commitment and passion for helping people.

I thought that visit was going to be a once-in-a-lifetime experience. I didn't anticipate that overcast spring day would turn out to be the first of many trips I would take to Nagoya to spend in deep conversation with Mr. Yoshino, and the beginning of what has become a profoundly important relationship in both of our lives. Over the course of the 18 months we lived in Tokyo, I visited Mr. Yoshino at least five times in Nagoya. I soon called these day-long excursions — 20 minutes via taxi to Shinagawa Station where I would grab a latte and pretzel croissant, followed by a smooth 90-minute bullet train journey covering 350 km (217 miles) to Nagoya, and a further 15-minute taxi ride to Yoshino's office — my "Yoshino-san commute." I would return the same evening — retracing my steps, this time with a dinner bento box procured at Nagoya Station.

A HABIT OF REFLECTION AND LEARNING TOGETHER IS ESTABLISHED

While I considered myself the learner and Mr. Yoshino the teacher during our earliest encounters, Yoshino told me that he too learned from me. In response to a thank you email I sent after our first visit, he replied:

> *You said that you have learned many things on lean concepts and practices from our conversation. I want you to know that I myself have learned many things from the questions you asked. Your questions and comments were all insightful and helped me to reconfirm the importance of the "TPS/lean concept" we have long cherished at Toyota.*

I couldn't have been more honored that he, too, felt like he had learned and gotten value from our conversations. This became the pattern of our relationship — two people, from different cultures, backgrounds, genders, and generations — coming together to learn, share, and help each other, through conversation and reflection.

This became the pattern of our relationship — two people, from different cultures, backgrounds, genders, and generations — coming together to learn, share, and help each other, through conversation and reflection.

A FRIENDSHIP — AND PARTNERSHIP — EXPANDS AROUND THE WORLD

In July 2016, my family moved back to our home in California, but Mr. Yoshino and I kept up our regular communications. Our relationship evolved, but never waned, despite the distance. During frequent return visits to Japan, I continued to make visits to his office in Nagoya via my "Yoshino-san commute." Soon, we began to collaborate professionally around the world to offer workshops, seminars, and talks to audiences across Europe, North America, and Japan. Mr. Yoshino has visited and stayed at my home in California several times. And, starting in 2018, I launched my executive Japan Study Trips (KBJAnderson.com/JapanTrips) — week-long learning experiences for leaders looking to deepen their knowledge of lean practices, the Toyota Way, and Japanese culture — in which Mr. Yoshino takes part.

While I may now call him "Isao" when we speak privately, I still refer to him as Mr. Yoshino or Yoshino professionally and in writing, as a sign of respect.

AN IDEA FOR A BOOK

At our first meeting, Mr. Yoshino granted me permission to write about our conversations in the blog I had just started (KBJAnderson.com/Blog). One article became many and turned into an entire series titled "Toyota Leadership Lessons," which generated a great amount of interest and feedback from readers.[2] Mr. Yoshino enjoyed my synthesis of our conversations — of what I heard and learned from him — and printed the blog posts for his university students to read. They, too, enjoyed these insights about their lecturer, and the articles gave them a chance to practice their English. It was this series of blog posts that ultimately became the inspiration for this book.

Mr. Yoshino and I continued our discussions in the year after I returned to the United States. He proposed the idea of creating a small "booklet" based on these initial blog posts and expanding to include more topics. As we

---

2 To read articles from the "Toyota Leadership Lessons" series or other blog posts including Isao Yoshino, visit KBJAnderson.com/Tag/Isao-Yoshino.

discussed this project, it morphed into the vision for a more comprehensive book framed around specific leadership principles supported by stories and shared insights.

In mid-2018, we started with purposeful interviews with the intent of creating a book. But, as we uncovered Mr. Yoshino's memories and rich layers of learning, and as I sat down to write, I realized that the format needed to change once again. Instead of structuring a book around "10 leadership principles" (or some other number) and then fitting stories within them, which didn't allow for the telling of complex experiences over periods of time, I knew that I needed to tell Mr. Yoshino's journey of learning and leading as it unfolded for him (true to chronology). I wanted readers to experience the *process* in which he learned and to let the leadership lessons come from these stories.

This book, which emerged from our early, initial conversations and my reflective blog posts, has evolved into a special way to document Mr. Yoshino's insights and stories about learning and leading — and share them with *you*!

THE POWER OF REFLECTION, PARTNERSHIP, AND SHARED PURPOSE

If you're like me, you enjoy a good conversation with an old friend — picking up where you left off, even if days, weeks, months, or years have passed. That's how Mr. Yoshino and I created this book, one conversation at a time, oftentimes revisiting stories and concepts to go deeper and learn more.

In looking back on the process of creating this book together, Mr. Yoshino often commented that our partnership has helped him learn anew about his life and his career at Toyota. He has rediscovered long-forgotten memories, smiled when recalling the leaders who made a positive impact on his life, unraveled complex periods in his career, and re-examined his earlier lessons from a different perspective. As he once remarked:

> *I am learning and re-learning more about my life. There are things that I knew then that I understand more deeply now.*

> **"I am learning and re-learning more about my life. There are things that I knew then that I understand more deeply now."**

Over the two years leading up to the publication of this book, we talked several times a month — in the evening for me after my kids were in bed, and in the mid-day for Mr. Yoshino. We found ourselves laughing intensely on video calls when Mr. Yoshino remembered some long-hidden stories — and we hope that they inspire some smiles from you as well. And there have been memories of more difficult periods that have caused us to pause and revisit, piece by piece, over time.

Through our discussions and friendship, we have both learned more deeply what it means to weave a full life of purpose and intention. We have discovered that we share a common fabric of purpose — to lead international lives, to help others discover their best selves, and to develop our best selves at the same time.

> **Through our discussions and friendship, we have both learned more deeply what it means to weave a full life of purpose and intention. We have discovered that we share a common fabric of purpose – to lead international lives, to help others discover their best selves, and to develop our best selves at the same time.**

Our conversations have led not only to a greater level of understanding for Mr. Yoshino about his own life experiences, but have led me to have deeper insights both on my own practices and on principles that I have known about from reading about Toyota. From hearing Mr. Yoshino's stories and perspective, I've also gained access to knowledge and insider stories that neither I nor you could have read in books. *Until now!*

WHO SHOULD READ THIS BOOK?

This book was written with a broad audience of leaders and aspiring leaders in mind — it was written for you!

What you are about to read is much more than a collection of Mr. Yoshino's personal experiences and stories. It is a book that highlights important people-centered leadership lessons, records historical moments in time from the perspective of a Toyota leader, and offers something for current and aspiring leaders that will help them reflect and learn about themselves.

This book is for you if you:

- Are interested in becoming a more effective people-centered leader
- Practice lean or continuous improvement methods in your organization
- Strive to develop a culture of learning in your organization
- Serve in an organizational development, coaching, or leadership role
- Want to learn more about Toyota's history and culture
- Are interested in reading some heartwarming stories about personal discovery and leadership.

Through the work I do as a leadership coach and consultant, I endeavor to help leaders live and lead with intention. It is vital for leaders to develop clarity of purpose and align their processes and behaviors in service of that purpose. As luck would have it, Mr. Yoshino provided me the opportunity to discover and refine my purpose as well. It's my honor to share his insights, intertwined with my own, in this book.

It is vital for leaders to develop clarity of purpose and align their processes and behaviors in service of that purpose.

LOOKING AHEAD

I invite you to be inspired by Mr. Yoshino's experiences of learning and leading, which he shares — from his generous heart and insightful mind — with the intention to help us all learn.

I feel so incredibly fortunate to have the friendship with this special person and inspiring leader, and to have the opportunity to talk with and learn with him regularly. This book is my tribute to Mr. Yoshino and a way to continue

Isao Yoshino and Katie Anderson, Nagoya Gakuin University, Nagoya City, Japan, January 2020.

the chain of learning that was passed down from his early schoolteachers and then leaders at Toyota, to his subordinates like John Shook, to me through our conversations, and now to you.

My hope is that you will be inspired as I have been from hearing Mr. Yoshino's reflections and lessons — inspired to be a better learner and a better leader.

I am excited to offer you Mr. Yoshino's stories of learning and leading, and our shared learning as he reflects on his experiences of a lifetime of continuous learning. I have no doubt you, too, will learn a great deal.

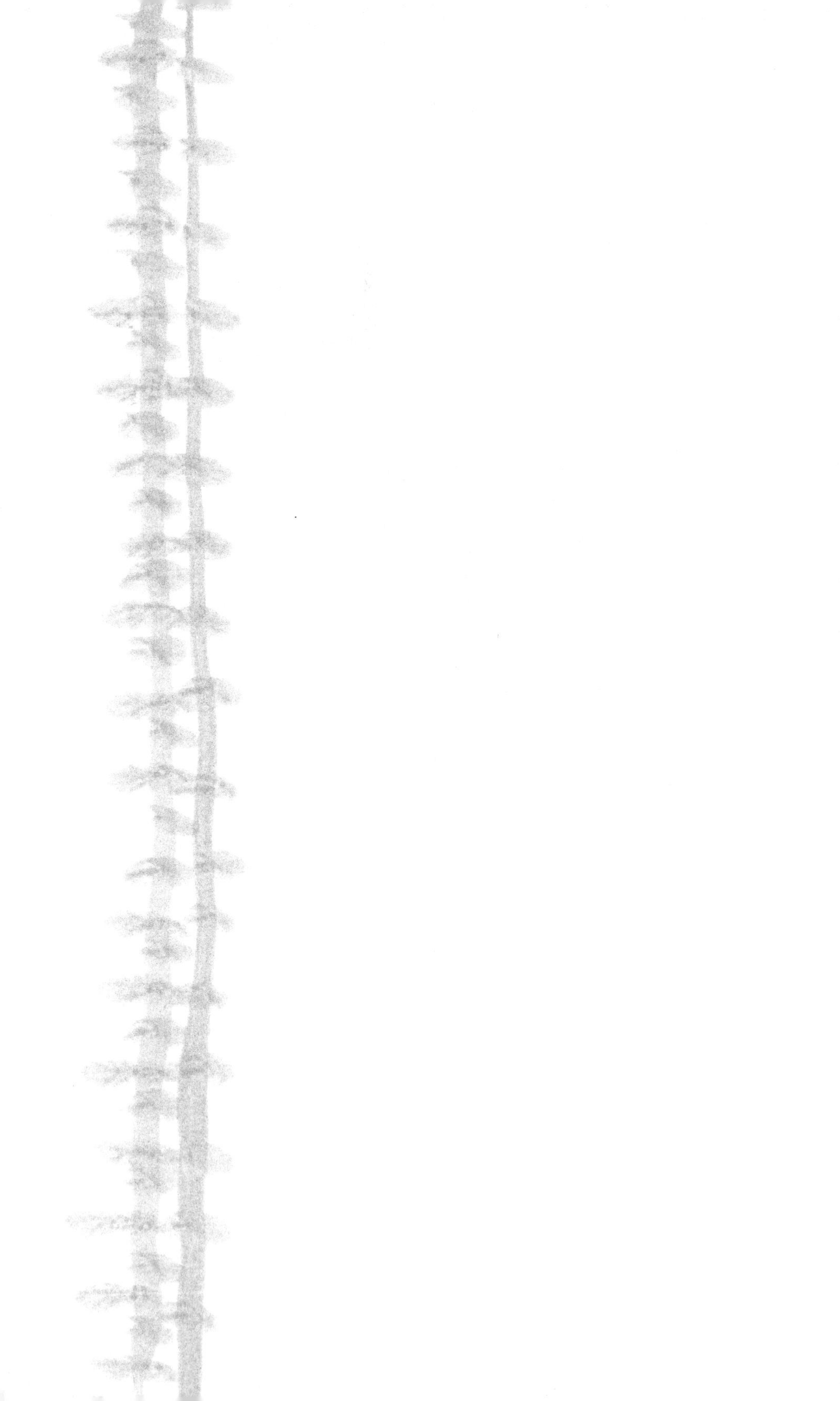

INTRODUCTION

"The only secret to Toyota is its attitude toward learning. We don't even notice and take it for granted."

– Isao Yoshino

Isao Yoshino once told me that the only secret to Toyota is its attitude toward learning: Toyota and its people are more patient, even more so than other Japanese companies, in reflecting, learning, adjusting, and continuing to try until they succeed. They are willing to experiment, and embrace failure and bad news as possible sources of learning.

LEARNING TO LEAD AND LEADING TO LEARN

Isao Yoshino's experiences spanning nearly four decades at Toyota Motor Corporation help us understand how Toyota intentionally developed the culture of excellence for which it is renowned today. Yoshino's career at Toyota is bookended by two seminal events in Toyota's history: when it was awarded the Deming Prize in 1965 for its Quality Control efforts and when the company published *The Toyota Way 2001* to codify its management philosophy across the organization. It is this nearly 40-year span of organizational learning and continuous improvement in which Isao Yoshino learned to lead and discovered the capacity to "lead to learn."

Few of us have had the opportunity to work in an organization that values learning and embodies people-centered leadership principles as fully and authentically as Toyota does. This culture did not happen magically — it required intention and purposeful choices by its leaders. Yoshino was there during these pivotal moments when a better way of leading and working was being more fully formed. And perhaps, most importantly, as he rose in the ranks of seniority at Toyota, he continued to put in place what he learned about leadership to develop his people at all levels.

Yoshino does not consider himself a technical Toyota Production System (TPS) expert — instead, his expertise is in the *people* side of Toyota's culture — the leadership behaviors and mindsets of the Toyota Way. While serving mainly in back-office positions until the final decade of his career, Yoshino held important roles in supporting and leading various organizational development programs and overseas operations functions. What's more, his years at Toyota coincided with critical times in the company's history during the last quarter of the twentieth century. As you will discover in the pages that follow, Yoshino was integral in supporting Toyota's senior leadership's decision, in the late 1970s and 1980s, to invest in and strengthen the mindset and behaviors that we now define as "lean leadership." He helped lead Toyota's Kan-Pro program, which re-taught thousands of senior managers fundamental management capabilities. And he served in multiple roles supporting Toyota's expansion to foreign markets and translation of TPS to other cultures, such as the New United Motor Manufacturing, Inc. (NUMMI), joint venture with General Motors (GM) and other manufacturing plants in North America. These events deepened Toyota's people-centered culture and management capabilities, as well as expanded its philosophy to the rest of the world.

Yoshino's personal evolution as a learner and as a leader parallels the evolution of Toyota's people-centered learning culture, which was built on a foundation of respect for people and a commitment to continuous improvement. His experiences demonstrate what it's like to work in an organization whose leaders truly embody the concept of "we make people." And his stories offer us lessons on how to create a culture focused on continuous learning — by investing in one person at a time.

A LEADER'S ROLE

As I mentioned in the preface, the first time I encountered Isao Yoshino was in 2014 when he and John Shook took the stage at a conference to share their experiences about working together as manager and subordinate. Something Yoshino said then about his role as John Shook's manager struck me as particularly profound:

> *My aim as a manager was to develop John by giving him a mission or target, and to support him while he figured out how to achieve the target. And as I was developing John, I was aware that I was developing myself as well.*

In this one statement, Mr. Yoshino summed up what I consider to be the essence of leadership. Throughout this book, you'll see me refer to this as a three-part framework you can commit to in your own work as a leader. I believe that great leaders:

1. **Set the direction:** Issue a clear challenge, goal, or target for your people.
2. **Provide support:** Help your people develop themselves as learners and leaders, and create the systems that enable their success.
3. **Develop yourself:** Constantly improve yourself as a leader and a learner.

> **"My aim as a manager was to develop John by giving him a mission or target, and to support him while he figured out how to achieve the target. And as I was developing John, I was aware that I was developing myself as well."**

I share Yoshino's words — and this framework for leadership that he and I both believe in so strongly — in almost every learning session I facilitate. It is a powerful construct — simple in concept, but more challenging in practice — for what it means to lead and learn to help your people, yourself, and your organization. These core concepts of people-centered leadership inspired the title of this book and are the threads interconnected through all the stories you're about to read.

THE "TOYOTA WAY" PRINCIPLES – THE FOUNDATION OF TOYOTA'S CULTURE

Throughout this book, you will discover how Yoshino learned, exemplified, and later amplified — through his role in teaching people around the world — the principles now known as the "Toyota Way." These were not written down during Yoshino's tenure at Toyota, and only around the time of his retirement did Toyota codify them in a document called *The Toyota Way 2001*,[1] never published but rather released as an internal document.

The Toyota Way 2001 document, of which Yoshino has retained his personal copy, makes *explicit* the implicit values, methods, and knowledge passed on for generations at the company. The two main pillars in the document — Continuous Improvement and Respect for People — are supported by five guiding principles, as follows:

Continuous Improvement

- ***Challenge*** - We form a long-term vision, meeting challenges with courage and creativity to realize our dreams.
- ***Kaizen*** - We improve our business operations continuously, always driving for innovation and evolution.
- ***Genchi Genbutsu*** - We practice *Genchi Genbutsu* ... to go to the source ... to find the facts to make correct decisions, build consensus and achieve goals at our best speed.

Respect for People

- ***Respect*** - We respect others and make every effort to understand each other, take responsibility, and do our best to build mutual trust.

1 *The Toyota Way 2001* document, prepared by Toyota

- ***Teamwork*** - We stimulate personal and professional growth, share the opportunities of development and maximize individual and team performance.

Taken together, the two pillars of the "Toyota Way" — Continuous Improvement and Respect for People — are about learning more deeply and helping each other improve. And as I came to learn about Toyota's commitment to these two pillars, I further understood Yoshino's own philosophies and actions, formed and taken in the context of these guiding principles from Toyota's highest leadership.

REFLECTION — *HANSEI* — IS THE KEY TO LEARNING

The concept of *hansei,* of reflection, is the foundation of this book — and of learning.

Hansei — a Japanese word that translates to "self-reflection" — represents the deeper learning that comes from examining the past and making corrections for the future. *Hansei* is a fundamental part of Japanese culture. *Hansei* is also an integral piece of the Plan-Do-Check-Adjust (PDCA) cycle of scientific learning that W. Edwards Deming (an American engineer, professor, and management consultant) and others introduced to Japan following World War II, and which Japanese business leaders, particularly at Toyota, advanced and ingrained into their company cultures. *Hansei* is the "check and adjust" part of the PDCA wheel and is a key tenet of what became known as the "Toyota Way."

Purposeful, honest self-reflection — in business and in life — can help us make better decisions and can allow us to lead ourselves and others more effectively. It is through reflection that we can learn, and then choose to adjust.

Learning is never perfect, and it is never complete.

Purposeful, honest self-reflection – in business and in life – can help us make better decisions and can allow us to lead ourselves and others more effectively.

WHAT TO EXPECT

I encourage you to read this book with an open heart and a curious mind — to be thinking about how the lessons discovered herein go broader than one person's story and what you can learn. This is not a book about the perfect organization or the perfect leader. It is a human story about imperfection, striving for a challenge, persevering despite failure, appreciating success, learning to learn more deeply, helping others, and making the effort to do things differently (and a bit better) over a lifetime. It is a story about the past, but it is also an opportunity to learn and shape our own future.

I encourage you to read this book with an open heart and a curious mind – to be thinking about how the lessons discovered herein go broader than one person's story and what you can learn.

In the following pages, you will follow Yoshino's learning journey — personally and professionally — and his reflections on what he learned then, and what he has re-learned now with a different perspective looking back at the totality of his career. You will also discover stories about critical pieces in Toyota's history in which Yoshino played a key part — including some well-known (such as the NUMMI joint venture with GM in the 1980s) and some lesser-known (like Kan-Pro — Toyota's leadership development program for senior managers from 1979 - 1980 — and Toyota's failed U.S. water-ski boat venture).

Throughout the book I offer you insights from what I have learned — from Yoshino and from my own professional experiences. My take on Yoshino's lessons and my further discussion will provide context for the stories and should help you reflect and learn.

What This Book Is Not

There are many books about the tools and technical skills that support lean thinking and practice. Technical "how-to" explanations are not our focus. While Yoshino and I may refer to tools, practices, and structures that can help you and your organization, our intention is not that you copy them directly, but that you come to a deeper understanding of the principles, thought processes, and behaviors that will allow your organization to develop its own people-centered culture of excellence.

> **Our intention is that you come to a deeper understanding of the principles, thought processes, and behaviors that will allow your organization to develop its own people-centered culture of excellence.**

Additionally, there are many books that provide a comprehensive chronicle of Toyota's history. We do not attempt to capture a breadth of experience and history here. Instead, we present one person's memories of key times in Toyota's evolution and his own leadership journey within that time and place, but like with all memories, they are subjective.

THE FRAME FOR THIS BOOK: WEAVING WARP AND WEFT

The Toyota Motor Corporation was originally founded in the 1920s as a weaving company — the Toyoda Automatic Loom Works, Ltd. — by Sakichi Toyoda, known as the father of the Japanese Industrial Revolution. The metaphor of fabric and weaving guides the structure for this book, paying homage to Toyota's origins. This framework is the loom on which Yoshino's stories "of a lifetime of learning" interconnect.

WEAVING FABRIC – THE RELATIONSHIP BETWEEN WARP AND WEFT

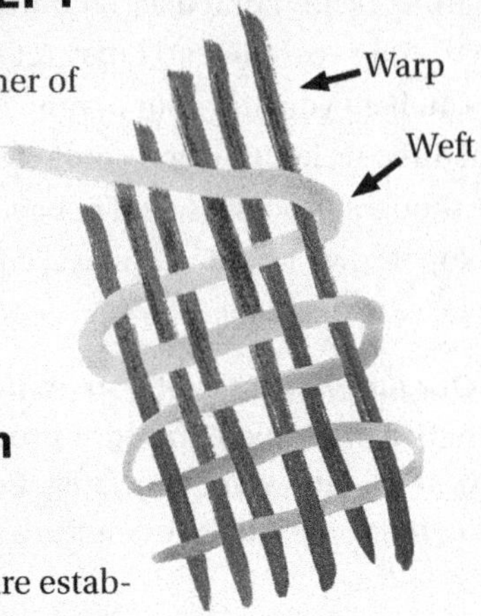

Fabric is crafted by the weaving together of two threads: vertical threads (warp) and horizontal threads (weft). Warp and weft threads are interdependent and cannot function without the other.

Warp

Weft

Warp Threads: The Known

Warp thread are strong and constant. As the foundation of the fabric, they are established from the outset and held stationary once set in their vertical pattern on the loom. They must be strong enough to withstand high tension.

Weft Threads: The Discovered

Weft thread are fluid and flexible. They can be variable or uniform. They can be fragile and break, or be thick and strong. Their colors can differ and change. Not immediately obvious at first, they are what create the pattern of the fabric. By being drawn through, over, and under — winding around the warp threads — weft threads reveal themselves and we discover their contribution.

Interdependence Between Warp and Weft

The interplay between these two threads creates the richness of the fabric's texture and design. Through a process of discovery, of experimentation and creation, and of mistakes and learning, the weaver creates a pattern. The original pattern may have been intentional, or created through discovery along the way, but the final product is only known at the end.

Yoshino shares a deeper meaning behind the weaving metaphor:

> *In Japan, it is believed that the vertical warp threads represent the fabric designer's strong belief, clear vision, inner spirit, and determination to attain the goal of the completed fabric. Warp threads are spiritual, powerful and consistent. The horizontal weft threads, on the other hand, represent something more practical and physical. At first, weft threads might not be as visible or obvious as the vertical warp threads, and may look plain or unspectacular before they are woven. However, once the weft threads join the warp threads, they bring a unique and rich pattern to the fabric.*

WEAVING A PURPOSEFUL LIFE FABRIC: THE JOINING OF THE KNOWN AND THE DISCOVERED

Just like fabric, our life story and the fulfilling of our life's purpose is the interweaving of the known and the discovered.

Just like fabric, our life story and the fulfilling of our life's purpose is the interweaving of the known and the discovered.

Sometimes, until we look backward — until we spend time in *hansei*, deeply reflecting — it's difficult to see how the known and discovered factors of our lives weave together. Only in looking back do we see the result of these interrelated threads, the unique and rich pattern of purpose that we have created through our lives.

Sometimes the direction we want to go is known from the beginning. We have a clear sense of purpose, a dream, or a goal that we want to achieve. Our warp threads represent a strong sense deep inside of us. Once known, they are like vertical threads on a loom — strong enough to withstand tension, setbacks, and challenges. We can hold onto this known goal or purpose, like a guide rope on a steep mountain or the North Star in the sky, to keep us on course, to help us get up and persevere, and to pull us back on track when we have gone astray. Warp threads guide us — and at times compel us — to move forward, deliberately and with intention.

Often, however, the other threads that we need to create our life fabric — to reveal our complete purpose — are not clear from the start. Instead, they are discovered. Like our choice of various colors, shapes, and textures to incorporate into the pattern of a fabric, in life we pick up different ideas and skills, experiment, learn, and discover as we go. These elements are connected to and visible from the outside. These are our weft threads. Our fabric of purpose is shaped by the relationship between the known and the discovered.

> **Our fabric of purpose is shaped by the relationship between the known and the discovered.**

As we move along our warp threads, in pursuit of realizing our known purpose, dream, or goal, we incorporate different weft threads into our fabric's pattern, threading them back and forth. We must take action to keep looping and entwining our threads together. Sometimes a thread breaks as we work, and we have to stop to fix it. Sometimes the weave becomes loose and we must tighten it. We pause, adjust. We continue, and we learn.

Some of the pattern we weave is planned far in advance, some of it is created by unexpected events, and some becomes known only by looking back at the finished product. For that reason, looking backward is just as important as looking forward. While we may have established a clear purpose or vision from the start, sometimes it is only when looking backward at our decisions and actions — some intentional, some random — that we can see how the pattern and texture has emerged.

Combined together, these two types of "threads" create the fabric of our lives.

YOSHINO'S WARP AND WEFT THREADS

After years of conversation with Yoshino to help him unravel, view, and revisit his past experiences from different angles, it became clear to me that two strong "threads" united to become his life tapestry: his warp threads — a known inner desire to broaden his perspective and know people of many cultures — and his weft threads — his discovered purpose of learning, leading, and helping other people fulfill their own purpose. These two threads, intertwined, represent Yoshino's life purpose.

Warp: The Known

Yoshino's warp threads, his known inner purpose, manifested when he was a young boy who first dreamed of going to the United States. That dream was finally realized through the setting of goals and interim targets along the way. Like warp threads, this dream of international experiences was Yoshino's inner determination — it was firmly established and able to withstand many tests, setbacks, and challenges.

His deep desire within to be connected to people around the world continues to be strong today. Yoshino reflects:

> *When I look backward on my life, my "warp threads" were a strong desire to go to different countries, particularly the U.S., to get to know different cultures and people, and to broaden my perspective. It started when I was a small boy and witnessed one young American soldier visit my house and ask my father for directions. It struck me immensely. Since then, my warp threads, just like vertical threads in kimono textiles, have kept their role as a core part of my life's target.*

Weft: The Discovered

Yoshino's weft threads, his discovered purpose — of helping to support and develop people to become their best selves through learning and leading — gradually became known to him as he moved along his warp threads. He picked up different threads — some thicker, some thinner, some bright, and some dull — and he learned how to weave them together through success and failure. While these weft threads — principles about learning and leading that we have long known — sometimes look common and ordinary when viewed alone, when woven together they create a rich pattern from which we too can glean powerful insights for our careers and lives. Yoshino describes his weft threads:

My "weft threads," my desire to help support and develop other people, started when I was a teenager studying English. My juku *[cram school] teacher always praised me on my abilities and personality, and it served as a great springboard for me to further advance my English study.*

When I started working at Toyota in the mid-'60s, my bosses and senior people around me kept giving me a lot of advice formally and informally. I wondered why they were so kind to a newcomer like me. I found out later that they helped me because they themselves were once given a lot of valuable advice and support from their superiors when they joined Toyota. They just wanted to pass on the tradition they had enjoyed. It was nothing special or outstanding what they did, but it made me so happy. I was secretly determined that I would do that myself for other people when the time came.

THIS BOOK'S STRUCTURE

This book is presented in two large parts, where the stories are organized in a way that allows you to follow Yoshino's learning journey along two dimensions — the known and the discovered.

Yoshino and I offer these stories to you and encourage you to enjoy them however they best fit your own learning. You can choose to read this book from front to back, in order, following Yoshino's learning and leading journey chronologically. Or, if there is a specific topic or period in history that you are particularly interested in, feel free to jump ahead.

Part I – Warp Thread Stories: Purpose Shapes Us

The stories presented in Part I are focused on Yoshino's warp threads — his internal desire to have broad world experiences. These are deeply personal stories about discovering a purpose, having a dream, setting a goal, and persevering until you achieve it. These stories present the arc of Yoshino's professional life and set the foundation upon which he wove in the weft threads of learning and leading at Toyota.

Part II – Weft Thread Stories: Discovery Defines Us

The stories in Part II follow Yoshino's journey of learning to lead and leading to learn across nearly 40 years at Toyota Motor Corporation. You will learn details of initiatives at key inflection points in Toyota's history, and experience one leader's reflections on success and failure along the way. You will learn how leaders at Toyota set direction and gave challenges, developed other people, and developed themselves. While also personal, these stories highlight broader leadership themes that you may already be aware of, as well as moments in history and insights you'll be hearing for the first time.

This part of the book is separated into three chapters, each following roughly one-third of the chronology of Yoshino's career of learning and leading at Toyota. Throughout this part, I have included supplemental sections to highlight historic influences on — and concepts related to — Toyota's culture, principles, and practices that Yoshino learned and taught along the way.

Learning to Lead – Foundational Leadership Lessons

Lessons learned from Yoshino's first 15 years at Toyota, presented as a series of eight vignettes and supplemental insights.

Leading to Learn – Helping Others to Develop

Career case studies from four significant roles in Yoshino's mid-career in which he was learning, leading, and learning more.

- **Case Study #1:** *Revitalizing Management Capabilities – The Kanri Noryoku Program*
- **Case Study #2:** *Changing the Culture by Helping People Change – The NUMMI Training Program*
- **Case Study #3:** *Focusing on the Good and Choosing Excellence – The San Francisco Liaison Office*
- **Case Study #4:** *Helping Others Broaden Their Perspectives – The "Change Yourself" Program*

Reflecting on Failure – Toyota's Water-Ski Boat Business

Recollections from the final third of Yoshino's career, in which he experienced the greatest failure of his career — yet learned deeply.

AIMING FORWARD, LOOKING BACKWARD, AND ALWAYS LEARNING

"These lessons we learned long ago can still work."

– Isao Yoshino

So, come along on this journey of what it means to be a learner and a leader. Learn from Yoshino's stories and our shared insights, more deeply discovered through our conversations and purposeful reflection — *hansei*. Then practice your own *hansei*. Reflect on what you learned from Yoshino's experiences by considering the questions posed at the end of each section.

Our intention in developing this book has been to help *you* weave together the threads of your own story — so that you can be a more intentional and better leader (and person) — no matter what industry, culture, or environment you are in.

Let's begin!

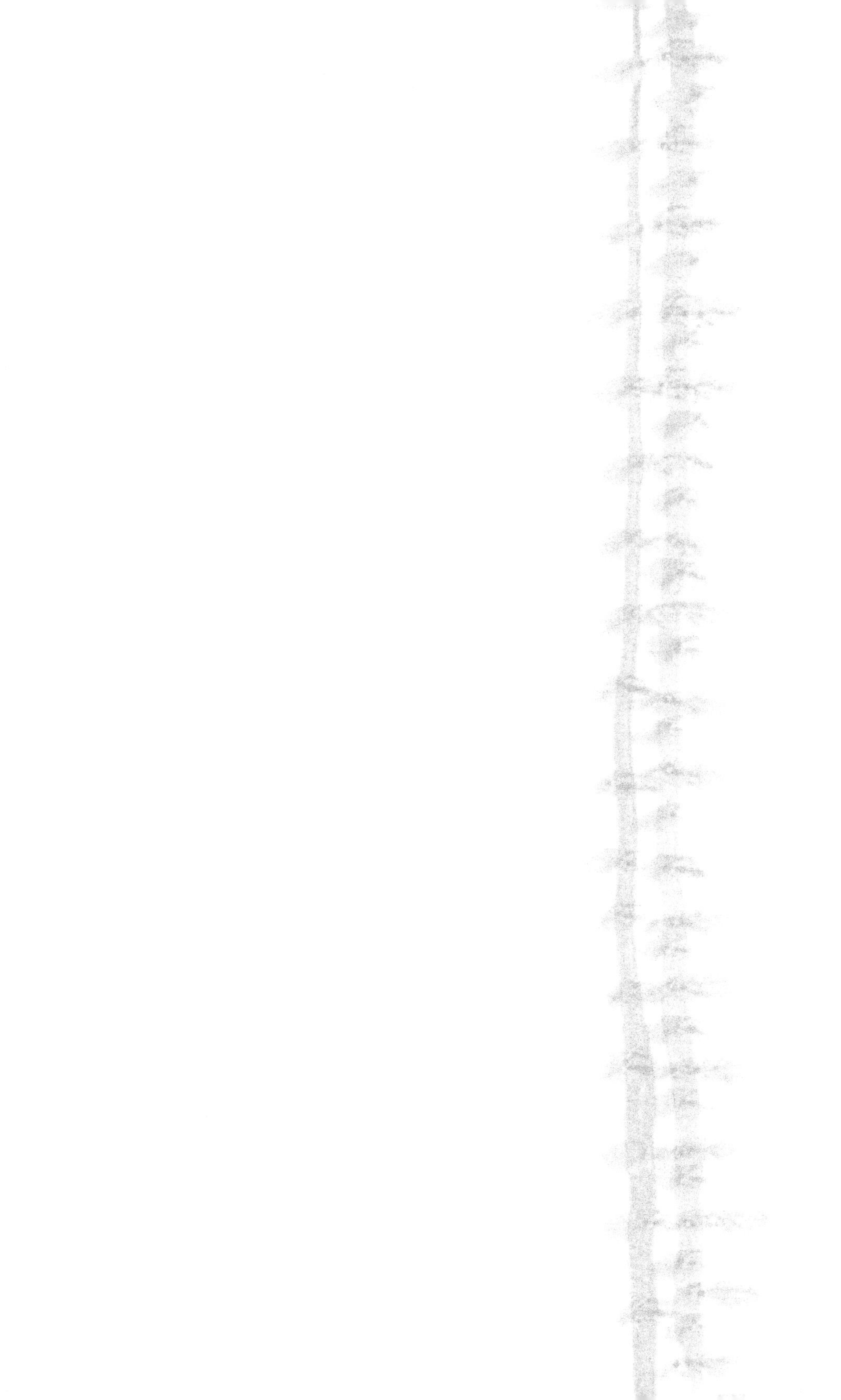

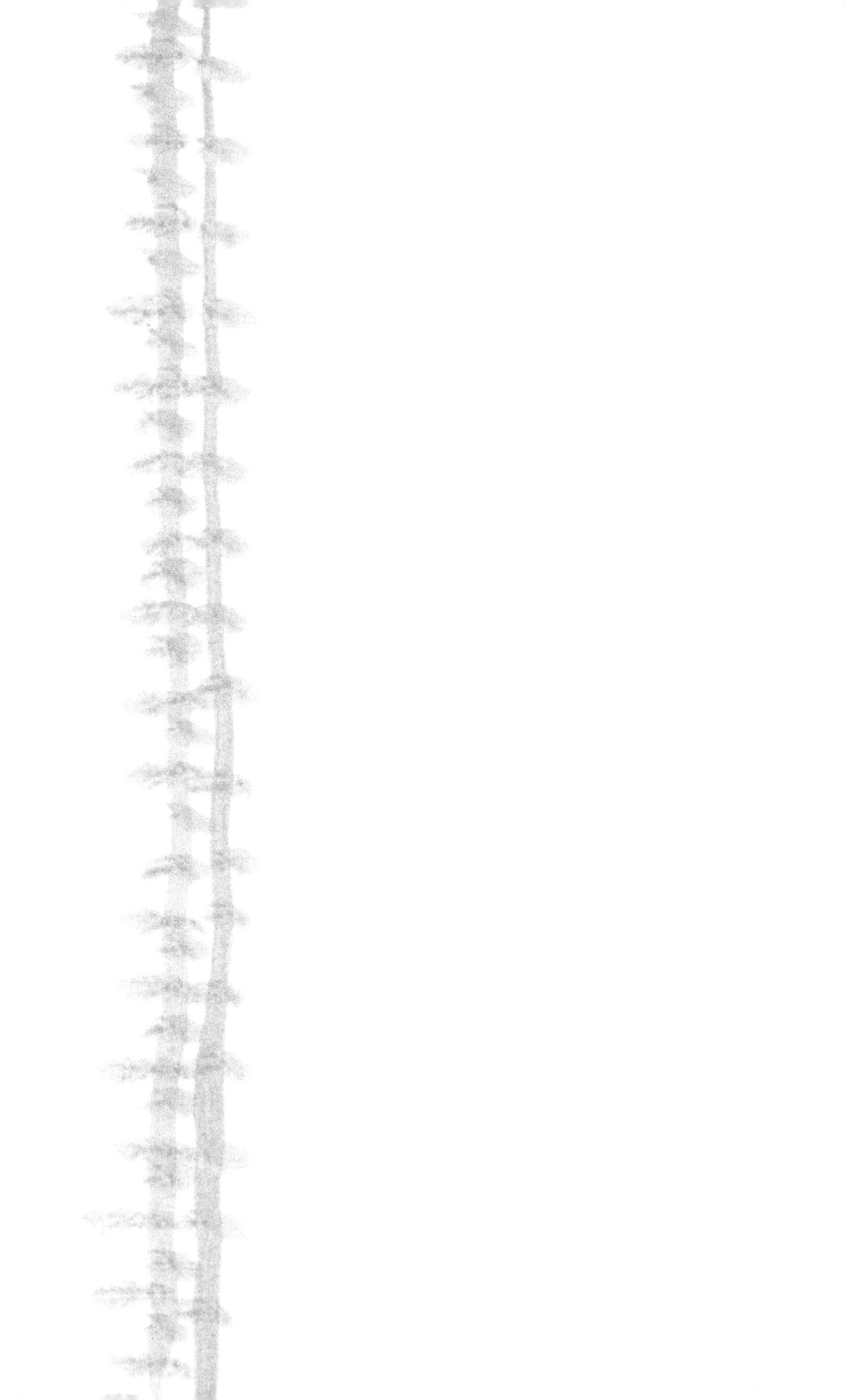

ISAO YOSHINO'S PROFESSIONAL TIMELINE

EMPLOYMENT

2014 - Present	Nagoya Gakuin University, Lecturer	Nagoya, Japan
2012 - 2014	Nagoya Gakuin University, Professor	Nagoya, Japan
2007 - 2011	Aichi Gakusen University, Lecturer	Nagoya, Japan
2004 - 2006	ECOTS Consulting, External Business Consultant (Fuel Cell Project)	Playa del Rey, CA, USA
January 2004	Retirement from Toyota Motor Corporation	
2002 - 2004	Toyota Motor Sales, USA: Fuel Cell Project	Torrance, CA, USA
1997 - 2002	Toyota Motor Sales, USA: Marine Division (Vice President)	Torrance, CA, and Orlando, FL, USA
1993 - 1996	Toyota Motor Corporation: Marine Department	Toyota City, Japan
1992	Toyota Motor Corporation: Human Resources Department	Nagoya, Japan
1987 - 1991	Toyota Motor Corporation: San Francisco Liaison Office	San Francisco, CA, USA

1982 - 1986	Toyota Motor Corporation: International Training Department	Toyota City, Japan
1977 - 1981	Toyota Motor Corporation: Corporate Planning Department	Toyota City, Japan
1972 - 1976	Toyota Motor Corporation: Research Department	Tokyo, Japan
1969 - 1971	Toyota Motor Corporation: Production Control Department	Toyota City, Japan
1966 - 1969	Toyota Motor Corporation: Export Department	Toyota City, Japan

EDUCATION

1962 - 1966	Osaka University of Foreign Studies (Major: Spanish)	Osaka, Japan

Isao Yoshino in his office, Nagoya Gakuin University, Japan, 2017

HISTORICAL NOTE

Yoshino's experiences at Toyota were at a time and place where most people in the workforce — and particularly in leadership roles — were men. This was especially true in Japan, and was still predominantly the case in the United States in the 1960s through 1990s at Toyota, when most of the stories you will read took place. As such, the pronoun "he" is used most often in this book.

Additionally, at Toyota during Yoshino's tenure, it was common to refer to direct reports as "subordinates." Yoshino does not use this term to be taken negatively; it is just the common term from his time at Toyota.

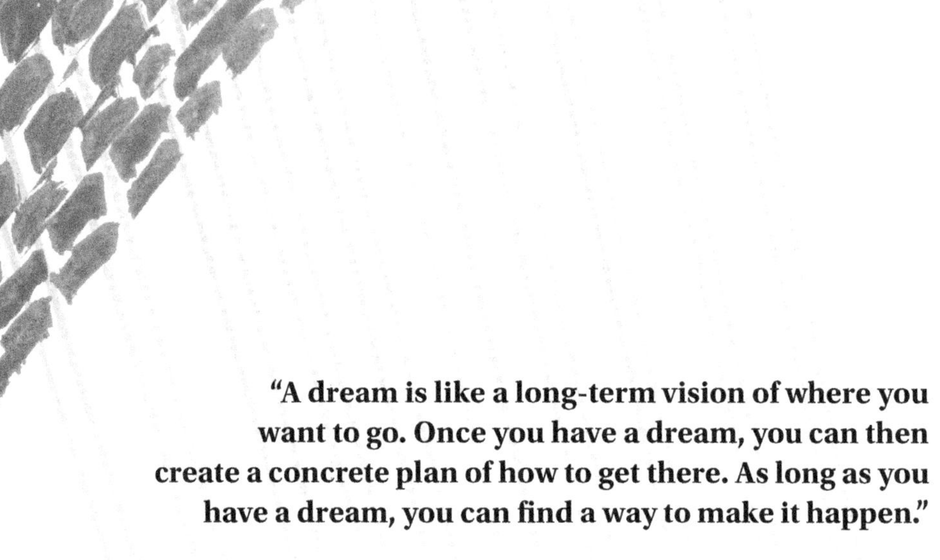

"A dream is like a long-term vision of where you want to go. Once you have a dream, you can then create a concrete plan of how to get there. As long as you have a dream, you can find a way to make it happen."

– Isao Yoshino

PART I

WARP THREAD STORIES: PURPOSE SHAPES US

Early in my friendship with Isao Yoshino, I was fascinated to learn that he had a clear sense of his life purpose from a young age. He has remained true to that purpose — never wavering and never giving up. As a young boy, Yoshino identified in himself a strong desire to broaden his perspective beyond the small country town in which he grew up and to have experiences outside of Japan. These warp threads of his life fabric have been the consistent force that guided and shaped most of the decisions he would make, personally and professionally.

In this portion of the book, you will follow Yoshino on his journey along these warp threads — the foundation of his life fabric on which he wove his lessons of learning and leading that you will discover in Part II.

- **First, a Dream**
- **A Clear Goal — and a Career — Takes Shape**
- **Patience and Persistence**

FALL DOWN SEVEN TIMES, GET UP EIGHT

There is a Japanese proverb:
"Fall down seven times, get up eight" ("*Nana korobi ya oki*").

While we are sure to face failure along the way, we must continue to get up and keep trying until we achieve our goal. It may take a long time, but if we are patient, resilient, and persistent — and if we keep trying — ultimately, we will get there.

Don't Give Up! *Ganbatte*!

There is a related Japanese saying that means "Don't give up." Coming from the verb *ganbaru* (頑張る), this concept represents the tenacity required to keep working toward a goal until it is achieved. The command form of the word, "*ganbatte,*" is used often in daily language to encourage others to "do your best" or "keep going" at work, athletic events, or exams. It is about trying hard and doing our best, of sticking with it, even if we don't always win. Through our spirit of *ganbaru,* we can continue to get up when we fall down. We can keep trying.

Daruma Dolls

In Japan, Daruma dolls represent both the importance of having a goal and the spirit of tenacity and perseverance needed to achieve it. Daruma dolls are hollow, lightweight figures of papier-mâché, made in various sizes, modeled after Bodhidarma, the founder of Zen Buddhism. The dolls are intended to be a visual representation of a goal — and a reminder of the perseverance needed to achieve it. Once you decide upon and set your goal, you fill in the left eye of the Daruma. The doll is weighted at the bottom so that when it is knocked over, it rights itself to its standing position: "Fall down seven times, get up eight!"

When you ultimately achieve your goal, you can fill in the right eye of the Daruma.

Ganbatte!

"Having that dream — like the North Star — in the corner of your mind is so important. Even if you don't take it out that often, it will guide you."

– *Isao Yoshino*

FIRST, A DREAM

DISCOVERING A DREAM

Born in 1944 in the rural countryside of Japan near where Toyota Motor Corporation was founded, Yoshino grew up in the years following Japan's defeat in World War II. It was a time of intense national focus on rebuilding and revitalizing the country, when Japan was relatively homogeneous. Few foreigners lived in the regions outside the major cities, and it was uncommon for Japanese natives to have traveled outside of the country. Yoshino did not have any experiences beyond his small town.

Yoshino's first interaction with anyone from outside of Japan occurred in the early 1950s, when he was about eight years old, and it set the trajectory of his life. He vividly recounts the moment that inspired his warp threads:

> *When I was a small boy, an American soldier came to my home to ask for directions. He was much taller than my father, even when he stood on a lower step leading to our door. I saw him smiling, talking nicely and asking questions politely, which was so surprising to me. I liked his attitude.*
>
> *That experience had a big impact on my life. Starting then, it was my dream to go to America someday and to experience cultures beyond Japan. Even as a boy, I started to think about what action plans I needed to take to go to America. I realized that if I wanted to go to the*

U.S. and be able to talk with people, I first needed to learn the language. Going to America became a dream — and my goal.

A STEP TOWARD THE KNOWN AND A FIRST GLIMPSE OF THE DISCOVERED

Young Yoshino's dream was now firmly anchored in his mind and, while he didn't know how he would achieve this seemingly faraway goal, he knew that the first step would be to learn English. Yoshino started studying English in middle school "just by the textbook," and, once a week, in the evening at *juku* or "cram school."

***Juku* Cram Schools** are private fee-based schools that offer supplementary classes and private tutoring for students. They typically operate in the evenings and on weekends to help students prepare for special secondary schools and for university entrance exams. *Juku* are common throughout Japan and, today, most Japanese secondary school students enroll in some form of cram school.

In the 1950s and '60s, in the rural countryside of Japan, it was a rarity to have access to native-English speakers or to encounter Japanese people with direct experience with the United States. Yet, Yoshino was fortunate to encounter three such teachers who furthered his English abilities — and intensified his passion for American culture. Yoshino's regular public school hired a young American teacher who spent time in his class several times a week and a native Japanese teacher who had lived in the United States for a year. Additionally, Yoshino's community had an English language *juku*.

While all three teachers helped him learn English, the most impactful of these three experiences was Yoshino's *juku*. In looking backward, Yoshino now sees that it was the very beginning of the development of his horizontal weft threads that he would incorporate into his life fabric — those moments of discovery that would strengthen and color his purpose.

The *juku* school in his neighborhood was run by a teacher named Mrs. Nagae, a divorcee (which was not common at that time) who had two daughters about the same age as Yoshino. Unlike most teachers who had learned English from other Japanese native speakers, she was different. She had previously worked at the U.S. military base, where she developed strong English pronunciation skills and had become "knee deep" in American culture.

In contrast to how English was taught at his regular school, where reading and grammar were the primary focus, his *juku* teacher concentrated on verbal communication. Mrs. Nagae spent time with her students to develop the correct pronunciation of the English "r" and "l" sounds (which sound the same to native Japanese speakers) by having them read sentences out loud and by having them talk with her in English.

Additionally, she exposed her students to a different way of thinking, which further intensified Yoshino's determination to find a way to move to the United States. Yoshino recounts:

> *Besides teaching us how to speak and write English, Nagae-sensei would also explain to us how American people think and talk. It was refreshing and new to me to discover a different culture and way of thinking. It was my first extended encounter with someone who really knew American people, which was very rare at the time in Japan.*

Yoshino's *juku* teacher helped bring him one step closer to his firmly established goal of having international experiences, and she also helped him start to discover the weft threads of his life: supporting the development of other people. Yoshino reflects how he was inspired by the way this teacher supported *his* development:

> *Everything Nagae-sensei taught us — and the way that she taught us — was totally new! I was so impressed with her — she was outspoken, positive, and confident, and she really cared about me as a student.*
>
> *I decided that I would always sit right in front of her and, even though there was no seat assignment, the other students knew that the front seat was mine. Even when I was late, the seat in front was always there for me.*
>
> *I studied every day and my English proficiency got better and better. It was a good starting point. I really appreciate my* juku *teacher who always tried to make me feel happy and praised me for the good work. Because*

> *of her support, I became comfortable in both writing and speaking American English.*

A VISION TAKES SHAPE OVER THE RADIO WAVES

While he was formally studying the English language, Yoshino's passion for American culture and the English language was intensified by access to American radio stations. The American military retained a strong presence in Japan following the end of World War II and had a radio broadcast — aimed at the Americans stationed overseas — called the "Far East Network" (FEN). Yoshino discovered the radio station and began a ritual of secretly listening to it every night.

When the U.S. government closed the base near Nagoya that was broadcasting FEN, Yoshino tracked down a shortwave radio so he could listen to other broadcasts from military bases further away. Late at night, every night, Yoshino would secretly run the wire of his shortwave radio into the hallway to plug it into the outlet outside his room. He'd stretch the cord under his door, and put in a single earphone so that he could surreptitiously listen to native American speakers on the FEN station. He discovered American pop music of the late 1950s and early 1960s, and he loved the talk of the disc jockeys. For teenage Yoshino, those late-night sessions were just like being in the United States!

MOVING TOWARD THE KNOWN AND DISCOVERING RICHER PURPOSE

Yoshino considers the convergence of his English teachers and access to the American military radio during his teen years as the catalyst that heightened his determination to move along his warp threads and find a way to relocate to the United States. Yoshino reflects on his teen years:

> *These experiences really exposed me to a new world. American culture was so different from that of local Japanese people, and I realized that this type of culture was what I wanted.*

FOLLOWING A PURPOSE, EXPANDING A DREAM

"Following my North Star has always been important to me."

– Isao Yoshino

As Yoshino progressed from high school to university, he continued to move steadily along his path, intent upon making his dream a reality. His desire to broaden his perspective, initially focused on the United States, expanded to a wider vision of experiencing many cultures around the world. With that expanded dream in mind, he chose to attend the Osaka University of Foreign Studies. When asked how he made a choice about his university experience, Yoshino reflects:

> *I was fascinated to go out and see other parts of the world, so I chose a foreign language school. I thought it might open up the doors for me to other foreign countries, not just the United States.*
>
> *People would laugh at me and ask, "You aren't just dreaming of going to Tokyo?" At that time, even going to Tokyo for one or two days was a dream for a country boy like myself. But I knew that I wanted to go overseas. I had a dream, and knew that I could make it happen wherever and whatever I studied.*

Although his older brother, Kazuhiko, had gone to Tokyo for college, Yoshino's family could not afford to send two children to private university. As the second son, Yoshino instead decided to attend a public university in Osaka, as it was less expensive and he didn't want to place further financial burden on his family.

By now, Yoshino's dream had expanded beyond the United States. He wanted to see and experience the world:

> *While living in the United States was the first goal that I wanted to go after, I had become fairly proficient in English, and exploring other foreign countries was now part of my bigger dream. I thought that no matter the language, knowing more languages would open the door for me to the world. I just wanted to go somewhere and see the other side of the world.*

Yoshino wanted a new challenge to broaden his world perspective: he decided to major in Spanish.

GROWING HIS AMERICAN "COUNTRY" ROOTS

And all the while Yoshino was gaining proficiency in Spanish, he did not lose sight of his original American dream. While living in Osaka for university in the mid-1960s, he discovered bluegrass music and decided to learn how to play the banjo! Yoshino recalls discovering his new musical passion:

> *In Osaka, I found out that bluegrass music (with guitar, flat mandolin, 5-string banjo, fiddle, and a bass guitar) instead of country music (with electric guitar, fiddle, and steel guitar) was popular in that area. Country was more popular in Tokyo, but Osaka people are more down-to-earth and like the "country flavor" of bluegrass.*
>
> *I found out about a radio program called "Midnight Jamboree," which played bluegrass music from midnight to 2:00 a.m. I didn't know until then that this genre existed. I was so struck by its simple and lonesome sound. I decided to learn bluegrass-style banjo playing.*

“A dream can be far-off, a blurry vision, or some kind of vague idea, but if you think of it often, then you can get a more concrete image. It becomes a clearer goal.”

– Isao Yoshino

A CLEAR GOAL — AND A CAREER — TAKES SHAPE

As Yoshino started his career at Toyota (the same year he graduated from university), he continued his steadfast pursuit — step by step — of fulfilling his known purpose of having a life with a broader perspective. During this time, Yoshino continued to discover his other purpose: a passion for helping people develop and grow.

While you will read detailed stories about Yoshino's four decades of learning and leading at Toyota in Part II, in this chapter you will see how his determination to achieve his initial dream (i.e., moving to the United States) crystallized into a concrete goal for an overseas assignment with Toyota. In turn, this goal shaped his life and provided the foundation on which he learned to lead and led to learn throughout his career at Toyota.

JOINING TOYOTA – A BET ON A DREAM

"I knew I wanted to work in the United States, but it seemed like a far-away goal. I had a hope someday Toyota would deal with other countries, and that I would get to be involved with that type of job overseas."

– Isao Yoshino

Following his university graduation in 1966, Yoshino had to choose what company he was going to join. This was a significant life decision because, as was typical in Japan at that time and is still mostly the case today, it would most likely be a decision for life. Ultimately, Yoshino joined Toyota Motor Corporation for two primary reasons.

First, he liked the people and its culture. Toyota headquarters was located near to where he grew up, in the Mikawa region outside of Nagoya, and its culture felt familiar to him. Yoshino liked what he heard about the culture at Toyota that was, in his words, founded by "country boys" like himself, rather than "city slickers" like many other automobile manufacturers, such as Nissan or Honda, located closer to major cities.

Second, and perhaps more important to young Yoshino (whose determination to have international experiences was strong), he thought there would be a good chance that he would have an opportunity for an international assignment in the future at Toyota. Joining Toyota was a good bet that his dream could one day come true. Yoshino recalls how the "dream in the corner of his mind" influenced his decision to join Toyota and crystallized into a goal of an international assignment:

> *The year I joined, in 1966, the Toyota Corolla was introduced to the market. It really was the dawn of the motorization of Japan. People started buying small-sized cars, such as the Corolla. I joined at a very good time, as it looked like there would be future expansion, including into overseas markets. The timing was great and I felt so lucky. I was so excited about being part of Toyota!*
>
> *At that time, Brazil was the only country in which Toyota was manufacturing cars outside of Japan. However, I had a hope that maybe someday Toyota would deal with other countries. I hoped that I would get to be involved in that type of job overseas.*
>
> *It took a long time, but 20 years later, it finally came true.*

Joining Toyota was a fortuitous choice for Yoshino. Driven by his known purpose and American dream (his warp threads), this decision shaped the entire fabric of his life in ways he never could have anticipated. In the coming years, he'd begin to weave the weft threads of people development

— a skill-set, talent, and mindset he learned from his superiors and peers at Toyota and ultimately taught others along the way.

SET A GOAL, MAKE A STEP-BY-STEP PLAN, AND REMAIN PERSISTENT

"I learned that if you have a dream, first you must set a clear goal to attain it. Then you can develop an action plan. If you start with thinking about an action plan without a clear goal or target, then you just start taking actions but they might not get you there. You may end up doing many things, but they might not really help you get to your dream."

– Isao Yoshino

Joining Toyota in 1966 was the first big step toward Yoshino's dream. But it would take 20 more years for Yoshino to achieve his goal of moving overseas with Toyota.

How did Yoshino remain focused and persistent even when experiencing setbacks? How was he able to define and take the steps that would enable it to happen, without the specific knowledge of how or when?

His warp threads — his strong desire, spirit, and perseverance — helped him stay the course. Like the Japanese saying, "Fall down seven times, get up eight," he continued to get back up even when he failed along the way because his determination to achieve his dream was strong. He was committed to where he was headed — and he had a plan.

Even though Yoshino had a good knowledge of both English and Spanish by the time he joined Toyota, he quickly realized that he would need to develop even more advanced English skills in order to make him a logical choice for an overseas assignment. His plan: he would position himself to be a prime candidate for an international assignment and set some interim targets for himself along the way.

Target #1: Advance English Proficiency Through Formal Certification

"I was very persistent. It was my target to get toward my goal. It was how I would achieve my dream."

- Isao Yoshino

The same year that he joined Toyota, Yoshino set a new target: pass the National English Proficiency Exam. Many companies, including Toyota, had started to use this test as their formal standard for English proficiency for employees to quality for overseas assignments. The exam tested for English writing, listening comprehension, and speaking. The challenge: it was only offered once per year.

Yoshino diligently applied himself to his studies to remember and strengthen his English after his four-year university immersion in Spanish, just like he did in his secondary school and *juku* days. In the evenings after work, Yoshino would pore over his textbooks and practice writing and reading to help him prepare for the exam.

Plus, as it turns out, a little friendly competition never hurts! Yoshino was not the only one studying for the exam. Yoshino's boss, who was also trying to pass the exam, issued a challenge to see who could pass it first. Yoshino recalls this competition:

> *My direct boss, an assistant manager of the Export Department at Toyota, was also studying English and wanted to pass the First Grade of the English Proficiency Test. He had tried to pass the test several times before, but unfortunately never succeeded. So, when I joined Toyota, he proposed that we — he, another newly hired subordinate who also knew English, and I — compete with each other to see who would pass the exam first.*

The three men would occasionally get together at work for informal study groups and to practice spoken English. Despite Yoshino's dedication and passion for his studies, and his desire to win the competition, Yoshino failed the test three times.

Yoshino ultimately won the competition — by being the first to pass the exam on the fourth try! Just like the proverb, Yoshino literally had to fall down many times, but he kept getting up and finally succeeded. He recalls:

> *By then, I was working in Toyota's Tokyo Office and my ex-boss was also working in the same office in Tokyo. I won the competition with him and he was a bit frustrated to be beaten by his ex-subordinate! Having some rivals was a big driving force to keep trying for many years.*

A little competition, comradeship, and pursuit of a dream helped him stay persistent. His long-established warp threads did not break under pressure.

Target #2: Learn "Business" English

"Because I had a clear target, I could stay committed."

- Isao Yoshino

When his boss proposed the National Exam competition, Yoshino also realized that he needed to learn "business English" or "*Shogyo Eigo.*" He discovered that business English differed from the conventional English language he had been taught and was studying, and would be important to know if he wanted an international assignment with Toyota:

> *At that time, there was no internet. The only way we could learn something new was at the library or the bookstore. One day, I was at the bookstore and I saw some books about shipping and international trading that included* Shogyo Eigo *business transactional terms for the industry. I thought to myself, "In the future, I might need this and it doesn't hurt to start learning this now."*

He set another concurrent target for himself: become fluent in business English.

In pursuit of this target, Yoshino would buy international shipping-focused magazines that used *Shogyo Eigo* as a way to expose himself to these new terms. One week, while browsing through the advertisements in a magazine, Yoshino learned that there was an informal group of international trading company workers that met in Tokyo each weekend to study and practice business English together. Every Saturday afternoon, the group would get together in Tokyo to review each other's written documents in English.

Yoshino wanted to join the group, but didn't know how it could happen practically. At that time, in the late-1960s, the newly developed Shinkansen, or bullet train, could get from Nagoya to Tokyo in three hours — a journey that now takes 90 minutes — but a one-way ticket cost roughly 10% of a new university graduate's weekly salary. Undeterred, Yoshino sent a letter to one of the leaders of the Tokyo-based group saying: *"I am in Toyota City and can only get to Tokyo about once every three months. How can I join you?"*

A group member wrote back to Yoshino proposing that he participate remotely by doing the self-assigned weekly homework and sending it by mail to the group each week. Yoshino was excited to be included and was inspired by the study group participants' shared commitment to help each other learn:

> *I was so surprised! They were so nice and they were helping each other. Although I was only able to join them in person every few months because it was so costly, I learned so much from those trading company people because they practiced their business English every day at work.*

Yoshino was a core member of the group for nearly three years, diligently doing his homework and making sure it got into the mail by Thursday afternoon so that it would arrive to the group before their Saturday afternoon meetings.

So, at the same time that he was taking, failing, and retaking the National Exam, Yoshino dedicated additional time to learning business-style English. Taking on this additional target meant that most of Yoshino's free time in the evenings was spent studying English. He was fulfilling his desire to broaden his world view by working with this group — and his determination to get an international assignment was strong.

Yoshino's dedication to his own learning and development, which started in his grade-school and *juku* days, was demonstrated in his achievement in his study group:

> *We gave ourselves nicknames instead of using our real names. My nickname was KE10 ("Kay Eee Ten"), which was the first Corolla's model*

code. I actually bought a Corolla to commute to my office. Every time that I sent in my assignments and we graded our homework, I was always pleased to see "KE10" toward the top of the list.

Every time one of the other group members happened to be in the Nagoya area, Yoshino would make plans to get together for a short time, even if it was just an hour or two. No matter the length of time, it was another opportunity for both to learn more about business English and to have a chance to practice speaking.

Yoshino's warp threads remained strong as he advanced in his plan to one day live and work in the United States. At the same time, his emerging passion for learning and development was augmented by his engagement with this peer group whose purpose was to support each other's learning and development, as well as his boss's encouragement to pass the National English Proficiency Exam:

When I look back and wonder why I could focus on those English studies so much, I found out that I became attracted to the eagerness and dedication to learn English, demonstrated by my Tokyo friends and my direct boss. I was so lucky to have run into those people at that early stage of my career.

Target #3: Learn More by Sharing Knowledge with Others

"When I look back, I realize that I always tried to do something new and different. I've always wanted to share knowledge and expand my network."

- *Isao Yoshino*

During his early years at Toyota, while he was studying for the National English Proficiency Exam and engaged with his business English study group, Yoshino also began to create unique ways to help other people learn the skills they needed to realize their own dreams and fulfill their life's purpose.

While still in his mid-20s, Yoshino received his second job assignment at Toyota, which was in the Motomachi Plant. Most of the employees had only a high school diploma and had received limited English training while in school. Most had likely not had access to or attended cram school like the university-bound Yoshino. On his nearly daily visits to the shop floor, Yoshino discovered that many of the Motomachi employees wanted to learn English, but they didn't have a way.

Yoshino decided to establish an informal study group, which he called the "Motomachi English Study Group." It would meet once per month, with Yoshino as the teacher and facilitator. Yoshino sent a flyer to the production engineers and others in the Motomachi plant, advertising that he wanted to share his English knowledge and invited anyone who wanted to join him.

The study group helped Yoshino begin to entwine his warp and his weft threads together. Not only would this group help develop the Motomachi plant workers, but it would provide him with ongoing practice in speaking — and now teaching — English. When reflecting on why he established the Motomachi English Study Group, Yoshino says that:

> *I was hoping that I would have a chance to be more involved with English and the United States in the future. And it helped me create informal relationships with the engineers who I would not have otherwise met at that point in my career.*
>
> *I learned that I wanted to share and expand my network. I didn't have a clear idea of my purpose for developing people at that time, but I thought that knowing and helping many people might be good.*

The group began in 1969, three years after Yoshino joined Toyota, and initially consisted of about 10 Motomachi plant workers, all many years older than Yoshino. Yoshino charged them ¥100 (less than $1.00) for each session to cover expenses for photocopying materials.

For each monthly session, Yoshino would prepare a simple topic that would be easy for the plant workers to understand. For example, for one lesson, he used pages out of a book about Volkswagen's marketing materials, which was a collection of advertisements that had images and captions with both English and Japanese translations.

Through this experience, Yoshino learned how to prepare training documents and instructional materials, which would play a key part in many of his future roles at Toyota. Yoshino recalls how the program ignited his love for teaching and the joy he got from helping others:

> *A few weeks after the start-up of the session, several college-graduate engineers from the Quality Control Department and the Production Engineering Department joined the group. They heard about my session from the shop floor workers, got interested in it, and decided to join us. It made me feel that I was making a small contribution to help people to grow.*

Looking backward, Yoshino now sees that the Motomachi Study Group was the beginning of combining his known purpose of having a broader world view — through learning other languages and living abroad — with fulfilling his discovered purpose of helping other people develop themselves. Through his Motomachi English Study Group, Yoshino was interweaving his horizontal threads of purpose along his vertical warp threads to create a rich pattern in his life fabric.

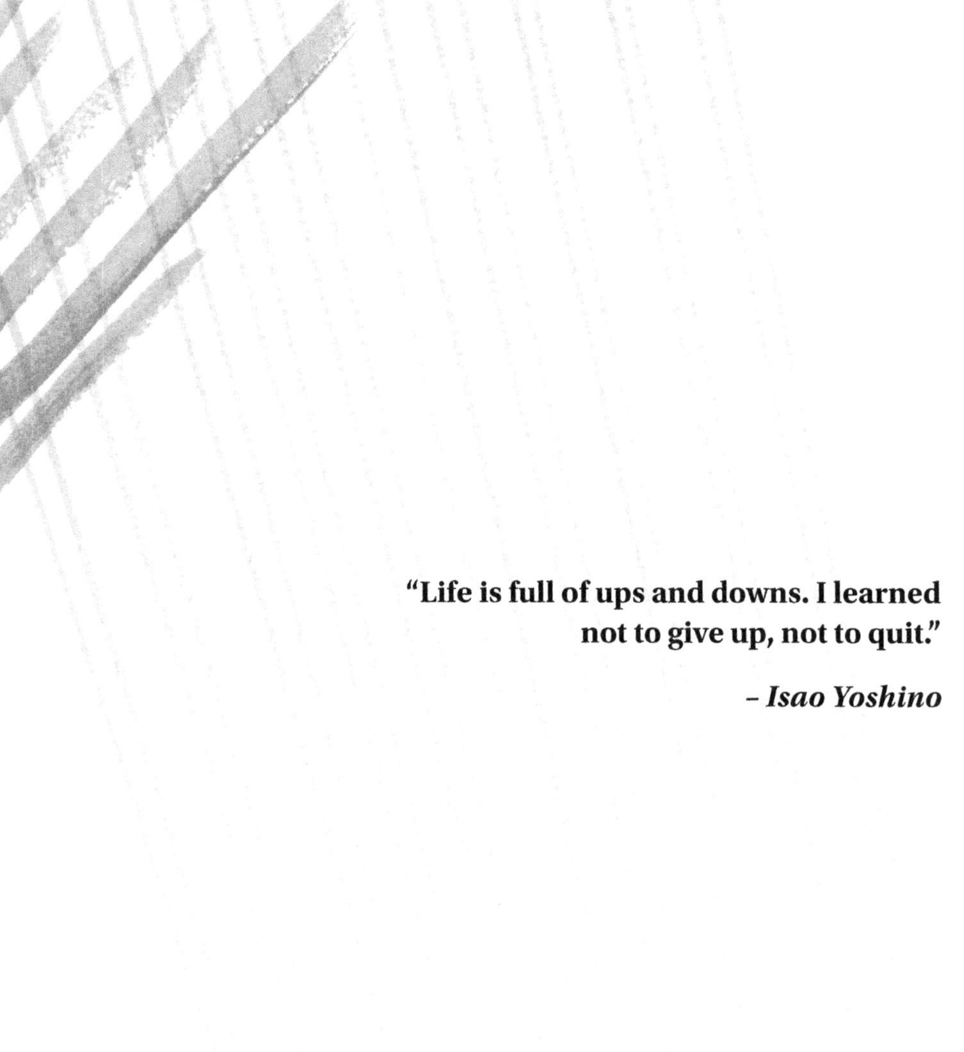

“Life is full of ups and downs. I learned not to give up, not to quit.”

– Isao Yoshino

PATIENCE AND PERSISTENCE

Fast forward a decade.

During the 1970s, Yoshino got married and had three daughters, all the while patiently holding onto his American dream while he was learning to lead in various assignments in Toyota City and Tokyo (which you will learn about in Part II).

Finally, in the early 1980s, Yoshino learned that Toyota was expanding internationally. It seemed that the bet he made in 1966 (when joining Toyota and hoping the company would eventually expand globally) was finally happening — bringing him a giant step closer to achieving his dream. In 1982, Toyota and General Motors (GM) agreed to a joint venture called New United Motor Manufacturing, Inc. (NUMMI), to be based in California. The former GM shop floor leaders would need to be taught Toyota's way of managing. Due to the English proficiency that he had worked so many years to develop, Yoshino was assigned to lead the training program for the American frontline leaders who were sent to Japan for three-week training rotations.

Although Yoshino didn't yet fully realize his dream of *living* in the United States during the NUMMI training program assignment, he continued along his warp threads and broadened his global perspective. He got to intimately interact with hundreds of American workers during each three-week rotation to Toyota City in Japan. He also hired John Shook (the author of this book's foreword) — the first non-Japanese employee at Toyota Motor Corporation in Japan — from whom he learned more about the American mindset and culture.

While leading the NUMMI training program, Yoshino redoubled his personal studies to deepen his knowledge of American language and culture. He revisited his shortwave radio obsession from his youth. He asked one of his staff members to record the American radio news that was broadcast during his usual working hours onto a cassette tape. Yoshino would listen to the news presenter — whose name, Robert Jefferson, is ingrained in his memory — every day during his 40-minute commute to and from work:

> *I would put the tape in the car and listen to it over and over again. It was difficult to understand at first because they talked so fast but, after about three or four months, I could understand most of it. It was a continuous effort to get better. There is always a learning curve and you have to be patient. I stuck with it because of my dream.*

"It was a continuous effort to get better. There is always a learning curve and you have to be patient."

Even though he had yet to leave Japan, being a multilingual international business professional and a global citizen was already part of his identity. And he waited patiently — continuing to position himself as a prime candidate — to achieve his goal of an overseas assignment.

ANOTHER STEP FORWARD (AND BACKWARD)

For Yoshino, realizing his dream of living and working in the United States was achieved one step at a time, with patience and persistence, and often the path included setbacks. One day, after having led the Japan-based NUMMI training for nearly two years, Yoshino was informally told by a colleague working out of Toyota's office in Los Angeles that he could be the next in line for a transfer to the same office. Yoshino was ecstatic!

However, even though everyone had informally agreed on the transfer, and the papers were nearly signed to make it official, Toyota leadership changed their minds. Suddenly, Yoshino was told that he would not be moving to the United States. Senior management had decided that they needed someone with Yoshino's English language proficiency and training skills for another important assignment: to set up the training programs for the opening of two new Toyota-run plants in North America — one in Kentucky, United States, and one in Ontario, Canada.

Instead of moving to the United States, Yoshino would remain based in Japan. Yoshino was initially devastated that the Los Angeles transfer did not happen. He recalls:

> *My dream of going to the United States was almost realized! And then I was told I had a different assignment. I was so shocked when my desired assignment didn't come through.*

Although an initial disappointment, this short new assignment gave Yoshino the opportunity to broaden his perspective and finally to see other countries. He traveled frequently during this period — six times in one year — to North America to lay the foundation for the opening of these two plants. At last, he was able to directly experience American and Canadian cultures. While not quite there — *living* in the United States — Yoshino was getting closer to his goal.

A GOAL, MORE THAN 20 YEARS IN THE MAKING, FINALLY ACHIEVED

Finally, at the end of 1986, Yoshino's long-held dream — and 20-year goal — finally came true when he received a three-year assignment to manage the new Toyota office in the San Francisco Bay Area. Yoshino was thrilled!

He was also surprised at the urgency of his transfer. Instead of the typical six-month notice given for overseas assignments, he was given less than three weeks to prepare for and make the move. While the short notice was a challenge for Yoshino (because by now he had a wife and three elementary and middle-school aged children), it didn't matter because his dream of an overseas assignment was finally going to come true! Yoshino left for California, and his family followed several months later.

Yoshino would soon learn that, in reality, dreams are not always what we envision them to be, but that our experience is what we make of it. Yoshino often remarks — to me and to others — that *"Life is full of ups and downs."* This proved to be acutely true when he finally moved to the United States and reality did not live up to his dream. Ultimately, he found a way to shift his mindset and create an experience that he now considers the most important assignment of his entire career. When asked to extend that assignment by a year, he accepted.

WARP THREADS REMAIN STRONG

After his four-year assignment in the United States concluded, Yoshino and his family returned to Japan. Within a year, he realized that he was not content living in Japan and working primarily on domestic projects. He longed for more international experiences; his dream was not over. He set new goals for how to return to the United States. His warp threads were as taut as ever, just further expanded and extended, allowing for more room to weave his growing fabric of purpose of integrating broader world perspectives with helping others develop.

Yoshino found a way to get back to the United States, as you will discover in Part II, where he ultimately lived for another decade. In this time, he learned even more about the importance of perseverance, and how failure can be the source of rich learning.

Only after retiring from Toyota did Yoshino finally return to Japan to live full-time in 2007, though his desire for international experiences continues to be the strong warp threads in his life. Today, he continues to speak and consult around the world.

NEVER WAVER

At a young age, Yoshino had a dream, which became the vertical warp threads of his life. He established goals and moved toward them step by step, through setbacks and successes, until he finally achieved each one. And it was his progress toward this dream — especially his choice to join Toyota Motor Corporation — that allowed him to discover his horizontal weft threads of purpose — of developing other people and himself. The lesson for all of us is that persistence, patience, and focus can lead us to our long-held dreams and color our lives with unexpected meaning along the way.

Persistence, patience, and focus can lead us to our long-held dreams and color our lives with unexpected meaning along the way.

Now that we have explored the concepts of warp threads — of pursuing a known purpose, setting goals and targets, and the persistence and patience it takes to keep getting back up when encountering setbacks and challenges, and how they apply to Yoshino's life — let's further explore the stories that make up the weft threads of his life fabric: What it means to be a people-centered leader and support others by learning to lead and leading to learn.

Let's continue!

PRACTICING *HANSEI:* REFLECTION QUESTIONS

- What is your known purpose or dream?
- Even if your purpose is not clear, what is something that guides you or is personally important?
- How could you draw your purpose or dream? What words can you use to describe it?
- What goals and targets have you set along the way?
- What setbacks have you experienced?
- How have you gotten back up when you have "fallen down"?
- What have you learned?

"I believe the concept of 'respect' has been passed from one generation to the next at Toyota. From the top-ranking leaders — like Mr. Toyoda and Mr. Cho — to a manager like me, every leader at Toyota puts a high priority on 'respect' to the people around us.

If I am asked what made Toyota one of the top-ranking automakers in the world, I would say, 'We make people while we make cars. It's our people who make cars, not machines. That is respect.'"

– *Isao Yoshino*

PART II

WEFT THREAD STORIES: DISCOVERY DEFINES US

As I came to know Mr. Yoshino more closely, our conversations went deeper into his discovered purpose of developing people. We uncovered rich memories from early in his career — where he was first led (and learned) — and later assignments in his career — in which *he* led (with a focus on helping *others* learn).

The stories that you will read here in Part II follow Yoshino's chronological journey of learning and leading over the course of his nearly 40 years at Toyota. These "weft thread" stories highlight how Yoshino started to incorporate a purpose for developing people and himself into his life fabric, as he steadfastly — and patiently — traversed his warp threads to pursue his strong inner desire to have broader international experiences. They are stories about developing people (and himself) that he picked up by learning, by teaching, by failing, by succeeding, and — perhaps most importantly — by caring deeply.

While these too are personal stories, Yoshino's experiences in Part II recount an insider's knowledge of Toyota's history and culture — about how an organization learned and led. These recollections and insights highlight the core leadership lessons Yoshino learned then — and more deeply has re-learned now — about what it means to be a people-centered leader and create a culture of learning.

LEARNING AND LEADING AT TOYOTA: "WE MAKE PEOPLE"

There is a saying at Toyota: "*monozukuri wa hitozukuri*," which means "we make things through making people." This fundamental leadership principle at Toyota means that supporting others to learn and grow — helping people learn how to think more deeply to solve problems and achieve their goals — is a vital effort in service of making a good product. This principle of people-centered leadership is illustrated by the mindset, behaviors, and experiences that you will discover in Yoshino's stories, which follow.

This part of the book is separated into three chapters, each following roughly one-third of the chronology of Yoshino's career of learning and leading at Toyota. Here's what to expect in the pages ahead:

LEARNING TO LEAD – FOUNDATIONAL LEADERSHIP LESSONS

This chapter is presented as a series of eight vignettes recalling Yoshino's memories of the first 15 years of his career. These stories of how Yoshino learned (and was taught) to be a people-centered leader — and the supplementary information offered throughout — highlight key lessons and leadership skills for readers.

LEADING TO LEARN – HELPING OTHERS TO DEVELOP

This chapter is presented chronologically in four case studies that describe how Yoshino subsequently taught others these leadership skills, while continuing to develop himself. Each case study highlights Yoshino's experiences during seminal points of time in Toyota's history in the late 1970s, 1980s, and into the 1990s, as the company solidified its people-centered culture and expanded its operations to other countries. Each period in Yoshino's career presented new opportunities for him to play a significant role in the development of others and in shaping the evolution of Toyota's culture.

REFLECTING ON FAILURE – TOYOTA'S WATER-SKI BOAT BUSINESS

This chapter documents Yoshino's recollections from the final decade of his career from the 1990s through early 2000s, during which he — and Toyota as a company — learned important lessons about pursuing new ventures and managing people across cultures. The water-ski boat saga unfolded over many years as Yoshino continued to chase his American dream, had a big idea, and ultimately led a failed business venture. Reflecting on failure, in addition to success, brought Yoshino to discover deep and meaningful lessons about leadership and learning.

LEARNING TO LEAD – FOUNDATIONAL LEADERSHIP LESSONS

While Yoshino was moving along his warp threads — steadfastly pursuing his dream of moving to the United States — he was discovering more fully what it means to be a people-centered leader. Yoshino's choice to join Toyota (made, in large part, in the hopes that it would offer him a way to realize his American dream) presented him with many experiences and role models of what leadership should — and should not — look like. As he worked through various roles at the company — sometimes navigating his way through challenging experiences and sometimes having incredible experiences — he was learning to lead. And as he learned, he incorporated these threads into his life fabric.

In this chapter, you'll hear eight stories from the first 15 years of Yoshino's professional career — all of which illustrate moments when he learned key lessons about people-centered leadership. Between and among these lessons, you'll find bonus information, designed to teach you key concepts and fundamentals about the history and culture of both Japan and Toyota.

- **Lesson #1:** Communicate Purpose, Every Day and in Every Way
- **Lesson #2:** Create the Conditions for People to Be Successful (and Take Responsibility When Mistakes Happen)
- **Lesson #3:** Go Out of Your Way to Help Others Learn

- **Lesson #4:** Go to See and Show You Care - Leadership Starts at the Gemba
- **Lesson #5:** Own the Thinking Process, Not the Thinking
- **Lesson #6:** Learn What Not to Be as a Leader
- **Lesson #7:** Be Curious, Always Keep Learning, Ask Questions
- **Lesson #8:** Set the Tone for the Culture You Want

JAPAN'S REBIRTH, TOYOTA'S PATH TO QUALITY, AND THE TOYOTA PRODUCTION SYSTEM

Before we dig deeper into Yoshino's learning journey at Toyota, it's important to have some cultural context about Japan's rebirth after World War II and about the development of Toyota's culture of continuous improvement.

After the end of the War in 1945, Allied forces, led by the United States, occupied Japan and brought drastic changes to the country. Japan was disarmed, its empire essentially dissolved, and its form of government changed from an imperial monarchy to a democracy. During this time, the Japanese economy and education system were also reorganized and rebuilt. By the 1950s, less than a decade after fighting against each other, Japan became a Western ally. American culture rushed into Japan and quickly became part of the Japanese landscape.

In 1950, the Korean War broke out on the Korean Peninsula and the special procurements related to the war stimulated Japan's economy and enabled it to recover quickly from the destruction of WWII. Yoshino recalls that:

> *The export of groceries and light industrial products soared. However, many Japan-made products were easily breaking down due to their low quality. Made-in-Japan products in the overseas market were considered "cheap" and "poor quality." Japan knew*

> *that it had to dramatically improve the quality of its products if it wanted to regain status as a global leader. It looked to both foreigners and Japanese thought leaders for ways to improve.*

In the 1950s, Dr. W. Edwards Deming, an American scholar and operations management consultant considered to be "the father of the third-wave of the industrial revolution,"[1] visited Japan four times to introduce Quality Control concepts to people in Japanese industry. From June to August 1950, Deming trained hundreds of engineers, senior managers, and scholars across Japan on concepts of quality, including the Plan-Do-Check-Adjust (PDCA) cycle. Yoshino recounts that:

> *Top executives from Japanese manufacturers were so impressed with Deming's practical theory that they applied it widely and experienced unheard-of levels of quality and productivity. In the area of Quality Control, the concept of "Quality Circles" started to prevail among Japanese companies, and took hold at Toyota in the early 1960s as it advanced what is now known as the Toyota Production System (TPS).*

Toyota itself was the recipient of the Deming Prize in 1965, the year before Yoshino joined the company.

Improved quality, combined with lower cost, created new international demand for Japanese products, which led to huge economic growth for Japan during the 1960s. The Olympic Games were held in Tokyo in 1964, the Shinkansen high-speed railway network ("bullet train") was built in time for the Olympics, and the Tomei Expressway connecting Tokyo and Nagoya was constructed before the end of the decade. By 1968, just over two decades after the end of WWII, Japan had become the second largest economic country in the world.

It was in this cultural environment — in Japan and at Toyota — that young Yoshino started his career in 1966.

---

1 https://deming.org/deming/deming-the-man

LESSON #1

COMMUNICATE PURPOSE, EVERY DAY AND IN EVERY WAY

Ask yourself: How long is the typical new-employee orientation process at your company? How did you learn about your company's purpose? When and how did you make the connection of that purpose to the purpose of your role?

Most formal orientation programs in Western companies are less than a week — many just one day — and are often led by Human Resources staff with a focus on topics like how to enroll in healthcare benefits or what you need to know about internal company policies. Orientation to the actual job and company culture is mostly ad hoc and dependent on each individual manager. *Purpose* might be mentioned at some point but, realistically, can something as important as an organization's deep, underlying purpose really be understood in one day, by an employee brand new to the company and the culture?

In contrast to what many employees find in Western companies, Toyota took a different approach. At the time Yoshino joined Toyota in 1966, orientation for new university graduates consisted of an intensive four-month comprehensive training program. As Yoshino recalls, it included both a month and a half of classroom training and two and a half months on the manufacturing shop floor — the "gemba."

WHAT IS "GEMBA"?

Gemba is a Japanese word that means "the place where something actually happens." It's a very active and engaging word! Japanese news reporters talk about "going to the gemba" to check on the weather in a specific location and, in detective books, detectives "go to gemba" to investigate the scene of a crime.

Yoshino explains how the word "gemba" is used in Japan:

> *In the police detective dramas on the TV, police bosses often say to their subordinates, "Go back to gemba 100 times. Then you would find what you might have overlooked." In that case, "gemba" actually means the scene of the crime or accident. We are not supposed to take "go to gemba" as just a limited area, but it should be interpreted as a broader meaning.*

Outside of Japan, "gemba" is more commonly known in a business context as "the place where the work is done."

At this point, you may be saying to yourself, "A four-month orientation program with two and a half months of doing actual frontline manufacturing work? Wasn't Mr. Yoshino hired for office work? What's the point of having him learn a manufacturing job for *more than two months*?" Simple: Toyota understood that teaching its culture took an investment of time — and direct experiences — to lay the foundation of understanding for new hires. And that started with teaching the new hires the real purpose of the company and how each of them personally connects to that purpose.

The objective of the shop-floor portion of the orientation was very specific and intentional: start with defining purpose and teach it through direct experience.

The objective of the shop-floor portion of the orientation was very specific and intentional: start with defining purpose and teach it through direct experience.

TOYOTA'S PURPOSE: WE MAKE GOOD PRODUCTS BY MAKING GOOD PEOPLE

Toyota's slogan since 1953, which hangs on banners throughout its plants, is "*Yoi shina, Yoi kangae,*" (よい品 よい考[2]), which translates to "Good Thinking, Good Product."

Even in an industry full of robotic assembly and sophisticated machines for manufacturing, it is the people — and their good thinking — that actually make good products. Yoshino says that Toyota's traditional motto is a constant reminder to all employees that "*It is important always to think about better ways to attain the goal of delivering good products.*"

It was during his orientation that he learned what this really meant — not just from banners hanging from the wall, but through time and direct experience.

We Make Good Products

The first objective of the orientation program that Yoshino completed was to convey to all new university graduates — all going into "back office" roles, such as public relations, human resources, technical development, legal, and purchasing — that their work was in support of the value-creation activities of the company: the production of cars. Yoshino recalls one of the training managers telling his new hire cohort: *"We are manufacturers. Our main responsibility is to manufacture a good product."*

We Develop People

The second, and perhaps more important, objective was to give the new hires exposure to the fundamental culture of the company — that developing people was the most important way to develop good cars. As Yoshino often says, which he experienced from the beginning of his orientation

---

2 Yoshino notes that, from a grammatical point of view, the character 考 should be followed by え. But because the original motto was written without the え), we have no choice but to use this imperfect expression here!

program at Toyota through to his retirement: *"We make people while we make cars."*

> **Developing people was the most important way to develop good cars.**

IMPACT OF EARLY INVESTMENT IN PEOPLE

Investing four months into an orientation program was one important way for Toyota to demonstrate its investment in "making people." One might think that the Japanese tradition to hire people for lifetime employment fully explains Toyota's investment (in time and money) of its new employees. However, not all Japanese companies have the same type of orientation program that Toyota does. The structure and length of the program demonstrates Toyota's commitment to its people, and the importance it places on ensuring that its culture is transferred and embedded from the beginning in its new hires.

Two and a half months on the shop floor not only gave Yoshino experience with the *process* of making cars, it also gave him exposure to the people-centered and learning *culture* of Toyota. He had opportunities to get to know the frontline workers and managers, and interacted directly with the people who his "back office" job would support.

Yoshino remembers this first exposure to Toyota:

> *At first, the gemba assignment was difficult because it was so different from office work. Although it was a little boring to sit in a room all day during our first month of classroom training, it seemed much like what I imagined office work might be like — even though I had not done much office work before either. When I moved to the shop floor, it was such a different environment.*
>
> *The older shop floor workers were not college graduates — most of them had just a junior high school or high school education and had not had the opportunity to go to university. They were warmhearted, hardworking, down-to-earth, and treated us well even though we knew*

> *nothing about making cars! In fact, I felt a little bit embarrassed because we had no experience and we didn't contribute to the company like they did.*

Several years after Yoshino joined Toyota, an additional hands-on sales training was added to the orientation program. The new hires were all sent to local Toyota car dealers across Japan for three months to actually sell Toyota cars. Yoshino is still jealous of those university graduates who had a chance to experience an even broader orientation experience than he had.

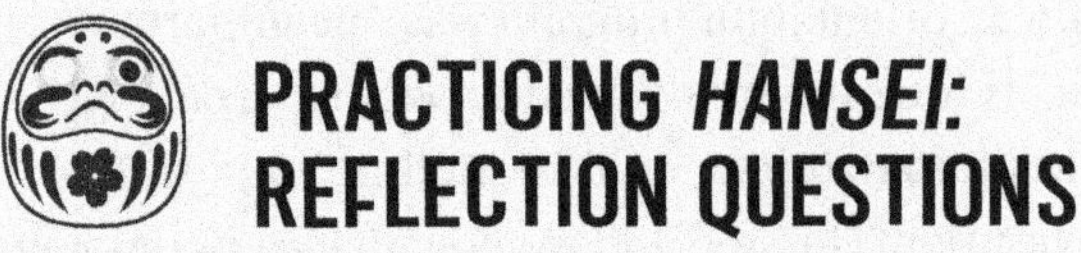

PRACTICING *HANSEI:* REFLECTION QUESTIONS

- What is your company's purpose? How did you learn it?
- What does the welcome and entry into a new company signify?
- What kind of orientation does your company provide?
- How did your orientation prepare you — or fail to prepare you — for understating the company culture? For understanding your role?
- How could your company's orientation process be improved? What could you do to influence or inspire that improvement?

INFLUENCES ON TOYOTA'S CULTURE

Yoshino considers the foundational principles of Toyota's culture — such as steadiness, humility, teamwork, perseverance, and patience — to be influenced in part by two significant factors: physical geography and historical context.

Physical Geography

The Toyota Motor Corporation is based in the Mikawa region in the Eastern part of Aichi Prefecture, where it was first founded at the Toyoda Automatic Loom Works, Ltd., in 1926 and later became a car manufacturing company in 1937. Yoshino explains the importance of this geography on the development of the area's culture:

> *The Mikawa region is a mountainous area with poor soil conditions, where people — for centuries — have had to work cooperatively to raise sufficient crops to feed the community. Other regions in Japan, particularly the cities such as Tokyo and Kyoto, did not have to manage through these same hardships. Out of these challenges to survive, the Mikawa people developed a culture of teamwork, diligence, patience, perseverance, and loyalty.*

Historical Context

One of the most influential leaders in Japanese history, Ieyasu Tokugawa, the founder and the first shogun of the Tokugawa shogunate of Japan, was born in the Mikawa region. Yoshino explains Tokugawa's significance in Japan and in the Mikawa region:

> *Taken as a hostage at the age of four years old by a neighboring clan, where he lived for 10 years, Tokugawa learned the importance of patience and perseverance. Years later, in 1600, Tokugawa won a decisive battle against an attacking army and achieved supremacy in Japan. The Emperor, a ruler only in name, gave Tokugawa the historic title of shogun (military governor) to confirm his preeminence. Japan was now united under Tokugawa's control. He worked hard to restore stability to Japan*

and established a rock-solid political system that lasted for more than 260 years. He is considered one of the greatest leaders in all of Japan. His family ruled Japan until 1868 (Meiji Restoration), when Japan finally opened its borders to foreign countries.

"Shogun Ieyasu Tokugawa," Artist: Utagawa Yoshitora, 1873, Source: Art Gallery of Greater Victoria

Leadership Precepts of Ieyasu Tokugawa

Yoshino sees direct parallels between Tokugawa's leadership precepts (in italics below), translated from the adjacent image, with his view of Toyota's culture (highlighted in bold below).

- **Steadiness and have a long-term view:** *"Life is like a long journey with a heavy burden on your back. Don't hurry."*
- **Diligence:** *"One who regards inconvenience as natural will never be discontented. When you want more than you have, remember the days when you were in need."*
- **Learn from failure:** *"If you only know what it is to conquer and don't know what it is to be defeated, it will be harmful to you."*
- **Patience:** *"Patience is the base of being safe forever. Regard anger as your enemy."*
- **Leaders take responsibility:** *"Blame yourself, not others."*
- **Humility:** *"Not being enough is better than being too much."*

These are some of the fundamental leadership principles that Yoshino learned — and taught — throughout his career and life.

To download a copy of Tokugawa's Precepts, visit LearningToLeadLeadingToLearn.com.

LESSON #2

CREATE THE CONDITIONS FOR PEOPLE TO BE SUCCESSFUL (AND TAKE RESPONSIBILITY WHEN MISTAKES HAPPEN)

"Managers need to create a culture where people are not afraid of making mistakes. Everyone makes mistakes. We can learn many things from the mistakes we make."

– *Isao Yoshino*

Most people come to work with the intention of doing a good job. And, more often than not, mistakes are the result of a bad process rather than malintent on the behalf of the person who made the error. But, even knowing that in theory, what is more common: blame the person or blame the process? Most of us probably answer that our first instinct is to "blame the person." What does it look like, instead, to work in an environment where leaders take ownership of failures in the system rather than blame people when mistakes happen? Where they see it as their responsibility as leaders to create the conditions for people to be successful in their work?

During his gemba orientation, Yoshino had his first significant experience with what the concept of "we make people while we make cars" actually meant. This encounter left an indelible imprint on Yoshino about the choices that leaders have in creating a people-centered culture based on respect and learning, and strongly influenced the type of leader he became.

YOSHINO MAKES A BIG MISTAKE

"Making mistakes feels terrible. However, when you make a mistake, you can learn so many things."

- Isao Yoshino

During an orientation rotation in the Motomachi Paint Shop, Yoshino was given the responsibility of preparing paint to be sprayed on the newly assembled car bodies as they came down the moving line. This task consisted of pouring products from two different cans — the paint and the solvent — into a giant mixer, and repeating the process every two to three hours as the tank started to get empty. Yoshino admits that waiting for the tank to empty was a pretty boring job ... that is, until one day when a shop floor worker ran into the mixing room shouting that the paint was not sticking to the cars. More than 100 cars were dripping with paint mixture and would have to be repainted! Shortly after, the Paint Shop manager rushed into the mixing room where Yoshino and a few others were standing to see what had gone wrong.

MANAGER'S CHOICE – BLAME THE PERSON OR TAKE RESPONSIBILITY FOR THE PROCESS?

"Blaming is your power as a boss. But if you start with blaming, it is hard to go back. It may make you feel temporarily happy, but is not good in the long run."

- Isao Yoshino

Yoshino immediately knew that he had made a mistake when doing his task. He remembers that first moment:

> *I was so scared. I thought, "Are they going to fire me?" My mistake created a huge problem — they would have to repaint all those car bodies!*

Much to Yoshino's surprise, instead of immediately shouting at Yoshino or blaming him for the 100 cars that would have to be repainted, his manager instead calmly asked, "What did you do?" Yoshino tentatively picked up the cans and demonstrated the process by which he had poured the mixtures into the tanks, holding up one can and then the next. It quickly became evident to both the manager and Paint Shop workers that while Yoshino had indeed mixed up the cans and put the wrong products into the mixer, it was easy to see how the mistake had happened. The cans looked nearly identical, and the writing on the labels was small and difficult to differentiate at a glance.

Upon seeing and hearing all of this, not only did Yoshino's boss not blame him for the mistake, he apologized for not setting up the work environment so that a mistake like this would not have been so easy to make! Yoshino describes his surprise about the Paint Shop manager's response:

> *My boss did not blame me directly, which made me feel so relieved. Instead he said, "Don't worry, mistakes can happen. You are just a beginner and you did your best. Thank you very much for making this mistake, as we are so familiar with the process here in the Paint Shop that we didn't label the area very clearly. I am sorry."*
>
> *At first, he probably thought inside of his head, "You screwed up!" But then he realized that, "We should have prepared a much clearer process for this newcomer so that he could not make any mistakes." It's only natural that I made a mistake as a new employee because the cans had such small labels.*

"Don't worry, mistakes can happen. You are just a beginner and you did your best. Thank you very much for making this mistake, as we are so familiar with the process here in the Paint Shop that we didn't label the area very clearly. I am sorry."

The response from the Paint Shop's manager was not one that Yoshino expected. When he recalled this memory for the first time in decades, during our first interview for this book, Yoshino exclaimed:

> *Can you believe it? My boss was not only not blaming me, he also said "I'm sorry" and "Thank you!" I was so surprised and happy! That was my first encounter with Toyota workers. It is a great memory and had a big impact on me.*

A SHARED CULTURE, NOT A ONE-OFF REACTION

Yoshino's experience in the Paint Shop was not an isolated experience. Many of Yoshino's friends made similar mistakes and experienced similar responses from their managers. When he shared his experience with his orientation cohort friends, he learned that:

> *Most of the other newcomers from university were making similar mistakes in the areas where they were assigned. I remember that one of them put the wrong bolt in the wrong hole on a car on the line. They all got the same reaction from their bosses as the Paint Shop managers had for me!*

YOSHINO'S LESSONS

Young Yoshino learned many important lessons from that experience. Yes, of course, he learned the procedure of how to put the right paint mixture in the tank, but, more importantly, he learned invaluable lessons from these shop-floor managers about how leaders are responsible for creating conditions for success — and for not blaming people when a system issue is to blame:

> *When I look back now to where I learned how to be a people-oriented leader, I realize that it started with this experience in my first months in the Paint Shop. It was my first encounter with Toyota leaders. Their reaction to my mistake showed me the Toyota culture — and the type of leader I wanted to be.*

Yoshino took this important lesson and incorporated it tightly into his own philosophies about how to lead and learn.

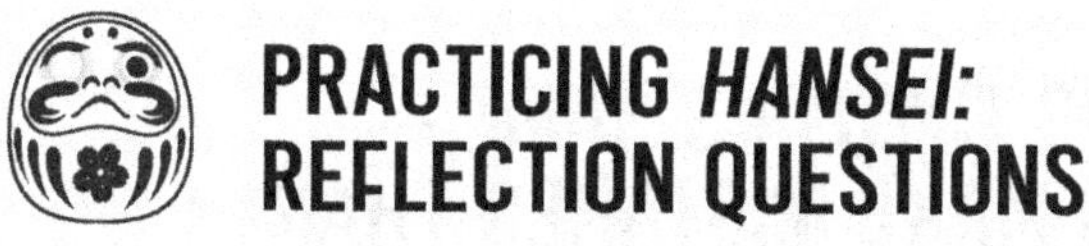

PRACTICING *HANSEI*: REFLECTION QUESTIONS

- Think of a time you made a mistake at work. What did you do? How did your manager or others around you react?
- Or, think of a time that someone made a mistake at work. How did you react?
- How would you or managers in your organization respond today if someone made a similar mistake as Yoshino?
- What do you think would have been different for Yoshino if the managers had responded by blaming him for the paint mistake?

THE HISTORY OF TOYOTA'S NAME – IT'S BETTER TO MAKE MISTAKES THAN BELIEVE YOU ARE PERFECT

"It is far better to know that we still have to improve than believe we know everything already."

- Isao Yoshino

Many people do not realize that the founding family of Toyota Motor Corporation was actually Toyoda, not Toyota.

Sakichi Toyoda founded Toyoda Automatic Loom Works, Ltd., in 1926, and his son Kiichiro Toyoda started automobile production as a division of the company in 1934. Four years later, in 1937, Toyota Motor Corporation was founded as a separate company, changing the original family name from ToyoDA (written with ten brush strokes in Japanese katakana characters) to the company name ToyoTA (eight brush strokes).

The official reason shared by Toyota Motor Corporation, on their factory tours in Toyota City and website, is that the number eight is considered to be a lucky number in Japan. When the number eight is written in kanji (八), the character spreads widely toward the end, which expresses a sign of success in the future as well as resembles the famous Japanese mountain Fuji-san.

Aim for Perfection, But Don't Ever Think You Have Achieved It

Yoshino likes to tell his own version of why the Toyoda family changed the name of the company from Toyoda to Toyota. He believes that having a name written in eight brush strokes instead of ten ensures that the company does not think it's on the top of the world — at least not yet. Ten is considered perfection, so by having only eight brush strokes, the company reminds itself that it still has more to achieve before it is perfect. There is always room to improve.

Yoshino explains why he likes his own unofficial interpretation:

> *We at Toyota all know that nobody is perfect and we often make mistakes, although we want to be perfect. Accepting that we are not perfect means that we can improve ourselves from the current position to a higher position by learning from the failure.*

Yoshino also likes this interpretation because it reminds him of what Tokugawa, Japan's first Shogun, wrote in the 1600s: "Not being enough is better than being too much."

LESSON #3

GO OUT OF YOUR WAY TO HELP OTHERS LEARN

"Make a small effort to give a little bit extra every day."

- *Isao Yoshino*

While a training program (such as the three-month orientation that Yoshino was immersed in when he joined Toyota) can have a significant impact in teaching new employees an organization's culture and providing them fundamental knowledge to do their job, the everyday things that leaders do can have the biggest lasting impact on developing their people. That's because the choices we make as leaders regarding how to invest our time and whether to go out of the way — outside of our official job duties — to show that we care about someone's development are critical.

YOSHINO'S FIRST ASSIGNMENT

Fresh out of his orientation program and the Paint Shop mistake, Yoshino's first official assignment was in Toyota's Export Planning Division in Toyota City, where he worked for three years. While he continued to learn about making cars, the foundational experiences he had with Toyota's culture of what he and I now call "learning to lead and leading to learn" was furthered by his direct manager and colleagues.

At the time Yoshino joined Toyota in 1966, Toyota Motor Corporation consisted of two separate companies — Toyota Motor Co., Ltd (TMC), the car manufacturer, and Toyota Motor Sales Co. (TMS). TMC was exclusively in charge of manufacturing cars and trucks, while all sales and marketing activities were handled by TMS, both in Japan and for overseas markets.

The two companies had different cultures, with the principles of the Toyota Production System more developed on the manufacturing side of the corporation. Only in 1982, as Toyota entered production outside of Japan, did the two companies merge. You will discover the difference in these cultures later through stories about Yoshino's final decade at Toyota in the chapter entitled "Reflecting on Failure."

Until the 1980s, all manufacturing happened domestically within Japan by TMC, with any foreign interfacing done by TMS for international exports. The only exception to this structure was a manufacturing company, Toyota do Brasil, located in São Paulo, Brazil. Toyota do Brasil — fully owned and operated by TMC in Japan — manufactured a 4-wheel-drive utility vehicle called the Bandeirante, known as the Land Cruiser in other parts of the world.

Yoshino's first official job responsibility was to communicate with the Brazilian subsidiary through letters or teletype. This opportunity to interact with a foreign country, even if in a small role, was an exciting first assignment for someone whose long-term dream was to have international experiences and who joined Toyota in hope of a future overseas assignment.

GO BEYOND YOUR ROLE TO HELP OTHERS LEARN

"An extra effort makes a difference."

– Isao Yoshino

Yoshino had multiple experiences in this first assignment in which leaders modeled the same commitment to people and their development as he experienced in his first months of orientation. He learned that "leader" is more than a role or job title — it is a way of being. The investment these leaders and colleagues made in him inspired Yoshino to craft a saying that became an integral part of his weft threads for the rest of his life: *"An extra effort makes a difference."*[3]

"Leader" is more than a role or job title – it is a way of being.

MAKE THE EXTRA EFFORT TO INVEST IN YOUR PEOPLE'S DEVELOPMENT

"The impact of the first manager is so huge. When I first joined Toyota, my image of what it meant to be a leader started from there."

– Isao Yoshino

Yoshino credits his first boss, Mr. Hideyo Tamura, with showing him what it meant to be a people-centered leader and to truly invest in your people. Yoshino directly reported to one of Mr. Tamura's assistant managers, but he recalls how his senior boss Mr. Tamura went out of his way to do small things every day to develop and support all the people reporting to him, unlike many other more traditional Japanese senior managers at that time.

Mr. Tamura was not a typical Japanese manager — or a typical Toyota manager — in the 1960s. Born in Hawaii while his father was a Japanese diplomat to the United States, he spoke proficient English and had developed an international worldview. Unlike more traditional Japanese managers whom Yoshino observed (who tended to be more strict and structured), Mr. Tamura was more open-minded and attentive to the development of his people. These people-centered leadership qualities were the ones that Toyota was starting to cultivate at this time in history.

---

3 Yoshino can't recall when he first heard or developed the English phrase, *"An extra effort makes a difference."* Yet over his lifetime of learning and leading, it has become his personal code. Yoshino says that every time his students ask him his favorite words or motto, he writes down this phrase on a sticky note and gives it to them.

Yoshino especially appreciated the extra effort Mr. Tamura took to share information and experiences that his junior staff did not have access to just yet in their lives or professional roles:

> *One thing that surprised me about Mr. Tamura was that each time he came back from overseas business trips, he would call all his staff members together to give us a briefing about his trip to the United States or Europe. At the time I joined Toyota, in the mid-1960s, very few businesspeople went abroad, as we often do now, and we had limited information about foreign countries. So, his briefings were quite informative and exciting, particularly for staff members like me who had never been abroad.*

Of course, to fresh grad Yoshino, who had set his dream to experience other cultures and a goal to live in the United States, the opportunity to be close to and learn from someone who had broader international experiences was that much more exciting.

GIVE CONSTRUCTIVE AND ACTIONABLE FEEDBACK

Yoshino also learned from Mr. Tamura the skills of how to help develop people by giving tangible, constructive feedback for improvement. He particularly recalls how Mr. Tamura would provide helpful feedback during the biannual performance evaluations, which was not the norm for most other managers, even at Toyota in those years:

> *No other managers disclosed their evaluation of their subordinates as openly as Mr. Tamura. When Mr. Tamura evaluated my performance, he would call me to the side of his desk and explain why he gave me those scores.*
>
> *He spent time to talk with me about both my strong points and my weaker points, and about how I could improve. I was so happy to know what expectations he had of me and what I needed to do to get better.*
>
> *I really liked Mr. Tamura's business style and I knew that I wanted to be just like him one day. I told myself that when I became*

a manager, I would be free and open to my subordinates just like him. He was my hero.

I was so lucky to be assigned to Mr. Tamura's department. If I was not assigned to his Export Planning Section, then maybe my life would be different.

Like his *juku* teacher, Mr. Tamura inspired Yoshino to focus on people development. As he was developed by people-focused teachers and leaders, such as Mr. Tamura, this weft thread started to become a more obvious and purposeful pattern in Yoshino's fabric.

DEVELOP A CHAIN OF LEARNING ACROSS THE COMPANY

"I felt blessed to have joined a company which has a tradition to promote the concept of the chain of learning across departments."

– *Isao Yoshino*

During the same time period, Yoshino had other early experiences that taught him the importance of supporting the development of people at all levels and the value of peer-to-peer learning. He recalls several instances of other young colleagues coming to share information and learning with him about Toyota principles and culture. One time stands out in particular:

One day a young man, a few years older than me, came to my desk and talked to me. He was not my boss or a direct senior to me, as he worked in a different department. His department and our department were located side by side in a big open room on the third floor at Toyota's headquarters in Toyota City.

He was very eager to talk about all the key Quality Circle (QC) concepts like Deming Circle (PDCA), which he had learned from his senior people at his department. I was wondering why a guy from another department would come up to a newcomer in another department like me and try to coach me on all those things so enthusiastically.

Within a few days, I came to know that he himself had been coached by his own senior staff on those key QC concepts and he was so happy with the sense of compassion he had received from these leaders. Looking back, I think that he got motivated to reciprocate and do the same thing to somebody else.

It was really a pleasant surprise for me to receive such a nice informal coaching at the beginning of my career. I thought it must be part of Toyota's culture.

These early experiences at Toyota contributed to Yoshino's chain of learning and added strength to the fabric of purpose he was beginning to create.

PRACTICING *HANSEI*: REFLECTION QUESTIONS

- Think back to your relationship with your first manager. How did that experience impact or shape your experience or definition of leadership?
- Who are some other influential people in your chain of learning? What did they do to go out of their way to help you learn to learn, and learn to lead?
- How have you contributed to your chain of learning? What are some the ways that you have gone out of your way to develop others?
- What are some of the seemingly small things that you can do, or extra effort you can make, that could have a lasting impact on someone?

"GO TO GEMBA" IS THE FOUNDATION OF LEARNING AND PEOPLE-CENTERED LEADERSHIP

"You can make a good decision only by a 'go to gemba' attitude."

– *Isao Yoshino*

One of the key tenets of the Toyota Way is "*genchi genbutsu*": "go to the source to find the facts." This is commonly referred to as "go to gemba." Leadership is not about managing from your office or reading data found in reports, but rather going to see to gather facts about what is actually happening — with your people, with your processes, and with your customers.

Mr. Fujio Cho, the former President of Toyota, is famously attributed with having said: "Go see, ask why, show respect." Leaders demonstrate respect by going to gemba to see what is actually happening, and asking questions to learn what people are actually thinking.

Yoshino elaborates on how "go to gemba" supports people-centered leadership:

> *In order for managers to be people-oriented bosses, it is essential for them to frequently come down to the shop floor and meet and talk with their subordinates face to face and see with their own eyes how manufacturing is being done on the shop floor. Leaders often don't know precisely what is going on at the worksite. Their subordinates work on the gemba from morning 'til night and see things firsthand, while leaders get to know the status mostly from the reports they receive or their occasional conversations with subordinates.*
>
> *Managers need to go to gemba and listen to their people carefully when making decisions, because the workers know their own jobs better than anybody else. Chief engineers, top executive officers, and departments' general managers are there only to help shop floor people make good cars. When they "go to gemba," managers can observe what is happening with their own eyes and ears rather than relying on the numbers or*

comments in a report. This attitude or behavior is deeply ingrained in the culture at Toyota. It is a regular habit.

Go to See with Purpose

"Going to gemba" differs from the traditional practice of "management by walking around" (MBWA) often espoused by leaders in the West, where managers conduct unstructured visits to the workplace. In contrast, leaders "go to gemba" with a purpose. They define *why* they are "going to see," and take a structured, intentional approach for *what* and *how* they will conduct the visit.

Going to gemba means:

- Getting out of the office or conference room to visit the actual worksite with purpose
- Deliberately checking on the status of specific work processes and outcomes
- Validating data and assumptions with observable facts
- Talking with the actual people involved — employees, clients, suppliers, partners — with an intention to learn their perspective and to show you care.

LESSON #4

GO TO SEE AND SHOW YOU CARE — LEADERSHIP STARTS AT THE GEMBA

"I discovered that you can learn so many things directly from the gemba because all things start from the gemba — not from the chief engineers or top executives or departments' general managers."

- *Isao Yoshino*

After three years working in the Export Department, Yoshino specifically requested that his next assignment be in a production support role for a plant in Toyota City. His reason? He wanted to learn how Toyota made cars directly by visiting the plant floor. In 1969, management granted his request and assigned Yoshino, now in his mid-20s, to the Production Control Department of the Motomachi Plant — the same plant where he had made the paint mistake in his orientation just three years earlier.

YOSHINO'S MOTOMACHI PLANT ASSIGNMENT

"While working at the Motomachi Plant, I learned how important it is to go to gemba to know what is happening there and to develop relationships with the people."

- *Isao Yoshino*

At the Motomachi Plant, where cars such as the Cressida and Crown (a model for the Japanese market only) were manufactured, Yoshino was charged with coordinating the model changes for the Cressida Mark II. His primary role was to ensure that the engineer's changes were shared with everyone in manufacturing. Yoshino explains his responsibilities:

I used to receive around 200 design changes each month, both on a big and small scale. I needed to make sure that the new parts with design changes were delivered to the shop floor and installed in the right cars at the right time. If the parts were made by outside suppliers, I also had to communicate with the suppliers to make sure the new parts would be delivered to the production line at the right time.

I was required to keep an eye every single day on the design changes documents I received from Technical Divisions, which they sent in A4-sized [letter] format every day. I also had to talk to all the related division people to make sure we were all on the same page.

I had to be organized not to make any small mistakes. Otherwise, it may happen that the car would come out of the plant with a wrong part on it.

GO TO GEMBA AS A LEARNER

"A 'go to gemba' attitude is so important. You may not know much about what is actually happening. You need to go see."

- Isao Yoshino

Always seeking to develop himself, Yoshino took the initiative to go beyond his official job assignment. While his back-office role did not require that he visit the plant floor daily, Yoshino had requested this assignment because of its proximity to the gemba. He made it a daily routine to get out from his desk, to "go to gemba" with the intention to learn:

Every day, first thing in the morning, I checked all the incoming model change documents for my job. In the afternoon, I made it a rule to go out to the shop floor to talk with the shop floor supervisors, group leaders, team leaders, and rank-and-file workers. I spent at least one hour on the shop floor every day, even if I didn't need to. In the evening, I came back

> *to my desk and did the rest of my desk work. That cycle became my daily working pattern.*
>
> *During the three years at this department, I learned the entire process of how a car is designed and manufactured with so many people and companies involved in a synchronized manner.*

Through his habit of "going to gemba," Yoshino met his goal of learning how to make cars. And he also learned an important lesson about how to "make people."

GO TO GEMBA AS A PEOPLE-CENTERED LEADER

"Going to gemba makes people feel like they are important."
- *Isao Yoshino*

During this time, Yoshino also learned that there is deeper — and perhaps more important — purpose of "going to gemba" to get the facts. He discovered that by going to the place where someone works, seeing what they experience every day, and talking with them directly, you demonstrate that you care about them. This is people-centered leadership at its core.

Yoshino first experienced the value of developing relationships in the gemba during his new-hire orientation in the Motomachi plant, but his three-year assignment in this same facility solidified this knowledge. He recounts the impact that his daily gemba visits had:

> *Most of the workers, including supervisors, did not go to university, but joined Toyota right after they graduated high school. They treated me very well just because I used to come out to the shop floor every day and spent time with them.*
>
> *Even when I had nothing important to talk to them about in terms of engineering model changes, I still tried to go to the shop floor every afternoon. I found out that the more often I went there, not only the more knowledge I learned about car making, but my relationships with them got closer because I knew more about them and they knew more about me.*

> *I believe I came down to the shop floor more often than anybody else who worked at my section.*

Yoshino discovered that the importance of "going to see" was not solely to validate facts and learn about processes, but to develop relationships and to show that you care about the people.

YOSHINO'S REFLECTIONS

People-centered leadership is the crux of what makes me and Yoshino — despite our many differences — so aligned personally and professionally. When I asked him to reflect on the importance of leaders taking the initiative to regularly "go to gemba," he remarked:

> *If you go to gemba and walk around the area or talk to the people there, instead of just judging things in your office, it will show that you chose to bring yourself to the gemba and see things by your own eyes and talk to the people face to face. It not only shows that "go to gemba" is the best way to get to know what is really happening, but also allows you to see how people at the gemba are working and whether they are happy with their work.*
>
> *Your decision to choose to bring yourself to the gemba will make people feel that their boss cares about the "go to gemba" concept and also cares about people working there.*

Yoshino credits his time in the Motomachi plant as one of the most impactful periods in his career in which he was "learning to lead." His experiences on the shop floor taught him the technical components of TPS — of how "we make cars" — and, more importantly, reinforced the people-centered management philosophy of how "we make people." Yoshino explains:

> *If I am asked which workplace or department influenced me most in my business life, I would definitely say, "Working at the Motomachi Plant made me who I am today." At the Motomachi Plant, people talked about all the concepts of TPS*

on a daily basis. But most importantly, I learned that it is people, not machines, that make cars.

At this very same time period in Yoshino's career, he started the Motomachi English Study Group, which you read about in Part I, to teach English to these shop-floor workers and supervisors. Yoshino was embodying "making the extra effort" as he started to weave his threads of purpose together. Without realizing it, he was experimenting with "leading to learn" while also focusing very much on his primary purpose of learning to lead. And his proverbial life tapestry of warp and weft threads was becoming more colorful as he gained awareness about how his enjoyment of mentoring and teaching others fit into his overall mission to live an international life.

PRACTICING *HANSEI*: REFLECTION QUESTIONS

- What does "go to gemba" or "go to see" mean to you?
- In your organization, how often do you "go to gemba" (to where the work actually happens, to your clients, to other departments, etc.)?
- Why is it important to have a clear purpose before "going to gemba"? What is your purpose when you go see?
- When you have "gone to gemba," what have you learned that was different from what you assumed you would observe? What impact did that make on your decisions or next steps?
- In your organization, how often do leaders get out of their offices to "go to gemba"? What is the impact when leaders don't go to see?
- What does "go to gemba" look like when you have distributed teams or work remotely?
- How do you "go see" in a knowledge or digital work environment?
- What are ways that you have taken the initiative to go beyond your official job assignment or role? What did you learn?

WHAT IS AN A3? A TECHNICAL AND SOCIAL SYSTEM FOR COMMUNICATION

"Writing and developing an A3 is only the starting point to solving a problem."

- Isao Yoshino

"A3" refers to a size of paper in Japan, Europe, and other countries (equivalent to 11 inches x 17 inches in the United States). At Toyota, A3 paper is used as a communication platform for many situations, including problem-solving, strategy (*hoshin kanri*), and project proposals. The format of the A3 changes based on the situation. Regardless of the format, an A3 is not intended as a template to be filled out, but rather a guide to tell a concise story about a situation, visualized on one piece of paper, and a method to communicate that story with others.

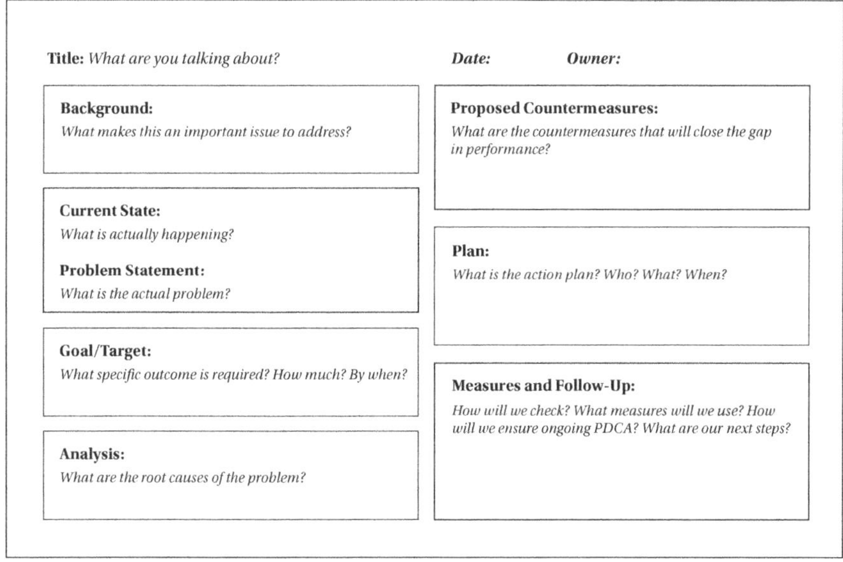

Title: *What are you talking about?* **Date:** **Owner:**

Background:
What makes this an important issue to address?

Current State:
What is actually happening?

Problem Statement:
What is the actual problem?

Goal/Target:
What specific outcome is required? How much? By when?

Analysis:
What are the root causes of the problem?

Proposed Countermeasures:
What are the countermeasures that will close the gap in performance?

Plan:
What is the action plan? Who? What? When?

Measures and Follow-Up:
How will we check? What measures will we use? How will we ensure ongoing PDCA? What are our next steps?

Here is one example of the basic flow of thinking represented on a problem-solving A3. Remember, it is not about the template, but the thinking process that it supports.

"A3 Thinking" has become synonymous with the *process* for articulating, summarizing, and sharing important information on one piece of paper. It is also a process for people development. The collaborative process of helping someone refining their thinking on an A3 report through going to see, getting input from others, and iteration, is one example of how Toyota managers lead to learn by helping others learn *how* to learn and how to communicate their thinking.

Deshi and Sensei – Two Roles in Developing A3s

Most of us know what the term *sensei* means from its wide adoption in other languages: "teacher" or "master." In Japan, *sensei* is used as an honorific to teachers, professors, coaches, doctors, and those with seniority. Yoshino's university students refer to him as "Yoshino-sensei," and one would refer to a physician as "*sensei.*"

The partner word to *sensei* is *deshi* or "apprentice."

In his book *Managing to Learn: Using the A3 Management Process to Solve Problems, Gain Agreement, Mentor, and Lead,* John Shook describes the technical and social components of A3s through a fictionalized story based on Shook's experience reporting to Yoshino and other managers. Through the book, the manager character works closely with his subordinate as he goes through the process of learning how to learn through developing a problem-solving A3.

Yoshino told me in one of our early meetings, which Shook later confirmed, that the Japanese word for "apprentice" was actually a reason that Shook called his learner character "Desi Porter" in *Managing to Learn.* I always thought it was a non-traditional American first name to choose! Shook modeled himself as Desi (the *deshi*) in the book, while Yoshino and some of Shook's other early managers were the inspirations for Sanderson (the *sensei*).

For more resources and information on A3 Thinking and related topics, visit LearningToLeadLeadingToLearn.com.

LESSON #5

OWN THE THINKING PROCESS, NOT THE THINKING

"One of the important jobs for leaders is to make sure that their people have a habit to 'go to gemba' to get firsthand information. It's a golden rule to make the right decision."

- *Isao Yoshino*

In 1972, six years after joining Toyota and working at headquarters in Toyota City, Yoshino was transferred to Toyota's Tokyo Office to work in the Public Affairs Department.

During this time, Yoshino had an experience with a senior leader that impressed upon him the importance of a manager's role in teaching his people the process of *how* to learn and to lead. The leader allows the learner to have opportunities for struggle and mistakes made while pursuing their goal or challenge, while at the same time provides enough support to build the learner's capability and confidence. The learner owns the thinking and the doing. A leader owns creating the conditions for learning.

The learner owns the thinking and the doing. A leader owns creating the conditions for learning.

UNDER TIME CONSTRAINTS, IT CAN FEEL EASIER TO SHORTCUT THE PROCESS

The senior officer in charge of the Public Affairs Department in the Tokyo Office believed it needed to become more efficient and strategic. He was considering changing the department's structure, and he needed some data and facts to help with his decision. The senior officer gave Yoshino a mission: collect basic information on how other well-performing Japanese companies, such as Nissan, Hitachi, and Panasonic, functioned and make a summary report on an A3.

Having spent three years at the Motomachi Plant, Yoshino knew the right process to go through to collect the facts and prepare an A3 report: "go to gemba." Yet, pressed for time, he skipped what he knew was an important step. He recalls:

> *I was given a short timeline to prepare the report, so I decided that I would just get data from the library in our Tokyo Office and a large nearby library in Tokyo. I had very little time to "go to gemba" and actually visit some of these corporations, but I assumed that the data on the books at the library was reliable. I put all the information I'd gathered into an A3 document and prepared to present it to the boss, along with the other eight or nine senior managers at the Tokyo Office who would be attending the meeting.*

Yoshino started to give his presentation to the senior leadership group, but was not permitted to proceed. Yoshino recalls:

> *When I tried to start my presentation, the "big boss" stopped me and asked, "How many corporations have you actually visited to make this report?"*
>
> *I replied, "As time was quite limited, I collected data from the books or documents that were available to me."*
>
> *The "big boss" replied, "You didn't go to any of the companies? How can you be so sure whether the data and information is true without directly talking to them face to face? You skipped a very important process. I will give you one more week to re-do the research work."*
>
> *He did not let me continue with my presentation.*

Yoshino was embarrassed. He knew the correct process to prepare the report — and he had shortchanged it. He acknowledges, in hindsight, that the "big boss" (who also had come from Toyota's manufacturing divisions) was correct to assume that Yoshino would have known to go directly to other companies to collect actual facts from the source rather than relying on secondhand information in older reports. Yoshino told me that he was ashamed for his own shortcomings, and that he was grateful for the opportunity to learn from his mistake. He believes that the senior officer's response was his way of teaching Yoshino how to learn.

LEADERS TEACH THE PROCESS OF LEARNING, NOT JUST THE RESULT

Over the next week, Yoshino made time to visit some of the companies in Tokyo to talk with them about the information needed for his report. His face-to-face interviews validated the data he had collected from the books at the library. When recalling this experience to me, he exclaimed, *"There was really no difference at all!"* Yet, as he acknowledges now, validating the data with facts was a critical part of doing proper and complete thinking.

Yoshino went back to the leadership team to present his revised report the following week. When he finished his conclusions, he was happy to hear the senior officer say: "Well done, Yoshino. That's what I had wanted to hear from you last time."

YOSHINO'S LESSONS

Yoshino reflects now that he learned — or re-learned — two important lessons from this experience: first, the importance of "going to gemba," and second, how leaders own the conditions for their people to learn:

> *Through this experience, I realized again how important it is to "go to gemba" to get all the necessary information directly rather than from secondhand information in books.*
>
> *Later on, I found out that the big boss did not use — or even consider using — any of the information that I collected from my face-to-face research. His main intention was to train me to learn how important it is to "go to gemba" to find out the true facts, even though we worked in the Tokyo office where our job was not directly related to the manufacturing segment.*

> *I felt ashamed for my narrow outlook and for not remembering the importance of the "go to gemba" concept, although I came from the manufacturing plant just two years before. At the same time, I felt blessed to have such a thoughtful boss who was patient and tried to train a young newcomer from the countryside.*

Yoshino remembers this as positive experience that reinforced that leaders should not focus only on the outcome of the assignment, but — perhaps more importantly — the process by which the learner completes the assignment. The senior officer was leading to learn, while Yoshino was learning to lead. This experience solidified Yoshino's understanding that a leader's role is not only to provide a challenge or target, but also to support the development of that person while he or she works to achieve the target. The process of learning is as important as the actual learning itself.

The process of learning is as important as the actual learning itself.

PRACTICING *HANSEI*: REFLECTION QUESTIONS

- As a leader, what is your role as it relates to supporting other people to complete their assignments or meet their targets?
- How much time are *you* given — by your boss or other leaders — to "fail" and learn? How much time do you give your direct reports for such failure and learning?
- How would you have felt if your boss asked you to do something and then didn't use the information?
- If you were this senior officer, how would you have handled a similar situation?
- Why do you think the senior officer didn't tell Yoshino exactly how to conduct the research for the report?

PUT A "HANKO" ON IT

In Japan, a *hanko* is a personalized stamp that serves as a signature on legal documents and other printed materials.

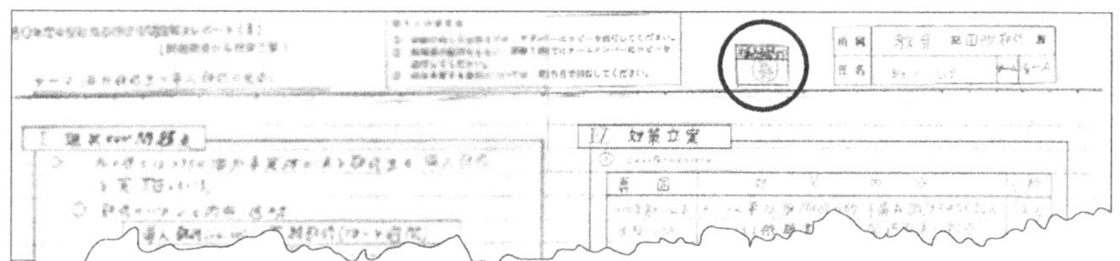

During professional conferences, John Shook often shares the first A3 that he wrote at Toyota, with Isao Yoshino's hanko *on it.*

At Toyota, a *hanko* represents a leader's role in coaching their subordinates to develop A3s or other assignments. As Yoshino learned from his boss in the Tokyo office and later demonstrated to John Shook and many others, a leader serves as a coach to a subordinate who is preparing a report, such as an A3. The manager's role is to ensure the completeness of his subordinate's thinking and oversee how the learner communicates that thinking on the A3 paper through multiple cycles of development. The leader stamps his *hanko* to "sign off" that he approves of the process the A3 owner took to prepare the document.

Yoshino describes the *hanko's* significance:

> *Putting your* hanko *on A3 report is evidence to show that you, as the boss, have gone through your subordinate's A3 and have provided necessary input or advice. If your subordinate's A3 is considered to be still immature or poor in its analysis, for example, it means that his or her boss has not done their job right.*
>
> *The* hanko *is a kind of testimonial to show that the boss is doing his or her own job. For example, as a manager when I gave John an assignment, I had to make sure that he has done enough analysis, focused on facts instead of assumptions, made the entire story flow smoothly in his own style, etc. The evaluation of my subordinate's A3 report was also an evaluation of my own coaching ability as a boss.*

Putting one's *hanko* on the document is the boss's formal acknowledgment in his or her role in developing the A3 owner's capabilities. As the saying goes, "the learner hasn't learned if the teacher hasn't taught."

LESSON #6

LEARN WHAT NOT TO BE AS A LEADER

"Having actual experiences is a great way for you to learn what is important and what is not."

- Isao Yoshino

EVEN TOYOTA HAS SOME BAD LEADERS

Of course, not every leader at Toyota embodies the Toyota Way values of humility, respect, and patience. While Yoshino had many wonderful experiences at Toyota that defined the type of people-centered leader he wanted to be, he also had interactions with managers and colleagues who were just the opposite. Yoshino's worst experience at Toyota was with a manager he calls "the bad boss" — one who lacked humility and patience, and who was downright mean.

Enduring two years of working for the "bad boss" while he was assigned to Toyota's Tokyo Office was an experience that still haunts Yoshino today. When he looks back at this time and what he wove into his life fabric, he sees it is made of darkly colored and broken threads. Yet Yoshino considers this period to be significant: he learned who he *didn't* want to be as a leader.

THE OPPOSITE OF PEOPLE-CENTERED LEADERSHIP

"Don't pretend to know more than you know. If you think that you know everything, and that you don't have to know more, that attitude will ultimately destroy you."

– Isao Yoshino

Yoshino describes the situation in which he was working for this manager, who embodied the opposite of people-centered leadership qualities:

> *Fortunately, or unfortunately, I have had several "bad bosses" in my company life. The worst was one for whom I worked in the Tokyo office for two years in mid '70s. He was a manager and I was an assistant manager in the division. This "bad boss" considered himself a smart guy and he often told us he graduated from one of Japan's most elite universities near the top of his class.*

It quickly became apparent that this boss was not like the previous people-centered managers for whom Yoshino worked. Yoshino recounts that:

> *At first, he was seemingly very nice, but it did not take too long for us to know he was self-centered and only cared about himself. He had so much self-esteem and always bragged about his accomplishments in his university life as well as at his past assignments in Toyota headquarters.*
>
> *When he gave us an assignment, he always told us what to do and how to do it. His approach to his subordinates was one-sided and made no sense to us all. He seemed to think that he knew all the answers.*
>
> *My boss's main concern seemed to be how to make himself look important to other people, particularly to the big boss in the Tokyo office. He did not appear to have any intention to develop or encourage his own people. We were so frustrated with working for a guy like him. It's totally opposite to what lean and the Toyota Way means.*

Yoshino found his boss's attitude went beyond the more "traditional" harsher style that many Japanese managers — even at Toyota — practiced at that time. Yoshino describes that beyond not developing his people, his boss bullied his subordinates, and Yoshino was frequently sick as a result of anxiety. Yoshino further elaborates:

> *All of us were very unhappy and hoped our boss would be transferred to another department. Finally, in 1976, I could not stand his unreasonable attitude and lack of respect, and decided to seek a more comfortable workplace. I talked my boss's boss, the general manager, and explained the situation.*
>
> *Fortunately, the general manager had been worried about my manager's problematic attitude toward his subordinates, and promised to relocate me to some other more peaceful workplace. I was so happy to know that this general manager had been worried about my boss and was watching the situation. After the extremely stressful and hectic two years, I was finally transferred.*

To the general manager's credit, shortly after Yoshino was reassigned, Yoshino found out that the general manager had transferred the "bad boss" to a non-management independent contributor position back at headquarters. He would work independently and not have the opportunity to "teach" this style of management to others.

KNOWING WHAT YOU *DON'T* WANT IS AS IMPORTANT AS IDENTIFYING WHAT YOU *DO* WANT

Yoshino experienced interactions with his boss that would not be acceptable in most office environments today. Yet he found some valuable lessons from this two-year experience, particularly a clarity about what he did and did *not* want to be as a leader:

> *If I am asked what was the worst experience, or who was the worst boss that I had worked for, in Toyota, I can declare for sure that this is it. Yet from this awful experience, I have learned very important lessons.*

> *I learned from this bad boss that when I found myself in the position to have many subordinates working for me, I would be fair, open-minded, patient, and always ready to help them. I would try my best to understand their personalities, characters, and abilities so that I could help to bring them to a higher level. If I had not been assigned to that ruthless guy, I might not have learned those important lessons.*

WHY DIDN'T THIS BAD BOSS GET FIRED?

When Yoshino shares his stories about this terrible "bad boss" with Western audiences, he almost always is asked why his manager wasn't fired. In anticipation of your questions, I asked Yoshino to elaborate. He offers a few possible explanations.

First, at that time in Japan — and even at Toyota — there was still a predominance of a domineering leadership style that was a holdover from a traditional Japanese apprenticeship mode. This was particularly evident with older managers who themselves were developed in a time where harsher interaction between boss and subordinate was the norm (though, in this case, Yoshino's manager was not much older than he was). Second, historically it has been difficult in Japan to fire anyone. Yoshino believes that, at that time, there would not have been a clear guideline in Human Resources about what was acceptable or not in terms of workplace conduct. In this case, Yoshino believes that it would have been difficult for the higher-level boss to have evaluated if his boss's management style was a violation of any standards, as these standards might not have been defined.

Toyota was in a state of transition from a more traditional Japanese "harsher" management approach to the more people-centered one with which we are familiar today.

PRACTICING *HANSEI:* REFLECTION QUESTIONS

- When is a time, if any, that you had a manager or colleague treat you disrespectfully? What was that experience like?
- What has been your experience when a manager (or someone else in a position of authority) who believed he or she "has all the answers"? What was your reaction when this person told you what to do and how to do it?
- What are some things that you have learned that you *don't* want to be as a leader? How have they helped you define who you *do* want to be?
- How have your challenging experiences shaped your life fabric?

HOSHIN KANRI AND CROSS-FUNCTIONAL MANAGEMENT AT TOYOTA

"Hoshin is an important tool to make sure that all the members in the organization can share the same goals and action plans to attain their own goals."

– *Isao Yoshino*

As we follow Yoshino's journey of learning to lead, and subsequently leading to learn, it is helpful to have some additional context of the leadership practices, organizational structures, and tools that he was learning and teaching.

Strategic Management in a Matrix Organization

In 1962, at the same time as Japan's intense focus on rebuilding the country and Toyota's intense focus on developing a quality management system, an internal audit at Toyota revealed many management gaps impacting its operations, including poor cross-functional communication, limited long-term planning, and weak practices of "go to gemba."

As a countermeasure, Toyota introduced two concepts that have become core to its management success: *hoshin kanri* and cross-functional management.

Hoshin Kanri

Hoshin kanri is a strategic planning and checking process that was developed in Japan in the 1960s. Yoshino explained to me that the *hoshin kanri* concept was developed in Japan as an integration of American management practices: management by objectives (MBO), popularized globally by Peter Drucker in 1954, and the Plan-Do-Check-Adjust (PDCA) cycle introduced to Japan by Dr. W. Edwards Deming in the 1950s.

The term *hoshin kanri* consists of two Japanese words: *hoshin* (方針) meaning "policy, plan, course, principle, objective" as well as "magnetic needle," and *kanri* (管理) meaning "control" or "management." In English, these words have often been translated as policy management, policy deployment, or strategy deployment.

Like a compass needle, *hoshin kanri* is linked to the concept of "true north." The strategy or policy plan is what sets the organization in the direction of true north. *Hoshin* is the organization's compass; *kanri* is the organization's plan on how to move in that direction.

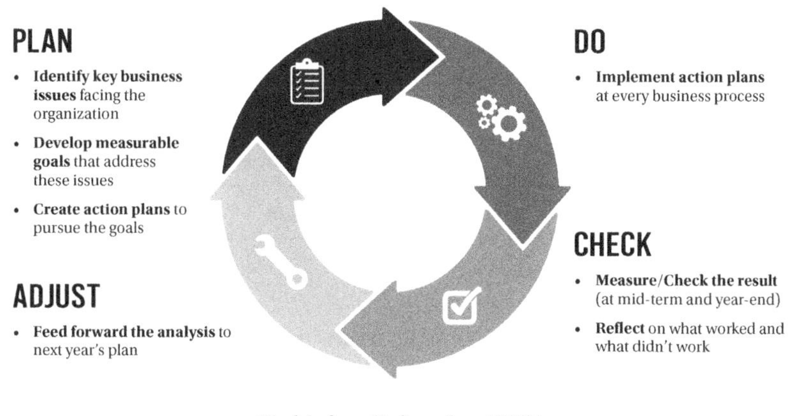

Hoshin kanri is based on PDCA.

Cross-Functional Management

Yoshino has shared with me that Toyota also created a system called "cross-functional management," which aimed to integrate different departments responsible for creating cars and bringing them to market (product planning, design, preparation, procurement, production, and sales) across different functions (quality, finance, technical development, HR, etc.).

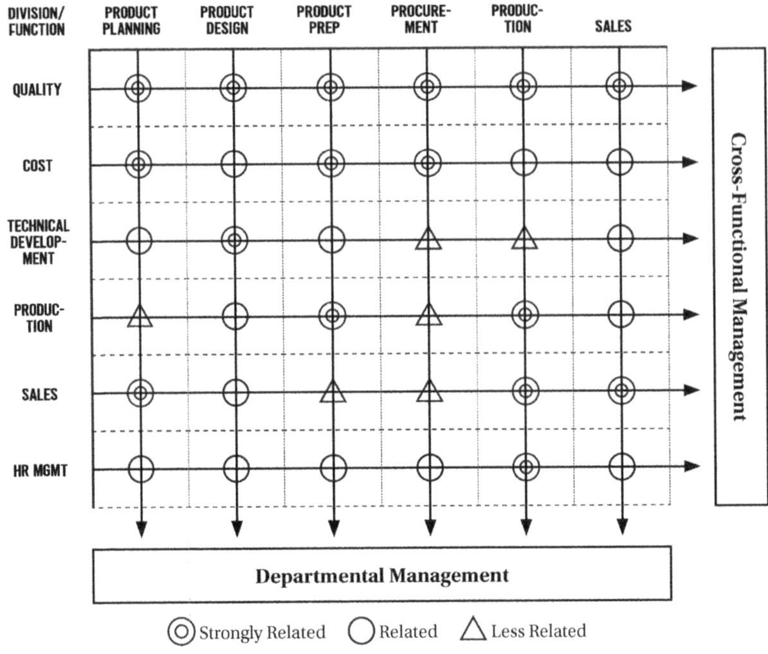

The process of *hoshin kanri* became the method for Toyota to align cross-functional departments and to connect strategy from the top leadership of the company to the frontline.

For more resources and information on *hoshin kanri,* visit LearningToLeadLeadingToLearn.com.

LESSON #7

BE CURIOUS, ALWAYS KEEP LEARNING, ASK QUESTIONS

"Asking questions is more important than telling the person your idea. When you ask a question, you get the person to tell you what they are thinking in their own words."

- Isao Yoshino

Following two years reporting to the "bad boss" in the Tokyo office, Yoshino stepped into a role back at headquarters in Toyota City, where he worked for the man who he considers his most important boss, Mr. Mikio Sugiura. Yoshino describes joining Mr. Sugiura's team as *"finding a buddha in hell"* — going from the worst manager he could imagine to one of the best leaders for whom he ever worked. Even at the time of writing this book, Yoshino, in his mid-70s, will journey several hours by train to meet with his former mentor, who is more than 10 years his senior.

This four-year assignment in the Corporate Planning Department was a tremendous learning experience for Yoshino. He grew as a learner and as a leader through direct access to senior leaders at Toyota and by assisting with the executive team's key initiatives. He supported the annual corporate strategy development and deployment process (*hoshin kanri*), helped develop the "Kan-Pro" training program (which you will learn about in detail in Case Study #1 in our next chapter), and handled any of top management's ad hoc requests. But, most importantly — for him personally — Yoshino learned invaluable lessons and skills about people-centered leadership from his boss, Mr. Sugiura.

ASK QUESTIONS TO HELP OTHERS LEARN

"Before working for Mr. Sugiura, I did not think that asking questions was an important skill, but I learned from him that it was very important."

- *Isao Yoshino*

Yoshino learned a fundamental leadership practice from Mr. Sugiura: ask questions as a way to develop others, and to maintain a "leading to learn" mindset. At first, Yoshino was a bit surprised that his boss — someone he personally considered to be an expert in many things — led by asking questions rather than giving his opinion. Mr. Sugiura didn't just tell people what to do, like his "bad boss" in Tokyo had done.

As part of their department's responsibility to oversee the *hoshin* process, Yoshino, his colleagues and Mr. Sugiura would review strategy plans prepared by company senior leaders on A3 paper and help align them to top strategies for the year. Yoshino discovered that not all the senior managers were as skilled at doing this. Because of his knowledge, it would have been easy for Mr. Sugiura to be directive in telling the other senior managers what he thought would improve their documents. Instead, Mr. Sugiura would ask questions to help them discover their own answers. Mr. Sugiura genuinely seemed interested in learning what each person was thinking. Yoshino recalls wondering: *"Why would this guy be interested in learning something new? He seems to know everything!"*

HOW YOU ASK QUESTIONS IS IMPORTANT

"One of the lessons I learned from Mr. Sugiura is that you need to adjust your pace to that of the people, not to expect other people to adjust their pace to yours. Your major role as a questioner is to make people happy to open up."

- *Isao Yoshino*

From observing Mr. Sugiura's interaction with other leaders, Yoshino also discovered there was skill and nuance in *how* to ask questions. Mr. Sugiura was particularly adept at connecting with people when he asked questions, regardless of whether they were his subordinates, senior-level peers, or his superiors (including Toyota's President). Mr. Sugiura would adjust his style of talking and the types of questions that he asked to be optimally effective for each individual. For example, as Yoshino explains:

> *When we talked to executives who were confident about themselves and eloquent in their speech, Mr. Sugiura would ask straightforward, direct questions, and ones that he believed those executives wanted to talk about. Those leaders, often engineers, didn't hesitate to speak up. We didn't have to push much, but rather just had to focus on keeping up the momentum of the conversation. He would ask his questions in a brisk pace, and the executives would respond in a brisk pace too. Sugiura-san then would dig down into more details and keep listening to them. Everybody feels happy if someone addresses topics that they want to talk about.*
>
> *On the other hand, when we talked with more quiet and reserved executives, who are not uncommon at Toyota, Sugiura-san would adopt a different approach. He would start with a general question and "small talk" to open their hearts. He didn't proceed too hastily, particularly when he didn't know much about the leader's personality and way of thinking. He followed the executives' own slower pace of talking. It's simple but it works.*

WHAT YOU ASK IS IMPORTANT

"You have to let the person you are helping explore ideas and fail. Telling them the 'answer' is shortsighted and does not help him or her develop critical thinking capability. It is only by understanding what the process was to get to the wrong answer that they might actually land on the right one."

– *Isao Yoshino*

Yoshino was also impressed at what questions Mr. Sugiura asked. He observed that his boss was adept at finding out what was important to each individual person and then asking specific questions related to that person's priorities. Mr. Sugiura would pick up immediately on the right topic for that person and then ask an open-ended question, such as: "What does that mean for you?" or "What is your opinion?"

By observing Mr. Sugiura's question-asking process, Yoshino came to appreciate that everybody has a different way of thinking and a different approach to each problem — a leader's role is to help someone *learn* to think. And Yoshino learned that Mr. Sugiura helped others to think by simply asking questions rather than telling people what to do. Yoshino describes that leading to learn requires that the leader gives others the opportunity to think, discover, and experiment for themselves:

> *Pushing people too much to exactly follow your advice takes away a chance for them to come up with their own ideas. You have to give enough room and capacity for them to analyze the problem and the solution.*
>
> *If, by luck, the boss's idea worked and fixed the issue, the person would be happy to see his problem solved. But if a boss gives the answer, it won't help the person learn in the same way as if they had accomplished the task by coming up with their own solution. Instead, they only borrowed an idea and applied it.*

Through his openness to always keep learning and his skill in asking questions, Mr. Sugiura was an invaluable model for Yoshino as he started to move into bigger leadership and training roles at Toyota.

For more resources on asking questions, including a downloadable coaching guide developed by Isao Yoshino and Katie Anderson, visit LearningToLeadLeadingToLearn.com.

PRACTICING *HANSEI:* REFLECTION QUESTIONS

- What is your experience with asking questions?
- What is your reaction when someone asks a question versus tells you what to do?
- Who in your life is good about asking questions? What have you learned from that person?
- How can you ask more questions to help others think about problems they own?
- Why as a leader or coach is it important to ask questions, rather than just tell people what to do when you believe you "know" the answer?

HOSHIN KANRI PDCA LEARNING CYCLES ARE BASED ON DIALOGUE AND REFLECTION

"*Hoshin kanri* is not just the boss saying 'here is the target, go do it.' There is a lot of conversation and discussion."

– *Isao Yoshino*

Yoshino teaches that one distinction between traditional strategy development (such as MBO — management by objectives) and *hoshin kanri* is the process of how the company pursues its strategies and goals. In *hoshin kanri,* managers' targets are aligned with corporate goals through discussion and collaboration, and each level or group in the organization then creates its strategies to reach the aligned goals. These conversations happen up, down, and across the organization to provide input into *how* everyone will work toward achieving the challenges set out by top management.

Framework of *Hoshin Kanri* at Toyota

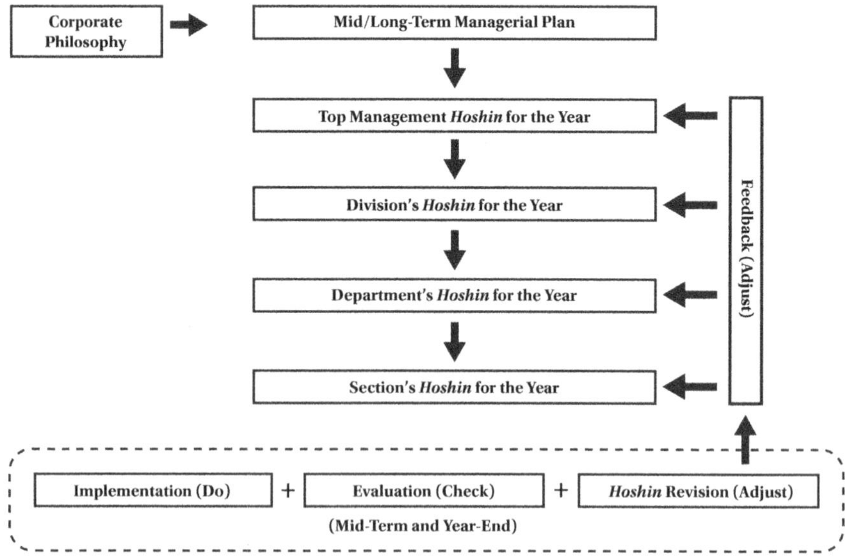

Yoshino explains that the process of *hoshin kanri,* as practiced at Toyota, is grounded in the Deming PDCA cycle and the dialogue that happens between people to align goals:

> *The process starts from the top level of the organization all the way to the lowest-ranking group in each section. Every group has its own* hoshin, *which means that each member of the group (theoretically at least) also has his or her own personal* hoshin *and goals to attain.*
>
> *At the end of each year, top management — the highest level — reviews the company's* hoshin *and its results. Based on the review, the new year's company* hoshin *(the President's hoshin) is developed. At this level, the company* hoshin *is naturally more strategic with broader goals.*
>
> *Then, based on the company* hoshin, *higher-level managers (e.g., general managers) develop their own* hoshin *A3s, and so do their subordinates (section managers). The general manager focuses on the activities of the entire department, while each subordinate manager writes their section's* hoshin. *They then need to check their* hoshin *with each other to ensure the targets and action plans are aligned.*
>
> *A lot of conversations and discussions take place between groups, and between bosses and their subordinates. The lower you go down in the company, the* hoshin *becomes more detailed with specific targets and plans.*

REFLECTION IS THE BEGINNING, NOT THE END

"At the end of each fiscal year, each division, department and section reflects on what they accomplished, and did not accomplish, and then starts to develop their *hoshin* for the next year."

- *Isao Yoshino*

Checking and adjusting (the C-A part of the PDCA cycle) at all levels of the organization is a critical part of effective *hoshin kanri.* Reflection and adjustment are the most critical parts to learning.

Yoshino explains that Toyota's practice of reflection runs deep at all levels of the organization and "*even top management turns the PDCA cycle*" — as demonstrated by senior management's annual one-week retreat at the conclusion of each fiscal year to reflect on the prior year and conduct PDCA cycles across all divisions.

For more resources and information on *hoshin kanri* and related topics, visit LearningToLeadLeadingToLearn.com.

LESSON #8

SET THE TONE FOR THE CULTURE YOU WANT

"Small things are not always small things."

- *Isao Yoshino*

Leaders' words and actions set the culture for their organization. Seemingly small choices when it comes to language and behavior can have a big impact in shaping the people-centered culture you want for your organization.

RESPECT: WE MAKE PEOPLE FIRST

One of the important lessons I have learned from Yoshino is that *"small things are not always small things."* To illustrate this, he has shared many examples from his early years at Toyota, when senior leaders took seemingly small actions to demonstrate respect and the philosophy that "we make people while we make cars."

Yoshino recalls a particular instance in 1979, which underscored the importance of how impactful a leader's words can be in reinforcing company culture. At the time that he was reporting to Mr. Sugiura in the Corporate Planning Department, Yoshino had opportunities to support Toyota's senior leaders on various executive projects. One of the many ad hoc assignments given to his division several times a year was to draft key speeches for the company president, Eiji Toyoda. Yoshino was often assigned this duty and has several stories about his interactions with Mr. Toyoda. Yoshino vividly recounted one of these encounters:

> *I was so thrilled at my boss's assignment to write the New Year Speech draft for the top leader of Toyota!*
>
> *The first thing that I had to do was to review the year's business conditions and figure out the next year's outcome, and then develop a draft of the speech. The second thing was for me and Mr. Sugiura to meet with our President in his office and show our first draft and ask his opinion.*
>
> *Mr. Sugiura and I visited Mr. Toyoda's office and showed our draft speech to him. Mr. Toyoda glanced over my draft and said, "This roughly looks like how I want it to be." He paused a moment, and then he said, "I just want to add a short comment on 'safety on the job site.'"*
>
> *Mr. Sugiura and I were puzzled at his comment because the company President's New Year Speech is like the U.S. President's State of the Union speech to Congress. We thought that adding "safety at the work site" would be too low in level for a New Year Speech by the President.*
>
> *So, Mr. Sugiura hesitantly said to Mr. Toyoda, "Excuse me sir, I am afraid that adding 'safety on the job site' might make your speech sound less refined."*
>
> *Mr. Toyoda responded, "My New Year's Speech does not have to be high-toned. I want to emphasize to all the employees that safety is the first priority at the job site."*
>
> *At that moment, my boss and I came to know that the highest-ranking person at Toyota was always thinking about his employees' safety. Mr. Toyoda did not say a word about "respect" at the meeting, but what he meant by adding these words about safety was definitely a sign of respect for employees.*

This subtle but important inclusion of a comment about safety — of demonstrating that people came first — was a testament to the people-centered culture of the organization: "we make people while we make cars." And that leadership and culture starts at the top of the organization.

PRACTICING *HANSEI:* REFLECTION QUESTIONS

- What does the top management at your company value most? How do they communicate this?
- Or, what is communicated by what the leaders don't say?
- In what ways have "small things" by leaders made an impact at your company or in your life?
- What are some seemingly small thing that you can do to help shape the culture of your organization or have an impact on others?

FOCUS ON THE PROCESS

"Attaining a well-balanced process is more important than attaining the goal itself."

– Isao Yoshino

Another distinguishing feature between *hoshin kanri* and management by objectives (MBO) is that Toyota's *hoshin kanri* focuses on the process to attain the result, rather than focusing on just the result itself. This focus on process is key to Toyota's learning culture.

The process is the roadmap for how you get somewhere. By understanding the process, we learn the factors that resulted in the outcome. We can then either try to replicate the outcome or know more how to avoid it. If we focus on results only, we only know if we failed or succeeded. We don't know what led to the failure or success.

We can then either try to replicate the outcome or know more how to avoid it. If we focus on results only, we only know if we failed or succeeded.

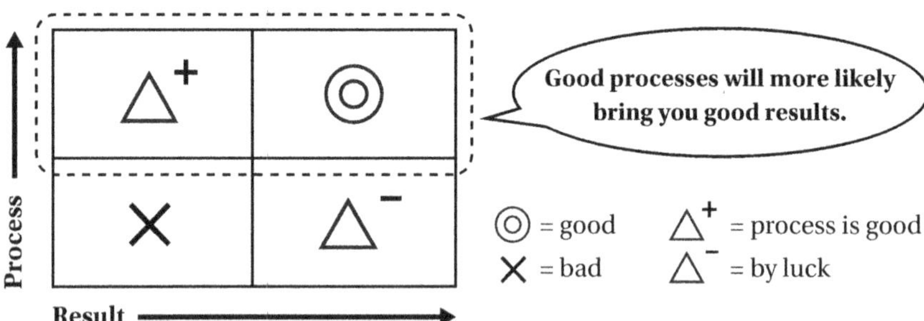

This difference between being process-oriented and being results-oriented is illustrated by the different actions taken in the *hoshin* process versus a more traditional results-oriented process.

	PROCESS-ORIENTED *HOSHIN*	RESULTS-ORIENTED TRADITIONAL STRATEGY
Plan	• Select a process to achieve the target	• Set a target to produce a result
Do	• Learn all steps of the process • Take action according to the process	• Take action and measure the result
Check	• Measure process performance • Assess the cause(s) of any defects in the process	• Check if the result matches the target
Adjust	• Take action on the processes that failed and succeeded to bring in good results	• Take action on the result that failed to attain the target

Being process-focused allows for greater learning. Remember, "the only secret to Toyota is its attitude toward learning."

"My role as a leader was to help others develop themselves."

– *Isao Yoshino*

LEADING TO LEARN – HELPING OTHERS TO DEVELOP

The previous chapter, "Learning to Lead," demonstrated how Yoshino was learning to be a leader at Toyota — a leader of people and projects and processes — through the day-to-day actions of leaders around him. In this chapter, you will follow Yoshino as he advances into the middle phase of his career at Toyota and continues the chain of learning as he takes on management roles. As Yoshino progresses through leadership levels within Toyota, you will discover how he incorporated skills of leading and learning — his weft threads — by leading others in a manner that helped both learners *and* leaders to learn and grow.

This chapter is organized into four chronological case studies spanning a period from the late 1970s through the early 1990s. In them, you will read how Yoshino served in integral roles for several initiatives that would turn out to be key inflection points in Toyota's evolution. You will also find "insider stories" and experiences — many not documented elsewhere before — about seminal moments in Toyota's history, as Toyota came to be known as the dominant car manufacturer in the world. Through each of these assignments, Yoshino contributed to developing other leaders' capabilities while continuing to grow and learn as a leader himself — through successes, failures, and reflection.

- **Case Study #1:** Revitalizing Management Capabilities – The Kanri Noryoku Program

- **Case Study #2:** Changing Culture by Helping People Change – The NUMMI Training Program
- **Case Study #3:** Focusing on the Good and Choosing Excellence – The San Francisco Liaison Office
- **Case Study #4:** Helping Others Expand Their Perspectives – The "Change Yourself" Program

CASE STUDY #1

REVITALIZING MANAGEMENT CAPABILITIES — THE KANRI NORYOKU PROGRAM

"Toyota's *hoshin kanri* — and the Kanri Noryoku Program — is one of the major reasons why Toyota continues to pursue its goals consistently with all the employees involved."

- Isao Yoshino

You might be surprised to learn that many of the leadership skills that we equate with Toyota today did not evolve solely through day-to-day coaching from leader to subordinate. What may have blossomed organically was often cultivated deliberately. The behaviors associated with the "Toyota Way" required significant organizational intention and investment in order to develop (and sustain) Toyota's culture through multiple leadership generations, and as the company expanded globally.

One such example of this intentional effort was the Kanri Noryoku Program (shortened to "Kan-Pro") in 1979 and 1980. Kan-Pro was a leadership development initiative, in which Yoshino was deeply involved during his early 30s, designed to re-teach and revitalize senior managers' leadership capabilities. Without this significant effort to reinforce leadership behaviors that Toyota considered fundamental, the mindset and practices we consider synonymous with the "Toyota Way" might not be as strong as they are today. Also, in Yoshino's assessment, Kan-Pro helped establish the use of A3 — as a thinking, communication, and leadership development process — as a standard across Toyota.

Yoshino was in the right place at the right time in Toyota's evolution to have this incredible opportunity to design and support this significant program. Through his role in Kan-Pro, he got to engage with and coach senior leaders, and, at the same time, deepen his own knowledge about *hoshin kanri* and practice critical management skills to be an effective leader himself. He was simultaneously leading to learn, while still learning to lead. And now, through Yoshino's recounting of this previously little-known part of Toyota history, and his personal leadership lessons, you too can gain insights into how Toyota reinforced and nurtured its people-centered learning culture.

TOYOTA HAD A PROBLEM

In the mid-1970s, Toyota experienced a decrease in sales and an increase in quality issues. Toyota's top management, including the Chairman and President, were concerned.

The executive team set out to examine the root causes for these issues and discovered both external and internal factors at play. Globally, the 1973 oil crisis was impacting automobile sales worldwide. Yet this didn't explain all of Toyota's problems. Yoshino explains that Toyota's top management also noticed that "enthusiasm" for the quality control and *hoshin kanri* practices introduced a decade earlier had diminished. In particular, they found that the management capabilities required for effective *hoshin kanri* (i.e., how to determine priority goals, create a plan, communicate through the organization, and synthesize information) had atrophied. Departments and divisions were not aligned. Leaders at all levels were losing sight of Toyota's top priorities and had begun to argue internally about how to achieve their goals. And critically, Toyota leaders were not passing on these core capabilities to their subordinates. The next generation of leaders were not learning the fundamental leadership capabilities of learning and leading that had been ingrained in Toyota's current top management in the early 1960s.

TIGHTENING THE SCREWS BACK TO STANDARD

Toyota's senior leaders determined that there was a need to *"tighten the screws,"* as Yoshino describes, and reinvest in the quality culture and *hoshin* practices that had been established at Toyota in the prior two decades. In short, Toyota needed a deliberate countermeasure to close the gap in management capabilities — to "retrain" managers and bring them up to senior management's standard. And to close the gap, Toyota's leaders would need to re-learn how to lead, in order that they could effectively lead to learn.

Toyota's President and top management team tasked Mr. Masao Nemoto, the senior executive in charge of quality and the *hoshin kanri* process, with developing the countermeasure to their management problem. Mr. Nemoto subsequently assigned his direct report, Mr. Sugiura — who you will recall was Yoshino's boss during this time in the Corporate Planning Department — to be the chief of the initiative. Mr. Sugiura was to pull together a small taskforce to develop the plan for (and subsequently support) a leadership development program. Yoshino was fortunate to be one of four junior staff from the Corporate Planning Department whom Mr. Sugiura chose to be part of this team.

MASAO NEMOTO: THE BIG PILLAR OF THE "PEOPLE SIDE" OF TOYOTA'S CULTURE

In Yoshino's eyes, Mr. Masao Nemoto is considered to be as influential (or even more so) as Mr. Taiichi Ohno when it came to developing the "people side" of Toyota's culture.[1] Both Mr. Ohno and Mr. Nemoto joined Toyota toward the end of World War II and played significant roles in shaping Toyota's culture.

Masao Nemoto

Mr. Ohno came to be known as the father of the Toyota Production System. Yoshino describes his leadership approach:

1 For more about Masao Nemoto's leadership philosophy, find a copy of his now out-of-print 1987 book, *Total Quality Control Management: Strategies and Techniques from Toyota and Toyoda Gosei.*

Taiichi Ohno

It is widely known that Taiichi Ohno established the foundation of TPS or lean concepts, primarily in the manufacturing-related part of Toyota. Mr. Ohno is considered to be "a big pillar" in Toyota's culture.

Mr. Ohno was a typical gemba-oriented engineer. As most of his time was spent at the production site (gemba), he knew every detail on the gemba. Because of his working style of focusing on the gemba, he was so good in finding the wrong way of doing things. So, when he found that something was wrong at the gemba, he could identify, right away, the root of problems that needed to be solved. He would then call the manager or supervisor of that site and ask them what the problem was. If the manager or supervisor could not find out the problem, Ohno would tell them to stand there and keep watching the process until they could discover the core problem.

Some people may view Ohno's coaching style as too harsh and that it looks like a kind of punishment to the manager or supervisor for their poor analyzing ability, but other people believe that it was Ohno's own coaching style to be patient until the manager or supervisor figured out the issues by themselves. Many of Ohno's admirers strongly believe that his coaching style may look stern on one side but you can see love on the other side.

In contrast, Yoshino explains Mr. Nemoto's leadership approach and his influence in shaping Toyota's people-centered culture:

I would presume that Mr. Eiji Toyoda wanted to create another "big pillar" — one more leader focused on the people-related side of Toyota. That leader was Masao Nemoto, who established another foundation of Toyota's culture in the area of "managers' role" at Toyota across all segments of the company, including manufacturing, administration, and sales and marketing.

Mr. Nemoto was a people-oriented leader who focused on the behavior and mindset of managers. He encouraged Toyota managers to be good listeners to their subordinates, to provide good coordination with other divisions or departments, to help subordinates to grow, to always review the result to improve further, and more. He tried to demonstrate what he himself would do and he expected his subordinates to understand what he meant and then encouraged them to develop their own style. His beliefs are all very basic and easy to understand, but not so easy to put into practice on a daily basis.

I would take the liberty of saying that Mr. Ohno was a traditional "harsher" Japanese-style leader and Mr. Nemoto was a "softer" people-oriented leader. Aside from whether my presumption is right or wrong, I believe the role Mr. Nemoto has played in developing Toyota's people-oriented culture is worth noting.

Yoshino explains that during Kan-Pro, Mr. Nemoto lectured to the senior managers about people-centered leadership and a manager's role at Toyota. Several years later, Mr. Nemoto documented his 10-point leadership credo, the principles of which are the foundation of the management concepts he taught during Kan-Pro — and which later inspired Yoshino to write his own credo.

For more information about Nemoto's Credo, visit LearningToLeadLeadingToLearn.com.

THE KANRI-NORYOKU PROGRAM WAS BORN

Toyota's leadership team called the initiative the "Kanri-Noryoku Program." The word "*kanri*" is the same as the word in "*hoshin kanri*," meaning control or management. "*Noryoku*" means capability or ability. "Kan-Pro" was exactly what its name represented: a management capability improvement program.

KAN-PRO'S TARGET AUDIENCE

After some debate (see "Behind the Scenes" on page 142), Toyota's executive leadership team determined the target for the re-training program. Kan-Pro would focus on *all* senior managers across Toyota's cross-functional management structure. This tier of leaders included the next future senior executives and directors in the company, and would be responsible for maintaining and nurturing Toyota's culture once the current top executives had retired. It was critical that their capabilities were revitalized and brought back to standard.

MANAGEMENT LEVELS AT TOYOTA

"The main job of higher managers is to set direction and then make sure people are happy and motivated. In other words, higher-ranking managers should be more 'people-oriented' than 'job-oriented.'"

– Isao Yoshino

Below is Yoshino's description of the management structure at Toyota at that time, which was typical for large Japanese companies. Understanding the management structure helps us understand Kan-Pro's context.

Senior Officers

The most senior level of the company was the executive leadership team, consisting of anywhere from 30-60 people. These "senior officers" or "Board members" had responsibility for the strategy and decisions of the company. In order of rank, the senior officers included the following titles:

- Chairman (one)
- President (one)
- Vice-President (usually only a few)
- Senior Managing Directors

- Managing Directors
- Directors.

Senior Managers

The next tier of management consisted of "senior managers," including general managers and assistant general managers.

Managers

The middle tier of management consisted of section managers, usually referred to just as "manager."

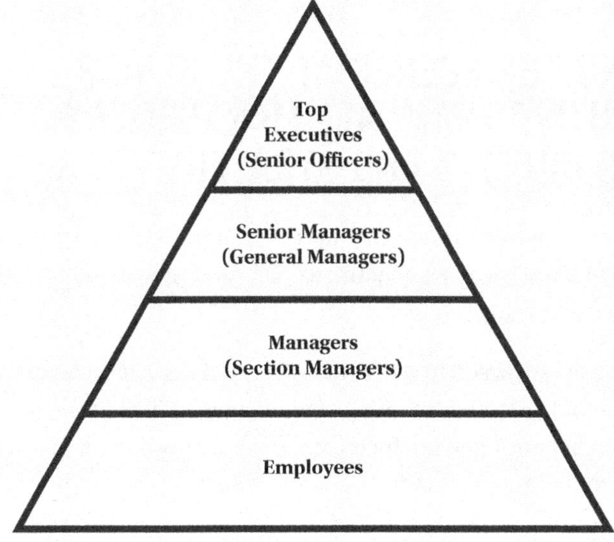

And, even though the Kan-Pro initiative focused on the 1,000 senior managers at Toyota, President Eiji Toyoda clearly laid out his expectation for the senior officers in his executive team. At his 1978 year-end executive meeting, as Kan-Pro was about to start, he announced: "While this program is aimed at managers at headquarters, I would expect that all of you senior officers will also develop your own management capabilities at the same time."

Mr. Toyoda was modeling the three leadership principles and role of a manager that Yoshino later laid out nearly 40 years later, that a leader's role is to:

1. **Set the direction:** Issue a clear challenge, goal or target to your people.
2. **Provide support:** Help your people develop themselves as learners and leaders, and create the systems that enable their success.
3. **Develop yourself:** Constantly improve yourself as a leader and a learner.

Mr. Toyoda set the challenge for his direct reports: he expected the senior executives to learn to lead, and, simultaneously, lead to learn.

BEHIND THE SCENES AT THE SENIOR EXECUTIVE TEAM: ALL MANAGEMENT OWNS QUALITY AND STRATEGY

Forty years after the initiation of Kan-Pro, in late 2019, Yoshino met with his older mentor Mr. Sugiura to visit their memories of working together on Kan-Pro.

Yoshino was surprised to learn that there had been intense discussion at the senior leadership meetings about what leaders in the organization thought should be the focus of Kan-Pro. This is the story that Mr. Sugiura told him.

Top management agreed that the people who had responsibility for Toyota's quality problems were not the frontline employees and their managers who were actually manufacturing cars, but rather the higher-ranked leaders in charge of the strategic direction and management of the company. They initially agreed that Kan-Pro would focus on these higher-level managers, as well as middle managers in the manufacturing areas because of their direct role in overseeing the quality of cars coming off the line.

However, some senior officers believed *all* senior managers across the cross-functional organizational structure should be included, not just in the manufacturing sector. For example, Mr. Matsumoto, who was the senior managing director in charge of the technical design division — the starting point in developing cars — advocated for his leaders in the technical design divisions to be included too. He believed that car design was also a factor in the quality of cars that came off the line. While other senior officers were concerned with overburdening the design engineers who were already working long hours, Mr. Matsumoto insisted that it was important for his people too to be re-trained.

What followed was a heated debate among all of Toyota's top leaders. Ultimately, they came to consensus that quality and success in the market hinged on not just manufacturing; all administrative departments and divisions played a role — either directly or indirectly — in the making of their product. Kan-Pro would focus on *all* senior managers across Toyota's cross-functional management structure.

Yoshino reflects on his surprise at learning about the behind-the-scenes discussion from Mr. Sugiura roughly 40 years after they created Kan-Pro:

> *It is amazing to me that top management had a heated conversation in the first place about what groups should be involved in the program! But what impressed me even more so, now looking back, is that higher management did not blame the workers on the shop floor for the defect problems in the market. They believed it was the responsibility of all management to own the quality of what comes out of the factory.*
>
> *So that's how Kan-Pro started: the senior management decided that "we all have to be on the same page."*

KAN-PRO'S TARGET: CLOSE THE GAPS ON SPECIFIC LEADERSHIP CAPABILITIES

"Setting goals and solving a problem by A3 is considered to be an important tool and an important skill to do 'things' right. Developing people, on the other hand, is considered to be an important qualification of a 'good' boss. Those are two different key elements to be required for managers. We need both elements to be a good boss."

– Isao Yoshino

Once the executive team had defined the audience for the Kan-Pro initiative, Mr. Nemoto and the Kan-Pro taskforce started to design the specifics of the program's structure. First, they needed to clarify what specific management capability gaps the program was aiming to close. Based on the senior leadership's initial assessment, they determined that the focus would be on developing the particular management capabilities related to *hoshin kanri*. They would focus specifically on the skills and behaviors needed to develop and achieve organizational goals within a cross-functional environment, including:

- How to have a kaizen (continuous improvement) mindset and use Plan-Do-Check-Adjust (PDCA) cycles
- How to cooperate, communicate, and negotiate with other divisions and departments, and how to get input from subordinates
- How to identify key issues and problems
- How to analyze root causes
- How to develop targets and goals
- How to reflect on progress, analyze results, and present barriers
- How to present and share their thinking on an A3 sheet of paper, including how to use A3 when making a presentation to management.

Other management capabilities — such as broad knowledge, judgment, and planning — were to be developed from manager to subordinate through daily operations, and not the primary focus of Kan-Pro.

HOW LONG DOES IT TAKE TO LEARN?

The two-year timeframe for the Kan-Pro re-training program was as intentional as the leadership skills it was designed to reinforce. Yoshino recalls that Mr. Nemoto and Mr. Sugiura spent many hours discussing the approach to the program. They believed that one year would be too short for people to deeply learn and create new habits — some would just comply until it finished but not really change their ways — and that three years would be too long for any leadership program because people might lose focus. They ultimately decided that two years would be the optimal timeframe to allow people to apply themselves seriously to learn and practice. Mr. Sugiura jokingly recounted in 2019 to Yoshino, "Two years is too long to fake it and try to pretend to work hard."

Over the course of the two-year program, roughly 1,000 mid-level and senior-level managers were assigned to participate in Kan-Pro. Twice a year in June and December, each of the managers were required to present their Kan-Pro A3 to a panel of senior officers for review purposes. In preparation for these senior management reviews, the participants engaged in many events together to learn and practice — both through formal training sessions and lectures by Mr. Nemoto, and informal monthly "study" sessions where managers and subordinates would develop, share, and improve their A3 documents together.

KAN-PRO COMPARED TO *HOSHIN KANRI*

Yoshino explains how Kan-Pro was built on the *hoshin* processes already in place, but had a different focus in terms of content and levels of management involved.

Kan-Pro focused on the senior management tier and select section managers, with the expectation that the senior officers — the top executives — would have responsibility for reviewing and coaching, the Kan-Pro participants.

Kan-Pro focused on each manager's own responsibility for developing their people and achieving their group's top goal.

Hoshin Kanri included all levels of the organization, from the top executives down to the managers and their employees.

The *hoshin kanri* focuses on achieving group targets and connecting them up, down, and across, the organization, in order to achieve the organization's top goals.

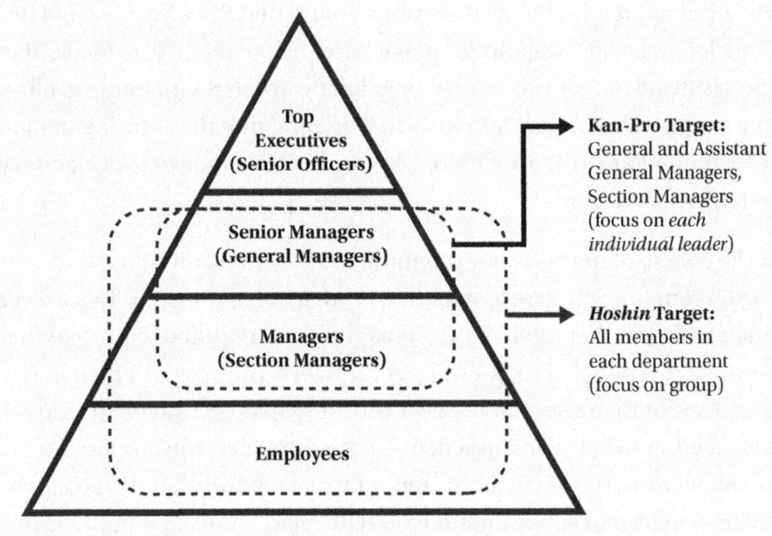

KAN-PRO'S IMPROVEMENT TARGET IS YOU, NOT JUST THE WORK

Kan-Pro built upon the annual *hoshin kanri* process in which the leaders were already engaged, but with shift in focus from how to achieve company and department goals to *their own role* in helping to achieve these goals. Specifically, the senior managers were asked to define how they themselves would develop others to be able to achieve their group's yearly outcomes. In Kan-Pro, each senior manager was tasked with choosing the top operational goal from his department's *hoshin*, and creating a specific *hoshin* plan on an A3 paper of the process he would use to support, engage, and develop his team as they worked to achieve the goal.

If during the review sessions a senior manager had not adequately addressed his own contributions to supporting the development of his subordinates, the senior officers would ask, "As a general manager, what did *you* do to help your subordinates?" This focus on each leader's actions reinforced that their responsibility as leaders wasn't only to achieve the business outcomes themselves, but also to define how they would support and develop their staff to achieve outcomes.

This focus on each leader's actions reinforced that their responsibility as leaders wasn't only to achieve the business outcomes themselves, but also to define how they would support and develop their staff to achieve outcomes.

THE TASKFORCE'S ROLE

Mr. Sugiura, Yoshino, and the rest of the taskforce had a significant responsibility to manage the logistics of the program and to coach nearly 1,000 senior managers on how to develop and present their Kan-Pro A3s.

One of the most important roles of the Kan-Pro taskforce was to get leaders excited about participating in a program that they might initially consider to be a burdensome addition to their daily work. The taskforce needed to inspire managers to believe that their participation would be advantageous to them. Over time, as Yoshino recounts later in this chapter, managers saw their abilities increase and realized that work actually became easier as they improved.

The taskforce members also played an important role in coaching senior managers on their A3s. Before each senior officer's review session, Mr. Sugiura and the other taskforce members — including Yoshino — would, by request, conduct an initial review of the manager's Kan-Pro A3s, and provide feedback on the content and flow of their documents. In each six-month cycle, the taskforce had more than 1,000 A3s to review. While it was a lot of work, Yoshino admits: *"It was a great learning experience for us!"*

In their A3 review, Kan-Pro taskforce members were looking for three specific elements of each manager's report, which they knew the senior officers would also be checking on:

1979 mid-year officers' review session[2]

- Had the managers put their top priority item from their annual *hoshin* plans as their Kan-Pro target? (Because the taskforce was part of the same department responsible for receiving and reviewing the corporate *hoshin* plans at the beginning of the year, they already knew what each manager's top priority goal should be.)
- Had the managers included and addressed items that they had failed to accomplish or had some difficulty with in the past?
- Had the managers added significant focus on developing their own people?

If any of these three areas was not addressed on the A3, Mr. Sugiura would follow up with the A3's author about how they could improve their document before presenting it to the senior officers.

REINFORCING KEY MANAGEMENT CAPABILITIES

Many of these management capabilities sound simple but, as Toyota found, they were not always put into practice. Even Toyota's leaders had to be coached and encouraged to practice the principles to ingrain them as habits. Below are just a few of the key concepts that the Toyota senior managers practiced — and that Mr. Sugiura and the taskforce helped coach — through the Kan-Pro initiative.

---

2 Photo from Toyota Motor Corporation Website: https://www.toyota.co.jp/jpn/company/history/75years/text/entering_the_automotive_business/chapter2/section4/item3.html (Accessed April 8, 2020)

1. Prioritize and Align Goals

"If you run after two hares, you will catch neither."

- Japanese proverb

The process of Kan-Pro helped leaders get better at prioritizing their goals and action plans. By having to choose their top priority item for their Kan-Pro A3 reports, the senior managers relearned the important lesson that the more targets and goals that you put in your plan, the less focused it becomes.

> **The more targets and goals that you put in your plan, the less focused it becomes.**

Kan-Pro also helped the leaders create alignment in their targets throughout the company, not just vertically from boss to subordinate, but also horizontally across often siloed departments. Yoshino recounts:

> *During the review sessions, officers would ask the general managers, "In your effort to solve your department's problems, how often have you discussed it with the general managers from other departments? This is one of your major responsibilities as a general manager."*

This expectation by the leadership team helped the senior managers understand their role in aligning priorities and goals across the organization. And, through relationships built during the informal Kan-Pro study sessions, they found it easier to talk to each other more frequently. Ultimately, these conversations — across divisions, and from boss to subordinate — ensured that Toyota's leaders were working on the same top priorities in the company.

2. Set a "Seemingly Impossible" Target

"It is what you learn from the lessons of not reaching your targets that make you smarter."

- Isao Yoshino

Targets should be determined by what is needed, not by what is achievable. One of the principles that Nemoto emphasized in his Kan-Pro lectures was the importance of setting targets that are higher than you think you actually can attain. As Nemoto later documented in his book, his philosophy was that: "Goals are only there to challenge people, and cannot be regarded merely as previews of things yet to come."[3] Toyota's senior officers encouraged their managers to set, as Yoshino calls them, "seemingly impossible" targets in their *hoshin* plans, and in their Kan-Pro A3s, rather than what they knew they could likely accomplish.

> **Targets should be determined by what is needed, not by what is achievable.**

3. Have a "No Problem Is a Problem" and "Bad News First" Mindset

"At Toyota, being perfect is not what is a priority. Failure is not important. It is the process that is more important. At Toyota, it is more important to 'check-adjust' and keep learning, than to try to be perfect."

– Isao Yoshino

Following from their belief that targets should be "seemingly impossible" rather than knowingly achievable, Toyota expects leaders to fail along the way. The twice-yearly reviews led by the senior officers further reinforced Toyota's culture that "no problem is a problem." It is by knowing the "bad news" that leaders and their people can work together to find solutions.

> **"It is more important to 'check-adjust' and keep learning, than to try to be perfect."**

---

3 Nemoto, Masao. *Total Quality Control Management: Strategies and Techniques from Toyota and Toyoda Gosei.* 1987. Page 46.

Yoshino recounts that during the review sessions, Nemoto and other senior officers would praise managers who were honest about their mistakes, not just success stories, and shared their thinking about how they were working to find a solution. Yoshino observed that senior officers would ask their senior managers directly about their failures if the manager had not included them in the presentation, and then would ask questions about what the manager was learning.

Yoshino explains this leadership mindset at Toyota:

> *Creating the atmosphere where bad news is welcomed is so important. If the big boss always carries a red pen to mark up a report or looks to blame someone, then people will make a fake report in order to make the boss happy. It does not happen within Toyota very much.*
>
> *If a manager only reports good news, then a Toyota boss will say, "Okay, that's great that things are going well, but you must have some bad news. Maybe it isn't something you are failing at, but there has to be something that you did not expect in the results. What are they?"*

Yoshino watched how Nemoto and the other senior officers reacted to the "bad news" the senior managers shared in the review sessions, and was equally impressed by the senior managers' sincere and proactive attitudes when they presented their problems. The interaction between bosses and subordinates at the review sessions created an atmosphere where the managers were even more willing to bring "bad news" forward at the next review cycle.

4. Use an A3 to Tell a Clear Story and Make Thinking Visible

"Writing an A3 helps make the invisible visible."

– *Isao Yoshino*

Using A3 as a communication process is a way to make the invisible — one's thinking and ideas — visible to others and to tell a clear story. By writing down their thinking, having to determine what was the most important information to include, and presenting their documents to their colleagues and the senior officers, the senior managers learned how to more clearly communicate. Yoshino likens the working through multiple iterations of an A3 report — writing, sharing, revising — as a process of "5Sing" one's thinking by "sorting" and "setting" the right information to tell the story.

WHAT IS 5S?

5S is a workplace organization process where the five Japanese S words are *seiri, seiton, seisō, seiketsu,* and *shitsuke,* which have been translated to English as Sort, Set in order, Shine, Standardize and Sustain. While more commonly referred to as a process of organizing visible objects and physical workplaces, Yoshino believes it is also an important concept in regard to communication and thinking.

Learn more about the concepts and history of 5S at LearningToLeadLeadingToLearn.com.

In the monthly informal study review sessions, managers worked together to share their ideas and get input from each other as they presented and reviewed their A3s. They rediscovered the value of talking with each other — boss to subordinate — and also communicating across the company to get alignment on their goals. The conversations that the managers and senior officers had in the review sessions helped uncover thinking and unspoken assumptions that previously had been invisible or unknown across groups. It was invisibility of thinking across and between groups at Toyota that had contributed to the quality issues coming out of the production line.

It was invisibility of thinking across and between groups at Toyota that had contributed to the quality issues coming out of the production line.

5. Check and Reflect: This Is Where Learning Happens in the PDCA Cycle

"The check process of PDCA is considered to be the most important part of the concept. Checking helps us to learn many important things from reviewing the result and its process."

- *Isao Yoshino*

One of the primary purposes of the review sessions was to reinforce the importance of the "Check-Adjust" cycle for learning — to remind managers that the process was more important than the result. Yoshino recalls that Nemoto emphasized this in his lectures to the senior managers:

> *Checking helps us to learn many important things from reviewing the result and its process. One of the things that Nemoto-san strongly suggested was that we need to include the check timing and check methods at the Plan Phase of the A3. By doing this, the boss and his subordinates can be on the same page and create a sense of unity within the team from the starting point.*

At the biannual review sessions, the senior officers would reinforce this point by asking questions about the check-adjust process and ensure that the managers were learning as part of their plan.

YOSHINO'S LESSONS FROM KAN-PRO

Playing an integral role in this special project was an incredible learning experience for Yoshino, still in a relatively junior role as an emerging leader in his early 30s. He had the unique opportunity to listen to Nemoto's lectures and attend the senior officer review sessions — aimed at much more senior managers than he. And, by reviewing thousands of the senior managers' A3s over the course of the two years, Yoshino refined his own capabilities for using A3 Thinking and expressing himself more succinctly. Not only was he developing his own leadership capabilities through exposure to senior leaders like Mr. Nemoto and Mr. Sugiura, but he was also learning valuable lessons through his coaching and support of the senior managers engaged in Kan-Pro. Yoshino was learning to lead while leading to learn through supporting higher-ranked managers to learn to lead as well. The chain of learning was strengthened.

Yoshino's First Lesson: Learning Cannot Be Delegated

"You can know A3 in theory, but you need to practice it yourself to really understand it."

- *Isao Yoshino*

One of the requirements in the Kan-Pro program was that every manager had to write his A3 by his *own hand* — not delegate it to a subordinate. Yoshino remembers one manager in particular who complained constantly to Yoshino that he didn't have time to work on an A3. This manager would call Yoshino on the shared office phone and say: "You are sending yet another requirement ['do an A3'] when I am so busy with my work!" Yoshino recalls that he and the Kan-Pro team would respond to these types of complaints from more senior-ranked leaders by saying something like: *"Yes, sir. We are asking you to do this. It looks like a waste of time, but it works."*

Even though many leaders grumbled about the program, they ultimately complied, and subsequently came to realize the importance of a manager's role in developing people and creating an A3 document. By working through an A3 with their own hands and minds (rather than delegating the task to a subordinate) and engaging others by sharing their thinking and getting feedback, they were actually solving more problems and getting their work done even more effectively. Yoshino reflects that, *"Strikingly, I discovered that managers whose A3s were excellent were also excellent managers at work."*

Yoshino's Second Lesson: Always Keep Learning

"The only secret to Toyota is its attitude toward learning."

- *Isao Yoshino*

One of Yoshino's most profound takeaways from this experience was the commitment these more senior leaders had to lifelong learning; they had truly embraced the opportunity to apply and develop themselves. While some initially complained, most took personal time once a month to meet together in "study groups" held outside of regular working hours, and worked on their A3s in the evenings. Yoshino told me that the impact of seeing these leaders commit to their development helped reinforce for himself that one's role — and growth — was what you made of it:

> *It was amazing to see managers in their 40s and 50s willing to give a lot of energy to work on* hoshin kanri *and A3 reporting. Over the course of Kan-Pro, I could see that they found that the program was practical, useful, and worth using to bring themselves up to a higher level. Seeing all this happen at work truly helped me grow professionally.*

Not surprisingly, leaders who took more initiative to develop themselves ultimately were better at developing others.

Yoshino's Third Lesson: It's Not About the Tool, It's About the Thinking Process

"Practical tools (such as kaizen and *hoshin*) and conceptual elements (such as respect and patience) are two wheels of a cart. If one wheel is missing, the cart cannot move forward."

- *Isao Yoshino*

Through supporting thousands of leaders in drafting their A3s and *hoshin* plans, Yoshino came to further appreciate that A3 and *hoshin kanri* are just tools that only are effective when coupled with management capabilities and mindset. The use of a tool did not translate to effective management capabilities.

In fact, for Kan-Pro, as Yoshino recalls, there was not a required format or template that the managers had to use for writing their A3s. In fact, the basic structure of the A3 was only a guideline to tell a concise story and to make one's thinking visible. In Kan-Pro, the senior managers were not being taught how to "fill out a template," as is often the case when A3s or other lean concepts are introduced in many other companies today. Rather,

Toyota leaders were learning the thinking process that the tool supported. Yoshino recounts how he realized this lesson during the taskforce's review of the various A3s:

> *There was one general manager who prepared a very simple A3 for his review session with his officers. His A3 was very simple with very short sentences and a lot of blank spaces. I thought he should have put more comments that supported his key points, and so I gave this feedback to Mr. Sugiura.*
>
> *He replied, "I understand what you mean. It is true that his sentences are very short and his A3 has a lot of blank space, but I can clearly see what exactly he wanted to say in his A3. He doesn't miss any important points. Everybody has his own style. Let's not force him into the format too much but let it go as is."*
>
> *Mr. Sugiura's comment was quite eye-opening to me. I learned that sticking to the rule or exact format is not necessarily help you to open up and communicate your thinking. Mr. Sugiura's comment was his own way of showing his respect to that person.*
>
> *This person who wrote the simplest A3 was later promoted to Vice Chairman.*

Yoshino's Fourth Lesson: You Don't Need All the Details to Support the Thinking Process

When it came to the A3 review sessions, Yoshino noticed that the senior officers didn't need to know the details of everything on their subordinate's A3 to be able to ask effective questions and coach their thinking process. A senior officer's key responsibility was to make sure that the divisions and departments that he was in charge of were heading in the right direction, with the right schedule and with everybody involved, to attain the higher-level goal. Senior leaders didn't have to be involved with the intimate details. This reinforced for Yoshino that senior leaders don't have to "poke their noses" into all the details — a term he uses to refer to micromanaging — but can set direction and ensure alignment.

WHAT WAS THE IMPACT OF KAN-PRO AT TOYOTA?

Looking back, Yoshino credits Kan-Pro with significantly strengthening the management capabilities of leaders across Toyota's entire enterprise and with establishing the A3 format as the communication standard.

At the end of the two-year program, Kan-Pro taskforce members and senior officers assessed that, while gaps still remained, overall management capabilities had improved across the board. Because of the program, Toyota's senior managers more clearly understood their roles and responsibilities as leaders, and they learned the importance of the *hoshin kanri* system. Mr. Sugiura documented in a project status A3 that the back-office managers' skills had risen up to the level of the manufacturing-related managers (who had started with a stronger foundation in these concepts). Yoshino said to me:

> *After the two-year campaign, managers recognized how important it was for them to understand their own role and to develop people.*
>
> *Of course, the results of Kan-Pro were not perfect. Many* hoshin *items still remained unsolved, and leaders still had opportunities for improvement, but we saw that the campaign had given all the managers a clear understanding of how important it is to set a target and follow it, as well as to develop people by utilizing the* hoshin *A3 process.*

After the Kan-Pro initiative, A3 thinking became an essential part of Toyota's culture. By developing and sharing their A3s, all leaders gained competence and comfort in using the A3 process when documented communication was needed, and they learned how to distinguish between what is important to report and what is not. And A3 became an important management and problem-solving process that has been exported around the world — as a way for all of us to "learn to lead" and "lead to learn."

To download a copy of Mr. Sugiura's mid-year and year-end Kan-Pro status report A3s (in both Japanese and English), visit LearningToLeadLeadingToLearn.com.

PRACTICING *HANSEI:* REFLECTION QUESTIONS

- What gaps in management capabilities exist in your organization?
- How does your organization invest in developing its managers and leaders? What happens "on-line" through daily work? What happens "off-line" through training classes or other programs?
- How often are your leaders asked to examine and define their contribution for developing their people in order to achieve the organization's business objectives?
- What are some features of Kan-Pro that you think were most effective?
- What elements of the Kan-Pro program might work in your organization? What would you adjust to fit your organization?
- Who is seen as being responsible for quality issues is your organization?
- What is one thing that you could do to invest in the development of your people?

CASE STUDY #2

CHANGING THE CULTURE BY HELPING PEOPLE CHANGE — THE NUMMI TRAINING PROGRAM

"Culture is created by the people who work there every day."

- *Isao Yoshino*

As we follow Yoshino's progress toward his dream of living internationally, we also follow Toyota's progress toward global expansion. In the late 1970s, as Japanese automobile manufacturers experienced global growth in demand for their products, they started to explore partnerships for foreign production of their cars. In the early 1980s, Toyota officially decided to enter the American manufacturing market.

Toyota now had a new challenge: how to translate and convey its culture and practices to a completely different environment — language, country, and company culture. Instead of jumping into foreign production with a plant it fully owned and operated, Toyota opted instead for a joint venture with General Motors (GM). This new venture — based in Fremont, California — would require a great deal of learning on behalf of both companies. It would be called New United Motor Manufacturing, Inc., or NUMMI.

WHAT'S IN A NAME: NUMMI OR "NEW ME"?

Yoshino says there was a lot of discussion among the newly formed company and the United Auto Workers (UAW) union about what to call the joint venture. He heard one story — which he likes as his favorite — related to the name's possible double meaning. When pronounced, the acronym "NUMMI" sounds like "new me." NUMMI was intended not only as an experiment to see if Toyota could translate and teach its ways of working to foreign workers. It was also an opportunity to inspire each person to improve and create a "new me" — for individual employees and leaders to be their very best, with new tools and management practices, and inside a new culture.

Photo of NUMMI plant. (Photo courtesy of John Shook.)

STRATEGIC SECRET: HAVE THE PATIENCE TO LEARN

"There is no real secret to Toyota. We are just more patient and willing to do things more thoroughly. We wait to make decisions because we want to consider everything and learn. We give more time and put in more effort to make sure everything is okay."

- Isao Yoshino

Toyota was not the first Japanese automobile company to enter the North American production market; Nissan and Honda started American-based manufacturing plants a few years earlier. Honda established its car production site in Ohio in 1979, while Nissan chose a location in Tennessee for their small-sized car production in 1980.

When reflecting on the timing of Toyota's entry to foreign production, Yoshino believes that Toyota's attitude toward learning — its patience to study as much as possible before making a decision — played a key role. He hypothesizes that Toyota's senior leadership made an intentional decision to delay its entry into overseas manufacturing until after its Japanese competitors, such as Honda and Nissan. Toyota wanted to watch its competitors' actions with the goal of learning from their mistakes and successes, using those insights to make an even better plan for their *own* entry into foreign production.

There was one important difference, however, between how Toyota and the other Japanese automobile companies that had started foreign production. Unlike Toyota, Honda and Nissan didn't begin their overseas production in partnership with union-represented employees. Yoshino recalls asking one of Toyota's senior officers:

> *"Why did Toyota top management finally choose the hardest option of overseas production by working with a unionized company like GM? Our competitors, like Honda and Nissan, chose non-union partnerships and they don't have to worry about it."*
>
> *The senior officer replied, "It is true that Honda and Nissan made a decision earlier than we did. I know our choice is not going to be easy. This will probably be one of the most difficult tasks we have ever had. However, if we can make it work with this joint venture, we will learn many things from this project that Honda and Nissan unfortunately could not afford, and then we can be a lot stronger."*

The senior officer's reply was eye-opening to Yoshino. He realized that the decision reflected Toyota's strong culture of patience and its ability to learn — which he considers to be Toyota's true competitive advantage.

ENTRY INTO FOREIGN PRODUCTION: OVERVIEW OF NUMMI – NEW UNITED MOTOR MANUFACTURING, INC.

"It was a great, new challenge for Toyota."

– *Isao Yoshino*

In preparation for this book, Yoshino imparted some behind-the-scenes history about the NUMMI joint venture to me.

Once Toyota was ready to enter foreign production, it first engaged in discussions with Ford Motor Corporation for a production partnership. However, Ford already had a series of smaller-sized cars in their car line-up just like Toyota's Corolla model, which it intended to be the focus of its international expansion. Because of this, discussions between Toyota and Ford ended, and the door opened for a partnership with General Motors (GM). GM already had a car-manufacturing plant in Fremont, California, with 5,000 employees who had been laid-off two years earlier. And unlike Ford, GM didn't have any small-sized car models in their line-up and they were looking to learn about small-sized manufacturing. The opportunities seemed mutually beneficial for GM and Toyota alike.

For GM, working together with Toyota would give them a chance to have a wider variety of car choices. Also, the new plant with Toyota would give the unemployed ex-GM workers a chance to return to work. For Toyota, the joint venture was a good opportunity to learn how to manufacture cars in the U.S. by using American workers as their workforce.

However, there were challenges. The Fremont plant was infamous for being the worst among GM plants: absenteeism was 20%, employees submitted nearly 5,000 complaints about management each year, assembly costs were 130% that of Japanese manufacturers, and production efficiency and quality was the worst of all GM production sites. It was known for its confrontational labor-management relations, and management separated themselves from workers (such as management having reserved parking spaces and a private dining facility and offices).

The arrangement for the Toyota-GM joint venture, as Yoshino recounts, included the following agreements:

1. GM's idle plant in Fremont would be used
2. Labor management relations would be based on "mutual trust and respect"
3. NUMMI would preferentially hire ex-GM workers (ultimately, 85% were ex-GM)
4. Toyota would send its managers (including a President and other managers — about 40 people in all) to California to support the Fremont facility
5. United Auto Workers (UAW) agreed to accept the Toyota Production System and to work with the company to improve efficiency, quality, and work environment
6. A broad range of job classifications (90+) would be reduced to three in order to develop a multi-skill workforce
7. UAW agreed not to strike as long as management did not practice "lockouts."

In 1983, with this agreement in place and the NUMMI plant scheduled to open in 1984, Toyota embarked on its newest challenge: translate its culture to a new environment.

"GOING TO GEMBA" IS THE BEST WAY TO LEARN

Drawing on their fundamental belief in the "go to gemba" concept, Toyota leaders knew that the best way to teach the Toyota Production System was to bring the former GM American workers to Japan to work directly in one of Toyota's plants. Yoshino describes Toyota's challenge and approach for translating its culture to a foreign environment:

The NUMMI joint venture was Toyota's first experience hiring American workers to produce Toyota-brand cars in the U.S. One of the first actions that NUMMI top management took was to send all American shop-floor leaders to the Toyota plant in Japan for hands-on training. We knew that these workers would need to understand Toyota's corporate philosophy and put it into practice when they were back to California. It was a great, new challenge for Toyota.

Toyota developed a high-level training plan. Cohorts of approximately 30 NUMMI group and team leaders, chosen because of their crucial roles on the shop floor, would travel to Toyota City, Japan, for a three-week immersive learning experience. Here, Toyota would teach its management practices to its newest employees — many of whom had never been outside of California, and most had not traveled outside of the United States.

Just like the orientation program that Yoshino and all other Toyota new hires went through, the training program for the NUMMI workers would include both classroom training and firsthand experiences on the shop floor. Only through "learning by doing" in the actual workplace could American NUMMI employees start to understand Toyota's culture and way of working. Toyota chose the Takaoka plant as the gemba-based training facility, as it was the plant that produced the same car that the NUMMI plant would make: the Toyota Corolla (though it would be marketed and sold in the U.S. as a Chevrolet Nova).

THE ROLE OF TEAM AND GROUP LEADERS AT TOYOTA

Frontline Management Progression at Toyota

Shop-Floor Worker → Team Leader → Group Leader → Supervisor → Section Manager

According to Yoshino, Toyota considers the group leader to be the most important role in the manufacturing process: 50% of the job is training team members on skills to complete their work, and 50% of the job is people management. Group leaders need deep knowledge both in "making cars" and "making people."

Yoshino explained the difference between the team and group leader roles to me:

> ***Team Leader:***
> *The team leader is the boss of the smallest team structure (usually between six to ten workers). Team leaders are called* "Han-cho" ("Han" *means team and* "cho" *means boss). Team leaders are selected from among team members who spend certain years of working experience at certain working areas. Team leaders are fully aware of all the working skills and processes in their own area.*
>
> ***Group Leader:***
> *After a certain number of years, team leaders are selected for promotion to the next level — that of group leader or* "Kumi-cho" *in Japanese). Group leaders manage a broader range of teams (usually around four to five) on the shop floor. Because they started as team members and then team leaders, group leaders have extensive technical knowledge and work skills, as well as people-management abilities.*

For easy identification on the shop floor, team leaders have two yellow lines on their caps, while group leaders have one yellow line.

YOSHINO'S ASSIGNMENT: DEVELOP AND LEAD THE NUMMI TRAINING PROGRAM

Toyota needed someone with both strong training experience and knowledge of the English language to manage the NUMMI training program — and they tapped Yoshino for the job. After four years in the Corporate Planning Department (supporting *hoshin kanri*, Kan-Pro, and other initiatives), Yoshino — now in his late 30s — moved to the newly created Training Department at Toyota's headquarters in Toyota City. The many years Yoshino spent positioning himself as the logical candidate for an American-based role was paying off. At last, an "international assignment" for Yoshino! Though still based in Japan, he was getting closer to realizing his dream.

Yoshino was excited by the role, and also knew his limitations. While he had years of experience developing and supporting training programs internally at Toyota, those efforts had been focused on Japanese mid-level to senior leaders and back-office staff who did not work on the shop floor. He admits that — despite his English language proficiency, love for American culture, and early experiences learning TPS in the Motomachi plant — he had no experience how to actually train foreigners or gemba managers leading frontline production teams.

ASSEMBLE THE TEAM

Yoshino knew that he needed support to create a successful training program, so he set about building his team. His first step was to hire an assistant manager, Ken Kunieda, who would help manage the team. His next step was to hire other Japanese staff members from inside the company who spoke English and had some experience with people from overseas countries. However, neither Yoshino nor top Toyota leaders thought this was sufficient.

In order for the NUMMI training program to be successful, Toyota — and Yoshino — believed they needed a native English speaker from the United States. This person could help the Japanese understand American culture, and help take care of the American-born NUMMI leaders while they were in Japan. At that time, there were some American employees at Toyota's offices in other locations in Japan — mainly in roles at Toyota Motor Sales, where they worked on non-manufacturing-related projects like developing service manuals in English for exported Toyota vehicles. But Toyota Motor Corporation did not employ any Americans at their headquarters in Japan who knew the shop floor. So, Yoshino's final step to complete his team was to find an American who could help bridge the cultural gap.

That person ended up being John Shook.

ONBOARDING JOHN SHOOK

"John Shook was one of several external candidates for our internal role to support the NUMMI training program. Everyone, including me, who was involved in the hiring process agreed that John was the right and the best one. Two key qualities that I highly valued about John: he was a good listener and he was very humble."

– Isao Yoshino

Shook joined Toyota in the autumn of 1983 to much interest across the organization. Yoshino told me:

> *John was a curiosity to everyone at Toyota's headquarters. They were all wondering how I, as John's direct boss, would train him or help him learn Toyota's culture and way of doing things.*

Yoshino describes three goals he had for managing the first American to work at Toyota's headquarters in Toyota City:

> *First, we wanted to learn about American people's mindset and way of thinking from John in order for us to prepare the best-fit training program for NUMMI shop-floor leaders.*
>
> *Second, we wanted to help John to learn Toyota culture — including TPS, and Toyota's key business concepts and values.*
>
> *And third, we wanted to develop a good practical training program for the NUMMI leaders, with John's input and involvement.*

Yoshino recalls a member of the Toyota Board of Directors pulling him aside and advising him not to treat Shook any differently from a Japanese new-hire employee. Yoshino agreed and put Shook into his own immersive gemba learning experience. The only difference was that the timeline was compressed from the multi-month orientation (that shop-floor new hires had) to a five-week training period. Shook's gemba training included learning a job in every section of the production line: stamping, body welding, paint, assembly, and production control and administration. Shook would be responsible for helping the NUMMI trainees learn how to work — and manage — the entire line.

LEARNING TO LEAD WHILE LEADING TO LEARN

"My role as a manager was to give John a target or goal, and then to support him while he attained that goal. And as I was developing John, I was aware that I was developing myself as well."

- Isao Yoshino

Yoshino and Shook shared a passion for bluegrass music and would play together at the NUMMI training program farewell parties — Yoshino on banjo, which he had started learning many years earlier, and Shook on guitar and vocals, which he had started when he lived in Nashville, Tennessee. (Photo courtesy of John Shook.)

Yoshino is often asked about his relationship with John Shook and how he helped train the first American at Toyota Motor Corporation in Japan:

> *When people become aware that I hired John Shook in 1983 and our NUMMI training program was a success, they say, "I heard that you trained John Shook. How did you train John? How was it?" But to be frank, I as a training manager didn't purposefully set out to "train" John. I needed him to be successful in his role, and I needed to learn from him about working with Americans.*

In his acknowledgements to his book, *Managing to Learn*, John Shook credits Yoshino and Ken Kunieda for being his first managers and mentors about the A3 process, though he admits "teaching me the A3 process wasn't merely an act of kindness on their part — they desperately needed me to learn the thinking and gain the skills so that I could make myself useful."[4]

While he was teaching Shook the A3 process and other important skills, Yoshino himself was learning to be a better leader. Specifically, Yoshino reflects now that he needed to learn about what it meant to work with Americans — including Shook — and find different ways to support them. Just like an experience that Shook fictionalized in *Managing to Learn* when the manager "Ken Sanderson" has to reflect each night how to best help and coach his subordinate "Desi Porter," Yoshino said there were many times that he went home at night to think about how he could adjust his style or devise a different approach to best help Shook, the other Americans, and his Japanese staff.

Even though he had a responsibility as Shook's manager to teach him (in the same way that Yoshino had been taught by his past mentors), Yoshino says that he also considered himself a learner in the process:

> *John also trained me to be a good manager. I always invited his comments and, through those conversations, I learned too.*

CLARIFY THE PURPOSE AND THE GOAL

"It is not our role to change their culture; they have to change their own culture. Our role is to help them change."

– *Isao Yoshino*

When Yoshino started his assignment of training the American NUMMI leaders, other Toyota leaders would come up to him and say: "Yoshino, congratulations on your new job. It sounds exciting, but I don't envy you

---

4 Shook, John. *Managing to Learn: Using the A3 Management Process to Solve Problems, Gain Agreement, Mentor and Lead.* 2008. Page iv.

because you've been assigned to change the culture of the NUMMI people. It is going to be very hard to change their culture."

Yoshino was daunted by this assumption that the training program for which he was responsible would result in NUMMI's culture change:

> *I was nervous and thought, "People expect me to change their culture right away? That is impossible!" I was worried that people thought I had to achieve an impossible quest. I was overwhelmed that people expected too much of me. I doubted myself and thought, "Maybe I'm not qualified for this."*
>
> *I wondered whether we could really help those American workers understand Toyota's core philosophy during the three-week training. Then I started to think a bit more deeply: "What is the purpose of this program? What is my responsibility?"*

"Changing the culture" of NUMMI was an important outcome for Toyota to achieve in order to learn how to successfully manufacture automobiles in a foreign market (the ultimate purpose of the joint venture for Toyota). But the three-week training could only be a foundational experience that would help the Americans see that there was a different — and hopefully better — way of working. Yoshino remembers thinking:

> *Changing the culture sounds like a great goal, but I am not looking after something great. I am looking after an important job of helping them start to change their culture. That is a more precise goal of what we need to accomplish.*

Yoshino talked with his team to get them on board with a shared understanding of their program's purpose:

> *We decided that we could not set out to change the culture, even though that is what people were expecting us to do. Our training department could not change the NUMMI culture for them. The people who would change the culture were the NUMMI people themselves — not us in Japan. But our training department could help them to change. So, instead, we would focus on how we can help each person learn.*

Isao Yoshino (far left), John Shook (top right), and other team members and cross-functional Toyota leaders, circa 1984. Yoshino comments: "The people in this photograph are just some of the many supporting members that made our training program a success. The smile on our faces show our excitement and commitment." (Photo courtesy of John Shook.)

A TARGET DOES NOT NEED TO BE PRECISE

"A practical style is more important than precision when setting targets. Precision doesn't matter in the beginning — you need the direction to go, and then you can learn and improve it. Spending weeks and weeks of doing nothing is worse."

- Isao Yoshino

During the program design, another Toyota manager asked Yoshino: "What is your target? How will you measure success?"

The ultimate outcome for which the training group — and each NUMMI trainee — would be evaluated was how well the trainees performed back at home, as assessed by NUMMI management. But Yoshino knew that his group needed some process measures — interim targets — to determine if they were on track.

Yoshino understood that having a target was important; it had been ingrained in him through his work in the Kan-Pro initiative and during his support of the executives' *hoshin kanri* process. However, he did not know exactly how he would measure success for the program in this case. Yoshino started to have conversations with his team to define how they would measure success. Yoshino recalls:

> *At first, we could not find any best-fit targets. The NUMMI people were not school kids; they were all plant workers, adults with different backgrounds. I thought a paper exam was inappropriate. So, we needed to come up with something else.*

Even if each three-week training program's success was not precisely measurable, Yoshino decided that they would evaluate it by two imprecise targets: impact of the program and participant satisfaction.

- **Target 1 – Impact of the Program.** Each trainee must be able to tell Yoshino at least one specific different concept he or she would implement when they returned to NUMMI. Yoshino would assess this at the farewell party — and more formally at the final training session — by asking what specific actions learned at the Takaoka Plant the trainees would use back home.

- **Target 2 – Participant Satisfaction.** When surveyed, more than 80% of the trainees would feel positively about their three-week experience. Yoshino would subjectively measure this at the farewell party too, by observing each person's attitude: did he or she have a smile on their face, or get teary when talking about it being a wonderful experience?

Yoshino admits that, even at Toyota, these were not typical targets, but knew that spending all his energy developing precise targets would take away from developing a strong learning program.

> *Many people laughed and asked, "Are those really your targets?" When I thought about it, I knew they were kind of strange targets that sounded too simple and kind of silly, but they were better than nothing.*

The targets helped Yoshino's team work in alignment and fostered a continuous improvement mindset to improve their processes between each cohort. Now, Yoshino reflects that:

> *It is important to set a target, whatever it is, and start working on it. It does not have to be too sophisticated or perfect. If it is too difficult to set*

a target, then use a ballpark target. That is better than nothing. You can then step forward with it and see what happens. Sometimes people try to create a best-fit target and spend a lot of time and energy. Many times, they fail to find the best one and ultimately give it up. Nothing happens if you don't start anything.

> **"Nothing happens if you don't start anything."**

EXPERIENCE IS MORE POWERFUL THAN BEING TOLD

"You cannot change a mindset without doing things differently first."

- Isao Yoshino

When Yoshino and his team started to design the NUMMI training program, other Japanese managers told Yoshino that the best training approach would be to tell the Americans exactly what to do during their gemba training. But Yoshino and his team believed strongly that Toyota should not force Toyota's way of doing things on the NUMMI leaders, but rather that they should give them experiences that would let them see the value of the process for themselves.

Yoshino's team set out to create the structure that would be the foundation of a mindset and behavior change for each NUMMI leader. To achieve their target, the program would need to give their learners exposure to the Toyota Production System and culture — and clearly demonstrate that Toyota's leadership behaviors were grounded in respect and mutual trust. For the native Japanese Toyota employees, treating team members with respect was already ingrained (think back to Yoshino's very first experience at Toyota in the Motomachi paint department when he put the wrong paint in the tank). However, this same mindset had not existed at General Motors in Fremont, California.

Yoshino determined that, to achieve his targets and help the NUMMI leaders change, they would have to show the NUMMI leaders what respect and Toyota culture was really about — including the problems, bad news, and opportunities for improvement:

> *In order to help them change, it would be our responsibility to give them an experience — in just three weeks — to see all the good things, the bad things, whatever they could experience about the Toyota way of working. We would not hide anything, and we would not force them to do anything. We wanted to let them experience it themselves.*

A Classroom Can Introduce Concepts, But It Can't Change Hearts

The NUMMI training program consisted of two parts. The first part was a one-week classroom orientation session, which consisted of a series of lectures. Yoshino's group invited key managers across Toyota to speak on eight topics:

1. Toyota's company history
2. Basic management philosophy
3. Human resources management
4. TPS (Toyota Production System)
5. Quality assurance
6. Quality control (QC) activities
7. Toyota's creative suggestion system
8. Health and safety.

Yoshino knew, just like his own experience two decades earlier at his new-hire orientation, that these classroom lectures would only give a foundation of knowledge. It was the gemba experiences that would provide the real learning.

Learning Happens by Doing

The second part of the NUMMI training program was practical shop-floor training for two weeks at Takaoka Plant. The team developed a hands-on training program for the NUMMI trainees, which would give them opportunities to experience and appreciate how Toyota people worked, thought, talked, and helped each other at the worksite.

What they developed was an on-the-job learning format that would later become standard across Toyota in its global expansion. Each NUMMI trainee was partnered with an equivalent Japanese group or team leader, and they literally spent their entire time together for two weeks.

Yoshino explained this partnership to me:

> *My staff and I would regularly go to the Takaoka Plant to see how they were doing on the shop floor. To our surprise, we witnessed NUMMI trainees and their Japanese partners communicating pretty well.*
>
> *We did not provide any interpreters for the NUMMI trainees. So, every morning when they arrived at the Takaoka Plant by bus, each trainee went to their workplace in the factory and would work all day with their Japanese counterpart. We knew that they didn't speak their partners' language at all, but they were able to use all kinds of communication skills they could think of: gestures, motions, smiles, facial expressions, and some basic words.*
>
> *Not only did they work together, but they cleaned their workplace together, had lunch together, took a short break together, joined all kinds of activities together, went to meetings together, and more.*
>
> *We all wondered why that happened in so short a period of time.*
>
> *The answer could be: Once you have established a strong relationship of trust and respect, language difference is no longer a serious barrier. You can communicate smoothly with heart-to-heart understanding. Most Toyota workers come from the Japanese countryside. They are good-hearted and didn't act snobbishly, and I believe that their down-to-earth character played an important role in communicating well with their American partners.*

Besides the language gap, we also could slowly see NUMMI trainees' way of thinking and attitude changing through their hands-on training at the Takaoka Plant.

First NUMMI training cohort on the first day of training — June 4, 1984 — at the Toyota Kaikan museum at headquarters in Toyota City, Japan. Isao Yoshino and John Shook are on the second to top row, third and second from the right. (Photo courtesy of John Shook.)

ACT YOUR WAY TO A NEW WAY OF THINKING

Moving from a mindset of hiding problems at all costs to "no problem is a problem" was a huge paradigm shift for the NUMMI leaders. In their past experiences, the only target they had known at the former GM plant was "production output" — with quality issues dealt with at the end of the line. Instead, at the Takaoka plant, they were being asked to address quality at the source and to sacrifice production output for quality output. In the first week of classroom training, Yoshino observed that the NUMMI leaders seemed to doubt the concepts of the Toyota culture presented to them — such as pulling the andon cable to stop the line or the role of the team leader (see on page 177).

As they experienced the Toyota mindset and actions first hand on the actual line, the NUMMI leaders started to see the possibilities of what a different set of behaviors — and ultimately company culture — could be. It was only when they experienced what happened when Takaoka Plant workers stopped the line (i.e., line leaders rushing in to support the work) that they truly understood how the system worked.

PULLING THE ANDON – SIGNALING A PROBLEM AND RESPONDING WITH HELP

One of the key principles that Toyota wanted to teach the NUMMI frontline leaders was that everyone on the Toyota plant floor — from workers to managers — shared the belief that "no problem is a problem." One tangible way that this concept was put into action at Toyota was by "pulling the andon" if a problem occurs.

"*Andon*" in Japanese means light or lamp. In this case, the worker triggers a light on the shop floor to signal that they need help to resolve a problem on the line.[5]

Originally at Toyota, andons were actual cables that workers would pull in the event of a quality problem or an issue impacting their ability to complete the task in the allocated amount of time. Later, at many factories, these cables to pull became buttons to press. The purpose of the "pull the andon" system is to make sure that the worker at each station will send only a good quality car to the next station. A key concept behind this practice is that a worker is also a quality inspector and has responsibility to not pass defects or errors down the line. And it also reinforces the importance of the team and group leader responsibilities to support the workers on the line and respond with help.

When line workers find a defect on the car, their responsibility is to try to correct it before it leaves their station. However, if they believe that they cannot finish the correction while the car is in their own area, the worker should pull the andon cable for help.

When the andon cable is pulled, a signal — often a light and/or sound — is made and the team leader is expected to immediately go to the station of the worker who is having trouble and help resolve

---

5 I am always inspired when I visit any Toyota plant in Japan and watch the coordination and teamwork of the production line. In every visit, in just a handful of minutes, I have witnessed multiple "andon" signals and the immediate response by team and group leaders.

the issue. When the problem is resolved, the team leader turns off the andon light.

LESSON: LITTLE THINGS ADD UP

To accomplish his targets, Yoshino drew on lessons he had learned from many of his past bosses about what it meant to be a people-centered leader, including how small things and making an extra effort can have a big impact. One small, but important, way that Yoshino set the tone of respect and teamwork for the NUMMI trainees was to learn each of the roughly 30 new Americans' names — both first and last name — by the end of the first day of each cohort. To Yoshino, this was an important way to demonstrate respect and to establish rapport with the Americans, most of whom were experiencing a completely foreign environment for the first time in their lives.

Also, every night during each three-week period, Yoshino would visit the dormitory building where the American trainees were staying, to check in on them and make sure that they were having a good experience.

Yoshino remembers:

> *In the daytime, from time to time, I would visit the Takaoka Plant to see how they enjoyed their work there. And in the evening, I would go to their dormitory to have an intimate talk with them. Our conversations were quite informal, and the Americans were so open in expressing their true opinions to me. We talked about our jobs, our families, our daily lives, our future plans, and our weekend plans. This greatly helped to strengthen the bonds between me and these good-hearted people from California.*

For Yoshino, who was obsessed with American culture and steadfastly working toward achieving his dream of living in the United States, a regular opportunity to speak English and intimately get to know "real" Americans was a delight. And, only in the later stages of working on this book, did Yoshino admit to me that one of the hidden benefits of going to the dorms in the evening was the "expensive thick-cut Kobe beef steaks" that were served in the meal halls. Shook had recommended that Toyota provide steak to the

Americans as they would not be used to many Japanese dishes, and Yoshino was a fan of the American-cut steaks![6]

Isao Yoshino (far back, right) and John Shook (not pictured as he is the photographer) taking a cohort of NUMMI trainees to a shrine in the mountains outside of Toyota City. Yoshino explains how he, Shook, and others would take each cohort on a sightseeing excursion during their first weekend in Japan before training commenced, which he believes "greatly helped us to informally deepen personal relationships with the NUMMI people." (Photo courtesy of John Shook.)

LEARN TO BE FLEXIBLE

The NUMMI training program in Japan was an opportunity for Yoshino and his staff to learn many things that they never thought they would. And for Yoshino, who long dreamed of living in the United States, it was eye-opening to see how other cultures approached communication and rules. These cross-cultural interactions were simultaneously a challenge and an inspiration — for him and his staff — to learn a different way of being.

For example, Yoshino was initially surprised by the level of diversity and outspokenness amongst the Americans (as compared to the Japanese culture

6 Shook himself doesn't recall the steaks, but he does remember having to jump into the kitchen to teach the line cooks how to prepare breakfast for an American palate. Instead of slightly runny scrambled eggs and raw-ish bacon, which is common even today at most Japanese breakfast buffets, he taught them how to cook fried eggs and crispy bacon.

where conformity is the norm and, as the Japanese saying goes, "the nail that sticks out is hammered down").

> *Every time we received around 30 NUMMI shop-floor leaders from California, I found out that each person was different from others. They had their own background, different way of thinking, different personality, different values.*
>
> *We were so surprised to discover that Americans speak so openly about their thoughts. This was one of the many new experiences for me, as we Japanese usually don't speak up so much like them, particularly when meeting for the first time.*

As much as the Japanese were surprised by the Americans' outspokenness, the Americans were equally not used to the rules and customs in Japan, leading sometimes to cultural conflicts. Yoshino elaborates that:

> *Sometimes the NUMMI trainees' requests were too personal [specific for just one person] or too demanding, and we could not accept their requests based on the Japanese common sense. But the Americans did not drop their requests so easily.*

Yoshino watched how Shook helped the Japanese learn to navigate the differences in cultures, and learned from Shook how to lead in a different culture:

> *I watched very carefully how John handled all those requests and demands from the Americans. He listened to all of them, digested their comments in his mind, and then responded to them with courtesy. Even when he had to tell them that we could not accept their requests, he explained the reasons in detail and his comments were convincing. He made sure that it did not hurt their feelings or dignity.*
>
> *When I came home and looked back at what had happened each day, I always wondered whether I could explain it in an easily comprehensible manner like John. I thought his style was something that we Japanese needed to learn.*

Importantly, Shook helped Yoshino and his Japanese colleagues understand that "common sense" can vary depending on cultural perspective, and invited them to see that they could be flexible in their approach and attitude to the Americans in some instances. Two experiences, in particular, stand out to Yoshino about how flexibility can help when working with different cultures or perspectives.

Flexibility Lesson #1: The Towel Incident

"Be flexible first"

– Isao Yoshino

Yoshino's first lesson in flexibility came during an early cohort. Each of the trainees was provided with one towel in their dormitory room. In addition, Japanese towels are quite narrow and thin, unlike the large fluffy towels that the Americans were accustomed to.

The NUMMI trainees wanted another towel, and openly said so, but Yoshino and his colleagues didn't understand this. It was the standard practice for Japanese-style hotels to provide customers just one towel for each person. As Yoshino says, *"one towel for each person"* was (and still is) the norm in Japan. The Japanese managers didn't understand why having a second towel was so important to the Americans and dismissed their request as trivial. However, Yoshino says that Shook helped the Japanese see that it was important to the Americans:

> *They had never been exposed to another culture in their entire life and it was not easy for them to be flexible to other cultures. John gave us a chance to understand that we Japanese needed to be flexible to the other culture first before we could expect them to become flexible to our culture.*

By being accommodating to their guests' cultural preferences, Yoshino felt that it invited the Americans to be more open to what the Japanese were offering to teach about the Toyota Way and TPS.

Flexibility Lesson #2: The Curfew Incident

"Being strict does not always bring you good results"

– Isao Yoshino

A second way that Yoshino learned the importance of being flexible was in regard to the well-intended, but not well-received, rules he set out for these American adults.

Starting with the first cohort, Yoshino imposed a curfew for the Americans to be back in the dormitory by 11:00 p.m. Yoshino said that he set this rule out of concern for their safety, as he didn't want them to get lost wandering around in the countryside. However, the trainees were sometimes invited by their Japanese partners for a dinner or drinks in the neighborhood and came back late at night, having gotten lost or forgotten the time, often missing the 11:00 p.m. curfew.

Yoshino remarks that:

> *My biggest concern was that they might be involved in some accidents or troubles with the local people due to the language gap or different mindset. But grown adults from California didn't respond well to having a curfew.*

Yoshino discussed this with Shook and they agreed that it was unrealistic to impose a strict curfew and force adults to obey it. They decided, instead, to be flexible and not enforce the curfew.

In addition, Yoshino took another action to meet the intention of his original rule to keep the Americans safe, but without imposing unwelcome restrictions upon them. Every time Toyota received new trainees from Japan, Yoshino would visit the local police department and provide them with a list of the NUMMI trainees' names and photos. Yoshino asked the local police to let him know immediately if they heard about any problems in the neighborhood that involved American workers so that he could help resolve any issues before they escalated.

To Yoshino's surprise, after he loosened the enforcement of the rule, the rate of being late for the curfew went down. Yoshino says that he learned that *"being strict does not always bring you good results."*

Yoshino (front, 4th from right) and Shook (front, far left) with one of the many NUMMI cohorts in 1984 outside of the trainees' dormitory near Toyota City. (Photo courtesy of John Shook.)

IMPACT OF THE NUMMI TRAINING PROGRAM

Despite neither the Japanese nor Americans being able to speak each other's language, and coming from different cultures, the training program was a success as evaluated by Yoshino's targets. At the end of each cohort, the trainees were always giving hugs, and had tears or big smiles on their faces, many of them saying what a life-changing experience it was. And everyone was able to clearly say something that they would do differently when they returned to California, as Yoshino recalls:

> *At the farewell parties, I would walk around and talk to each of the trainees, asking "What is the number one thing you have learned from this training and how do you want to apply it to your workplace back in California?"*
>
> *All the trainees gave me a clear-cut answer like: "I want to create a QC circle in my team," "I will clean my workplace with my people every day," "I will listen to my subordinates more often and more carefully," or "I will try the 'Creative Suggestion System' with my team." It made me so happy.*

Yoshino's process metrics were achieved! The foundation for culture change at NUMMI was established. Now the real test would be how the NUMMI trainees performed back in Fremont.

A NUMMI trainee, Isao Yoshino, and John Shook at one cohort's farewell party. Yoshino describes how each cohort would bring gifts with them from the United States. He says, *"I was surprised to find out that many of their gifts were handmade by the NUMMI trainees themselves. We were moved by their warmheartedness."* (Photo courtesy of John Shook.)

DEVELOPING CULTURE IS NOT A "ONE-AND-DONE" TRAINING EXPERIENCE

Toyota leaders wisely knew that a single three-week training program would not be sufficient to create new habits. When the NUMMI trainees got back to the plant in California, their training and support continued in the gemba with the Japanese Toyota group and team leaders with whom they had been partnered in Japan. Their Japanese counterparts traveled to Fremont for three months to make sure that the NUMMI trainees' learning in Toyota City took root at their plant in California.

NUMMI TRAINING OUTCOMES

The results of NUMMI are well known. In less than one year, the NUMMI plant went from being GM's worst plant to being heralded as its best. Incidences of employees who were AWOL (absent without official leave) went down from 20% in the GM days to 2% in the first year of NUMMI. Assembly costs went down to almost equal to Toyota's Japanese plant average. Productivity got two times better than the GM average. Quality became top level at General Motors overall. Employees became responsible for their work and proud of what they did. The former GM employees demonstrated that, given the opportunity to see a different way of working, and given the right support, they could change their own culture.

In December 1984, the first car — a Chevy Nova — came off the line at NUMMI in Fremont California. Just beside the Nova (standing in suits), from right to left, are: Mr. Kan Higashi (Toyota Vice-President, and NUMMI President), Joel Smith (UAW), Mr. Tatsura Toyoda (Toyota President), and Mr. Kosuke Ikebuchi (NUMMI Plant Manager). John Shook is on the 4th row second from the far left. (Photo courtesy of John Shook.)

FURTHER EXPANSION FOR TOYOTA – AND YOSHINO – TO THE UNITED STATES

Less than two years after launching the NUMMI joint venture with GM, Toyota invested in its first fully owned and operated plant in the United States, in Kentucky, and a second in Ontario, Canada. The NUMMI training program in Japan became an important base experience for Toyota's global expansion. Before NUMMI, Yoshino says that the Training Department within Toyota was not well known. However, after Toyota's expansion into foreign markets, and the success of Yoshino's gemba training program, the Training Department's function became critical to Toyota's success in translating its culture and principles to its new manufacturing sites. And Yoshino, having been part of creating a successful foundation to NUMMI, found himself pulled into another new assignment — to establish a successful foundation for these two North American Toyota plants in 1986.

As you learned in Part I of this book, Yoshino was initially disappointed about this assignment because it meant he didn't get approved for a role in which he'd be living and working full time in the United States. But he got back up after falling down and took on the role (which would last approximately a year) with enthusiasm and his best effort. Still based in Japan, Yoshino continued to get closer to his dream of living in the United States. For this new assignment, Yoshino traveled regularly to North America to talk with local government officials in Kentucky and Ontario to explain the importance of supporting an immersive learning experience for the new plants' group and team leaders. Yoshino recalls that the Kentucky government representatives didn't understand the importance of gemba learning or the role of the team leaders, and told him, "We have training manuals; why do the workers need to go to Japan?"

Yoshino and others convinced the officials to come to Japan and judge for themselves:

> *Every time I visited Kentucky, I tried my best to explain the key role that the shop-floor leaders like group leaders have, but it was so difficult for them to really understand it because they had never seen it with their own eyes before. So, we advised the local government officers to come over to Japan to visit our plant and meet with our people. Their visit to the Tsutsumi and Takaoka Plants was very successful. The "go to gemba" concept worked!*

After that, the government decided to establish a roughly $7 million training facility in Kentucky to be modeled after the program that Yoshino, Shook, and others had developed in the Takaoka plant for NUMMI.

LESSONS LEARNED – YOSHINO'S REFLECTIONS ON THE NUMMI VENTURE

"It works!"

- NUMMI Trainee

Through the NUMMI partnership and training program, Toyota learned that it could successfully translate its famed production system and support the development of its corporate culture outside of Japan.

Several years later, when Yoshino was living in California near the NUMMI plant, he regularly visited the NUMMI shop floor and talked with many of the Americans who had come to his training program in Japan. Yoshino remembers talking with a foreman who had been in the first group of American trainees to Japan. Yoshino asked him, now back at NUMMI for several years, how he found the Toyota Production System and Toyota culture. The foreman replied, "It works!" This was the greatest compliment that Yoshino — the person who set out to help them to change their culture — could hear. Yoshino told me: *"I was so very happy. Two years of hard work was paid off by one short, small comment."*

INTERWEAVING WARP AND WEFT

"I learned more from the Americans than they learned from Toyota."

- Isao Yoshino

Let's not forget what an incredible time these three years — two with the NUMMI training program in Toyota City and one traveling often to North America — must have been for Yoshino, who had been long working toward his dream of living in the United States. While still not actually *living* in the United States, his dream of having broader international experiences was partially fulfilled through these assignments to intimately work with so many Americans every day.

During this assignment, Yoshino integrated what he was learning about leading — through directly influencing the development and expansion of the Toyota culture globally — with his interest in expanding his world view and experiencing other cultures.

When reflecting on the impact of his experience leading the NUMMI training program in Japan, Yoshino humbly told me: *"I learned more from the Americans than they learned from Toyota."* One of the most important things he learned from the Americans was a positive "can do" attitude. This would prove to be a critical lesson that would help him in a difficult time shortly thereafter, when he finally achieved his goal of an overseas assignment to the United States — and realized that reality does not always match up with one's dream.

By every measure, the NUMMI joint venture was a huge success. It changed two companies, created a new one, and provided renewed job satisfaction to hundreds of men and women on two continents. It had, indeed, challenged every participant to become a "new me" for the betterment of the team, and to produce high-quality cars as a result of creating high-quality workers.

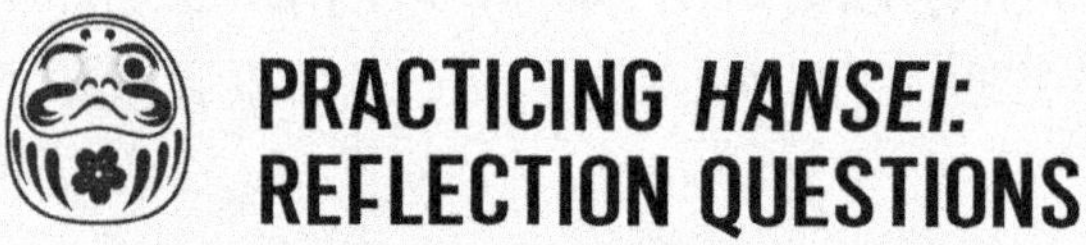

PRACTICING *HANSEI*: REFLECTION QUESTIONS

- How does your organization approach "culture change"? What has worked well? What has not been effective?
- How is your experience with programs to "change culture" similar to Yoshino's? How was it different?
- What do you think about Yoshino's measurement targets for the NUMMI training program?
- What stands out to you about how Yoshino led and supported his team? About how Yoshino and his team structured the training program? About how Toyota supported the NUMMI leaders when they returned to their plant?
- When you have had to work across cultures (company cultures, national cultures, regional cultures, etc.), what cultural gaps have you experienced? What did you do to try to bridge these gaps?

- What are ways that you can "be flexible first" when working with others?

CASE STUDY #3

FOCUSING ON THE GOOD AND CHOOSING EXCELLENCE — THE SAN FRANCISCO LIAISON OFFICE

"If you are too focused on the bad, you will only see the bad side of things. If you decide to focus on the good, you can learn so much more."

- *Isao Yoshino*

Two decades after joining Toyota, Yoshino had a pivotal life experience — one that tested his mindset, ego, and dreams. It proved to be one of the most important assignments that he had during his entire career at Toyota — all because he was able to change his mindset from the negative to focus on the good and to choose excellence.

OUR EXPERIENCE IS WHAT WE MAKE OF IT

Few people have the tenacity, patience, and discipline to chase a dream for as long as Yoshino chased his aspiration of living and working in the United States. Each life experience (like the English-language classes and study groups) and work experience (like the NUMMI training program) brought him one step closer. He amassed a great deal of cultural insight, a fluency in speaking and writing in English, and an even stronger desire to relocate to America.

Finally, after 20 years of persistence, of falling down many times and getting up — now in his mid-40s — Yoshino's patience had paid off. Toyota gave him the opportunity to achieve his goal and realize his dreams of an assignment in the United States! But reality (at least initially) didn't match the vision he had dreamed.

We have a choice, in work and in life, of how we respond to our circumstances. While we may not always have control of our conditions, we have control of our mindset and our reactions. Indeed, our happiness, our growth, and our experience is what we make of it. Yoshino, ever patient and introspective, realized early into his American adventure that he had a choice. The conditions of his "dream" were not what he expected. He could view his situation from a lens of negativity or he could choose to reframe it from a positive angle. Yoshino decided to choose to focus on "the good," and he kept moving forward by setting a new challenge for himself. Through this optimism and future focus — and reframing of his situation — Yoshino created a new reality and a different, positive experience. But first would come the challenges.

> **Our happiness, our growth, and our experience is what we make of it.**

YOSHINO GETS HIS "DREAM" ASSIGNMENT

With the launch of the NUMMI joint venture, Toyota opened a "Liaison Office" in the San Francisco Bay Area to support the Japanese Toyota executives running the plant and the frontline leaders serving as coaches to the Americans. They planned to open other similar Liaison Offices to support any new overseas plants as they opened. The San Francisco office was Toyota's first function of this kind in the U.S.

Mr. Kan Higashi, the President of the NUMMI plant, asked Yoshino if he wanted to be the next head of the Liaison Office. Yoshino explains how a friendship with the first manager of the San Francisco Liaison Office, who had gone to the same Osaka university and joined Toyota only two years before Yoshino, opened the door to finally achieving his dream assignment:

> *When Mr. Akada got into his third and final year of his assignment in California, Mr. Higashi asked him, "Who would be the right guy to succeed you?" As Akada knew me very well, he right away recommended*

> *me as his successor. Mr. Higashi was well aware of my work on the NUMMI shop floor training and he agreed with Akada's suggestion.*

Like Mr. Akada, Yoshino would be responsible for a small group of staff charged with ensuring that operations ran smoothly between Japanese headquarters and California. Yoshino describes the opportunity:

> *We called it the "San Francisco" office even though it was located in San Mateo and the NUMMI plant was in Fremont, 40 miles away over the Bay. I did not know exactly what kind of responsibility I would have, but I was hoping that the Liaison Office role would be very important.*

Yoshino was ecstatic and jumped at the opportunity for this three-year assignment in the United States. Finally, he would be achieving his long-held dream that he had patiently worked toward! In addition, Yoshino was also looking forward to the chance to follow up with the many NUMMI leaders he had helped train at the Takaoka plant a few years earlier:

> *I also thought the assignment would be great because I wanted the chance to see the NUMMI people who had come to Japan and who were now back in Fremont. I wanted to compare how they were before they came to Japan and now how they are back in Fremont. I would be able to see the changes in them, and what kind of changes were taking place around them.*

Surprisingly to Yoshino, Toyota management gave him short notice about the relocation. He clearly recalls the dates because it was such a sudden move. Even though he knew about the likelihood of the assignment, he only received formal confirmation from the Human Resources Department on December 22, 1986. Less than three weeks later, on January 8, 1987, he arrived in Burlingame, California, just south of San Francisco. When telling me the details of his transfer for the first time, Yoshino exclaimed, *"Can you believe it?"*[7] Yoshino's family — his wife and three school-aged daughters — moved out to California to be with him several months later. It was a whirlwind for all of them.

---

7 Typically, Yoshino explains, Toyota would give at least six months formal notice regarding overseas transfers.

REALITY SETS IN

Soon after arriving in California, Yoshino discovered that the specifics of his assignment did not equate to the "important role" he had imagined. While Yoshino knew he would be responsible for a variety of tasks to ensure the smooth operations of the NUMMI facility and bridging communication with headquarters, he instead found himself a glorified "gofer" or personal assistant to NUMMI's president, to the Japanese Toyota employees, and to their spouses. Yoshino recalls responding daily to seemingly mundane tasks, from helping get cats out of trees to arranging for gardeners and pool cleaners for the president's residence. Yoshino was disappointed and frustrated. This assignment was, at least at first, neither an opportunity to lead nor a chance to learn.

Over the first six months in California, Yoshino steadily became more frustrated and depressed. The gap between his dream assignment and his actual experience was a chasm. To add to his upset, his family was having a challenging transition living outside of Japan. This assignment in the United States — the warp thread that guided his life — was a disappointment. The dream was fraying before his very eyes.

MINDSET IS A CHOICE

"A change in mindset can be very powerful."

- Isao Yoshino

After six months of complaining about his situation, Yoshino realized that his ego and frustration with his assigned role were getting in the way of fulfilling his responsibilities — and enjoying his American experience. He hit his lowest point about six months in and had a realization: he was going to be in this role for another two and a half years — so he could either wallow in his frustration and complain every day, or he could change his mindset and find something positive about his job. He had a choice: be miserable or be happy.

He chose happiness. Putting his ego aside, Yoshino set a new challenge for himself: to be the best "gofer" and "Jack of all trades" that he could be. He would seek excellence. This new goal gave him renewed vigor to create a better reality. He reflects on how he came to this realization:

> *I had learned from Americans during the NUMMI training experience to judge yourself against yourself, not others, which helped with changing my mindset about my new assignment. Even if the requests I was getting were nothing special or important, I realized that I had to do these tasks anyway, whether I liked it or not. I could not afford to keep arguing with myself about whether they were important.*
>
> *I realized that somebody had to do these things, and I was in charge of the Office. So, it* was *important. I could either complain for another two and a half years, or I could find something good about the job. I decided that I would set out to be the number one "Jack of all trades."*

"Judge yourself against yourself, not others."

LETTING DOWN MR. CHO

About six months into his tenure in the San Francisco Office, Yoshino had a turning point. An interaction with Mr. Fujio Cho (who years later was promoted to President in 1999, and later to Chairman in 2005) inspired Yoshino to shift his mindset and see the broader importance of his role in the Liaison Office:

> *Mr. Cho, who was at that time the President of Toyota Kentucky, visited my office in San Mateo. In our short conversation at my office, Mr. Cho asked me, "Yoshino, I want to get in touch with Senator Pete Wilson. I think he is from this area. Do you have any contact with him or his office?"*
>
> *As I was still relatively new to the San Francisco Bay Area, I said, "I am sorry, Mr. Cho, I have no connection or contact with Senator Wilson. Yes, I know he comes from this area. Do you want me to find somebody who knows the Senator?"*

> *Mr. Cho said, "Thanks, but I am in a hurry. I will try to get somebody else who can introduce me to him. Never mind."*
>
> *I was so sorry for not being able to comply with Mr. Cho's request. I also felt very embarrassed to know that Mr. Cho had expected me, as the manager in charge of the San Francisco office, to have some connection with a "big shot" like Senator Wilson and be able to make an appointment for him.*
>
> *It was that moment when I recognized the main responsibility of our Liaison Office was to establish a wide range of connections in the Bay Area. So, although I could not help Mr. Cho to meet with Pete Wilson that day or that week, I decided to expand my human network as much as possible so I could make important introductions in the future.*

This interchange with Mr. Cho helped Yoshino see that he had a choice in how he viewed and fulfilled his assignment. He could find ways to make seemingly mundane requests of his job responsibilities take on a different importance. Becoming the number one "gofer" — and exceeding his customers' expectations — would require that Yoshino approach his role and responsibilities differently. He needed to view his work from a different perspective, and he was up for the challenge!

LEADERS INSPIRE OTHERS

Yoshino was not solely focused on a personal challenge. He was in a leadership role in the San Francisco office, managing a small staff, and recognized that he had the responsibility to set the tone for the office and help develop his people.

He set forward this challenge of excellence to his team as well. And as he was learning about his own leadership skills, he was also leading to help his people learn.

Yoshino determined that he and the rest of the Liaison Office would henceforth never be in a position to say "no" to special requests from executives like Mr. Cho — or seemingly unimportant requests, such as calling plumbers and helping get cats out of trees.

I also told my staff members, "Okay, this is the goal for you guys too. I want us to be the best Liaison Office at Toyota. We will be the number one 'Jack of all trades' in the company! Whatever requests they ask us, my policy is that we are not going to say no. We will say, 'Yes sir!' And we will make it happen!"

AIMING FOR EXCELLENCE

"If you change your mindset and decide to become the number one in a particular area, it helps you feel better and you can also have a sense of accomplishment."

– Isao Yoshino

While he never personally described his actions at this time this way, Yoshino was starting to bring the Japanese spirit of *omotenashi* to his every interaction. He does describe how — once he shifted his mindset and set the challenge for him and his team to be the "number one" at their jobs — that his entire experience changed, and so did the experience of everyone around him.

OMOTENASHI – JAPANESE CUSTOMER SERVICE AND HOSPITALITY

Visitors to Japan are often wowed by the level of service offered to them — from small details of design and comfort, to friendly greetings, and going out of one's way to help or serve others. This is the spirit of *omotenashi*!

"*Omote*" means "public face" — or what you want to present externally. "*Nashi*" means roughly "nothing" or "doesn't exist." Put together into one concept, *omotenashi* means that all your actions come from an honest and genuine place in your heart to serve and do your best for someone. It is about respecting the people you are serving, taking pride in your work, and doing your job to the best of your ability.

Yoshino found himself inspired to go above and beyond the expectations of requests that came his way. He laughed heartily while telling me stories about the many elaborate experiences he created for visiting Japanese Toyota executives who came through San Francisco. He would research the best (but little-known) restaurants so he could wow senior executives by taking them out on special evenings in the city. He learned about California wines so he could recommend the best wines to his guests, and he escorted visiting executives to special events like concerts and festivals to ensure they felt relaxed and had a good time without worrying about speaking English all day. At one such event, country music fan Yoshino was thrilled to sit in the front row at a John Denver concert and then go backstage!

Isao Yoshino with John Denver, backstage after a concert in 1987. Be sure to visit LearningToLeadLeadingToLearn.com to get the full story of this experience and how Yoshino earned and then lost John Denver's autograph. (Photo courtesy of Isao Yoshino.)

EXPANDING HIS NETWORK AND REDEFINING HIS ROLE

"An extra effort makes a difference."

- Isao Yoshino

Yoshino expanded his role to represent Toyota in the local community and created important relationships locally. He would never have to say "no" to a request like Mr. Cho's again. He challenged himself to redefine his role:

> *Instead of seeing each request as a silly lower-ranking job I had to do, I would take it as a great opportunity where I could expand my connections and establish an extensive network with local community people in the San Francisco Bay Area and at Toyota.*

Yoshino recounts how he started to expand his network by reaching out to business leaders in the Bay Area. From another Japanese friend, he came to know the ex-chairman of Alameda County Business Association, Gene Trefethen, who was an executive at Kaiser Permanente and owned a winery in the Napa Valley. Through that connection, he was able to arrange private wine tours, including one that featured a private train journey from San Francisco to Sacramento through the Napa Valley for Toyota executives and their spouses. And he came up with the idea to plant a special tree in honor of a Toyota executive at Trefethen Winery. His connections, and his shift in mindset, helped him create experiences of excellence for *his* customers — the Japanese expatriates and visiting executives. Yoshino was living the motto he considers his personal code: *"An extra effort makes a difference."*

He recalls that one frequent request of the Office was to help the children of new Japanese expatriates relocating to California get into local schools. He recounts one experience during which his "number-one gofer" mindset and the relationships he cultivated — and his spirit of *omotenashi* — paid off:

> *Many Japanese expatriates brought their elementary school-age children to the United States and wanted to have their kids smoothly transferred to the local school classes in San Mateo County. It was difficult to find any open slots for Japanese school children to be transferred to the local schools because they would arrive mid-school year. So, I visited the Board of Education Office in San Mateo often to ask them to let me know as soon as a new open slot came up. Because I visited them so frequently, I quickly became acquainted with the key people in the office.*
>
> *One day, I received a call from the Board of Education saying that they had one open slot for a transfer student and asked me if I still wanted it. I was so happy and rushed to their office to show my appreciation that I got the slot. I found out that there was a long waiting list for*

the open slots and I was just one of them, not necessarily the first one. I asked them why they had ignored the sequence on the waiting list and chose me instead.

They answered, "You kept visiting our office so frequently to get just one open slot for your people. I know it's your job, but we noticed that no one else comes to our office as often as you do. We all are impressed with your effort to make it happen. We all agreed to give this slot to you, as we know this is the right decision for us."

Viewing this American experience through a Japanese cultural lens, my visit to their office can be considered "go to gemba" and their decision to give me the slot could be "show respect."

Yoshino also handled some challenging and less glamorous requests, which he also did to the best of his abilities. In one tragic case, Yoshino was asked to help a Toyota executive in Japan, whose son died in a "shabby hotel" in downtown San Francisco during a trip in the U.S. Yoshino visited the coroner's office to confirm the cause of the son's unexpected death. It was an assignment like no other. And, more times than he can remember, Yoshino had to bail Toyota expatriate employees out of jail when they were caught on the freeway for drunk driving or other run-ins with the law. All this Yoshino handled with respect and decorum.

The list of requests that Yoshino received — and fulfilled beyond expectations — goes on and on.

A NEW VIEWPOINT AND A NEW ATTITUDE

"Through this experience, I learned how to view things from different angles."

- Isao Yoshino

Yoshino's mindset shift helped him reframe what he could get out of the experience of leading the Liaison Office and how it could benefit him. I asked Yoshino what happened for him internally — emotionally and in terms of his attitude — after he shifted his mindset and set the challenge of excellence. He told me:

> *I started to become more confident and positive. That triggered me to look at things from a different angle and to look at the big picture. There were many benefits that I could get from this role.*

Ultimately, as his original three-year assignment was nearly up, Yoshino said "yes" when his boss, Mr. Higashi, asked him to stay on another year. Yoshino's family was also happy for them to stay in the United States for one more year. Yoshino says that during the three years they had lived in the San Francisco Bay Area, his wife and daughters had also come to feel at home in California. Yoshino admits, *"I was so relieved to know that they had no problem with staying and agreed with my decision."*

Reframing his assignment and challenging himself — and his team — to achieve excellence not only made a positive impact on the people he served, but resulted in positive outcomes for him personally and professionally. He made the choice to make his original American dream a reality by embracing "the good." And by seeing every opportunity as one to exceed his customer's expectation, he cultivated relationships with most of the senior executives at Toyota as they passed through California. These relationships opened professional doors and turned out to be invaluable later in his career.

Yoshino now reflects upon how the lens through which you look at your circumstance shapes whether your experience is bad, ordinary, or extraordinary:

> *If you keep complaining about the job you were assigned to do, then you'll end up with a just an ordinary job. You can attain something, but in an ordinary manner.*
>
> *But if you decide that you want to be the best of that area, then you can make it a rewarding experience for yourself, and you can make a big difference.*

When looking back on this four-year assignment in the San Francisco office, Yoshino considers it pivotal in his life and career:

> *Ultimately, I was so lucky that I was assigned to all those tasks and I was so happy to be in my position. Living in California for four years opened the door to the next phase of my career. It was an important assignment to me — probably one of the most important assignments to me in my entire company life.*

At last, Yoshino achieved his dream of living in the United States. And during the adventure, he developed a professional maturity regarding his ability to shape and own his reality. In issuing his "number-one Jack of all trades" challenge to his entire team, he was constantly learning new ways to lead. And in embracing the newness of community relations, event planning, and concierge services for visiting executives, Yoshino was leading with a deliberate intention to learn.

PRACTICING *HANSEI:* REFLECTION QUESTIONS

- Think back to a time when you shifted your mindset from negative to positive. What helped you do this? What was the outcome?
- When, in your career or your life, was the reality of a role, opportunity or situation a disappointment compared to your expectations? What was your reaction? What did you do?
- What is a current challenge that you are facing? How can you reframe this situation to see it from a different angle?
- What are ways that you can make an "extra effort" for your customers, colleagues, family, or friends?

CASE STUDY #4

HELPING OTHERS BROADEN THEIR PERSPECTIVES — THE "CHANGE YOURSELF" PROGRAM

"REHABILITATION" IN NAGOYA

After four years in the United States becoming the best "Jack of all trades" at Toyota, and now in his late 40s, Yoshino returned to Japan in March 1991. He was reassigned to the Human Resources division where he had worked prior to the California role. However, instead of being placed in headquarters in Toyota City, he was assigned to an interim role in a smaller office in Nagoya.

While the Nagoya Office needed temporary leadership, Yoshino also believed that Toyota's senior leaders *"thought I needed to rehabilitate after spending four years away from Japan."* Toyota leadership wanted Yoshino to relearn a more "Japanese way" of thinking and acting. Yoshino was informally told that he would be in the Nagoya office for at least one or two years during this repatriation period.

This assignment ended up being less than one year — just a short period in his nearly 40-year career at Toyota — but is perhaps the moment in which Yoshino most fully exemplified the idealized "Toyota Manager." He assessed the situation, set a challenge, helped others develop, and continued to challenge and develop himself at the same time. What Yoshino created — and how he inspired his people to improve themselves — is an incredible and heartwarming story of leadership. Yoshino was exploring, experimenting, and continuing to develop his leadership style, now at a more senior level. He was leading to learn and still learning to lead at the same time.

A LEADER MAKES HIS "CREDO" VISIBLE

It was December 1990 when Yoshino was preparing to wrap up his American dream and heard the details of the new assignment that awaited him back in Japan. Just prior to his departure from the United States, Yoshino decided that it was time to document his leadership "policy" or "credo" and share it with the new team that awaited him. Inspired by Mr. Masao Nemoto's 10-point leadership credo published in the early 1980s and Tokugawa's precepts from the 1600s, Yoshino sat down with pen and paper to set out 10 leadership principles that he led and learned by. He wanted to make his expectations clear to his team — both about what to expect from him and what he expected of them. He wrote it by hand and sent by fax to the Nagoya office.

A month after starting his role as Manager of the Nagoya Office, he revised the document into "Yoshino's '10 Principles' as Manager of the Nagoya Office" — a copy of which he found buried in his files as this book was in its final stages. In explaining to me the leadership principles that he documented as his credo nearly 30 years ago, Yoshino exclaims: *"They still work!"* And I can see why; the principles are timeless, thoughtful, strategic, and people-centered.

YOSHINO'S LEADERSHIP CREDO

Yoshino has translated his handwritten credo, written on April 18, 1991, and pictured here (with his *hanko* in the upper right).

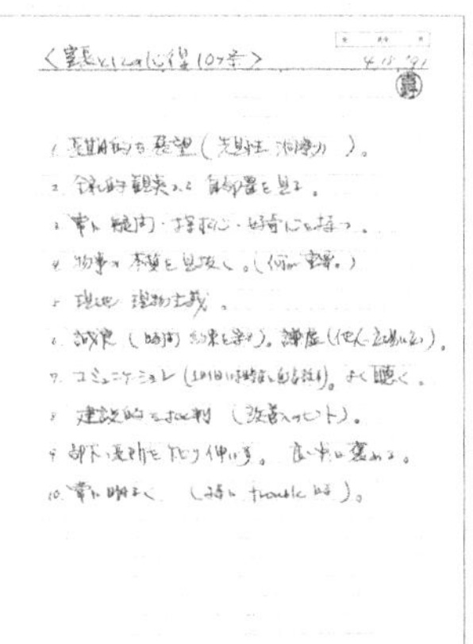

Yoshino's "10 Principles" as Manager of the Nagoya Office

1. Take a long-term perspective and have foresight.

2. Look at your own job from a company-wide view.

3. Always carry a questioning mind and a sense of curiosity.
4. Try to see through the true nature of things.
5. Practice *genchi-genbutsu-shugi* (go to gemba).
6. Be conscientious (keep your promises, be punctual) and humble (take someone else's view).
7. Communicate (talk to subordinates at least once a day). Listen to them carefully.
8. Give constructive criticism (a clue to kaizen).
9. Try to find out your subordinates' strong points, give praise, and develop them.
10. Stay cheerful (particularly when you are in trouble).

To download a copy of Yoshino's Credo, visit LearningToLeadLeadingToLearn.com.

ASSESSING THE CURRENT CONDITION – AND ISSUING A CHALLENGE

When he arrived in the Nagoya Office, Yoshino spent his first few weeks assessing the current conditions of the people and the work he was assigned to manage. And, of course, he did this by going to the gemba, observing the work, and talking to his people.

He quickly determined that this would be a vastly different assignment from his recent one in the United States. Instead of managing interactions across cultures and managing a small team with unique requests to fulfill (as he did in the San Francisco Liaison Office), Yoshino would now manage a large group of about 50 people that had regular, routine tasks, primarily focused in Japan.

Yoshino saw this assignment as an opportunity to explore his management style and institute all the people-centered leadership skills he had been developing over the past two decades. Yoshino determined that — while the actual work of the group was under control and his managers were doing a good job in managing the work — his people's growth and development needed his attention.

In looking back, Yoshino reflects on his initial assessment and how it led to his decision to focus on people development:

> *First, I didn't know anything about the work that the job group was doing, so I felt that I could do a better job as a manager just to watch and support them. Second, I also had about 50 people working for me, which is kind of a big group. I knew I could not manage everyone myself. Third, it was a very regular, routine job — nothing creative — mainly word-processing tasks. I thought that this assignment would be a nice opportunity for me to take time and learn something other than just doing the "job." I really could focus on the people.*

The challenge that he needed to tackle was not in managing the work but managing each person's personal development and challenging himself in how to support them. This would be a time to fully explore his leadership approach — now at a more senior level.

A LEADER SHOULD HELP BUT NOT MICROMANAGE

One of Yoshino's first actions upon arriving in Nagoya surprised his two assistant managers. Their previous boss had been a more traditional Japanese leader, an older man with a command-and-control style, who would, as Yoshino describes, *"poke his nose into the details all the time and tell them what to do."*

Because the work was under control and his assistant managers were doing a good job at managing the work and the people, Yoshino decided to take a different approach:

> *Right after I was assigned, I talked with my two assistant managers and said, "I'm new here and I am sure that you know everything about how things should be run. Even though it is my job to oversee everything, it's your area and you know better. I trust you and respect you as managers. You should do whatever you need to do. If you do your job,*

> *I won't poke my nose into what you do. Don't expect me to give you any good advice because I don't know the work like you do. But, please come to me when you have trouble or if you cannot handle everything by yourself — then I will do my best to help. But other than that, you can do whatever you believe is right."*

When Yoshino told the assistant managers this, they were completely surprised! They had never had a manager who had trusted them to do their job, even at Toyota. Yoshino was coming in with a totally different approach and way of thinking. Yoshino recalls their shock:

> *The assistant managers asked me, "Are you really giving us the freedom to do whatever we want?" I replied, "Yes, that is right. In this first week, I spent a lot of time in the office and could sense that you are trusted by your people. So, I give you the authority to do whatever you believe is the right thing to do."*

TEACHING OTHERS HOW TO WEAVE THEIR WARP AND WEFT

As Yoshino observed his employees in the first weeks of his new role, he discovered that they had limited world experience or opportunities for growth. He explains:

> *I discovered that they were all very nice people, who were very loyal to regular daily practices. Yet I didn't see them excited about much in their lives. Every morning they would come into the office and in the evening they would go home. Many of them took the bus a long way as they lived far outside the city. They didn't really have opportunities to get out and talk to other people and take advantage of commuting to a big city like Nagoya.*
>
> *I asked myself, "Are these people happy doing the same thing every single day, Monday through Friday? Coming into the office at 8:30 in the morning and leaving at 5:30 or 6:00, and then coming back the next day?" I decided to find a way to help them have more opportunities in their business and private life, to become more outgoing and to have a broader view.*

Yoshino assessed that there was a gap to be closed — not in the work, but for his people. He set his personal challenge: facilitate the growth of his people. And he set a challenge for his people: attain a broader worldview and define their greater purpose in life.

Early in this book, I introduced the weaving metaphor — the way in which we have stable, foundational "warp threads" (like Yoshino's life purpose to live internationally) between which we eventually weave "weft threads" based on our newfound passions and experiences. Yoshino had discovered that his love for developing people was one of his own weft threads and that, in developing people, he could help others understand their warp threads and find their *own* weft threads too.

Having a challenge — and a commitment to lifelong learning — was fundamental to the culture Toyota was cultivating. Yoshino realized that there was a gap to be filled for his people, and that as their boss, it was his responsibility to give them a challenge and create the conditions for their learning. Yoshino determined that he would spend his time developing his people and provide them with different experiences beyond their daily jobs and routines. He was going to help them understand their own warp threads — their dream or purpose — and teach them how to weave their weft threads by helping them develop themselves.

START WITH PURPOSE

Yoshino knew — from his own experiences in life and leadership — that having a purpose (i.e., a long-term vision, a dream to attain, or a goal to achieve) is essential. These are the solid warp threads on which our lives are based and our life's fabric is woven. Our warp threads give us the framework to develop ourselves and develop others. He did not sense that his people had embraced or even articulated expansive goals — beyond life essentials, such as going to a job to get a paycheck. Yoshino recalls telling his staff shortly after he started:

> *You have to develop your purpose. You need a dream to guide you. You must set up your goal to attain. Whatever it is you believe, it is important to develop yourself, to expand your viewpoint or perspective.*

Yoshino's own warp threads — his long-term dream and purpose — had shaped his life and had given him strength to persist. He wanted to help these young people tap into their own greater sense of purpose, and have the opportunity to see beyond their day-to-day lives. He wanted to continue the chain of learning — of life and leadership — that he had experienced throughout his years at Toyota.

Yoshino now reflects on how he set out to go beyond the assigned duties of his role and embrace a new challenge of people-development:

> *It was a great experience because I didn't do any of the actual human resources management work of my division; I let my assistant managers to do that. I just developed a training program for my own 50 people.*

While "just developing a training program" may seem like something small, it had a huge impact on the 50 people reporting to him. He made developing his people his number one focus.

DEVELOPING THE "CHANGE YOURSELF" PROGRAM

Even the casual observer is apt to acknowledge that Yoshino went above and beyond the expectations of his temporary assignment to manage the Nagoya Office Human Resources Department. Beyond simply managing the office, he set out to create opportunities for his people to develop themselves. Drawing on his years of leading formal training programs (such as Kan-Pro and NUMMI), Yoshino was inspired to create a special initiative for his people. He designed a program called the "Aesthetics" Program in Japanese, or the "Change Yourself" Program (as Yoshino translates to English). The purpose of the Change Yourself Program was to help people expand their perspectives and learn how to develop themselves. And Yoshino challenged himself on how he could best support his people in achieving this challenge.

THE SIX-COURSE "CHANGE YOURSELF" PROGRAM

Yoshino's "Change Yourself" Program consisted of six "courses," which he documented in a booklet for his staff. Each course included a didactic component that Yoshino taught, as well as an experiential learning assignment. The six courses reflect the mindset and skills — the weft threads — that Yoshino believes to be important to be able to achieve one's dreams (one's warp threads).

Yoshino translated the booklet into English, the high-level outline of which is directly quoted below.

Purpose of the "Change Yourself" ("Aesthetics") Program

Everybody wants to make more progress today than yesterday, and more tomorrow than today. Why don't you break out of your shell and change yourself to a "New You"?

Course A: "Widen" Your Human Network

Talk with more business colleagues. Know more about them. Let them know more about yourself.

Course B: "Broaden" Your Perspective

Observe things from many different angles. You will find that things now look different.

Course C: "Enhance" Your Power of Expression

Develop an ability to express yourself clearly. It will help you to become more persuasive.

Course D: "Enhance" Your Ability to Take Action

Go to gemba and talk to the people and watch things with your own eyes. It will make you become an "on-the-go" person.

Course E: "Experience" Different Cultures (in Your Backyard)

Visit places (in Japan) where people think differently and act differently. Placing yourself in a different culture is a great chance to explore the differences between others and yourself.

Course F: "Experience" Different Cultures (in Overseas Countries)

Visit overseas countries where values and the way of thinking is very different. It will help you to consider ways of changing yourself.

To download the complete translation of Yoshino's "Change Yourself" Program, visit LearningToLeadLeadingToLearn.com.

Be Available

First, Yoshino opened up his calendar for several evenings each week and invited pairs or small groups of staff to join him for dinner at a restaurant of their choosing, paid for out of his own pocket. Just like his first boss, Mr. Tamura, had done in taking the extra time to share his experiences with his staff, Yoshino now took extra opportunities to connect with and share his own broader world perspective with his young staff members.

Share Your Knowledge

Second, every week for several months, Yoshino drafted a small essay on personal development topics. In the end, he created more than 40 different essays, all written on A5-sized paper (half the size of A4- or letter-sized paper). Yoshino would choose one concept that stood out to him from his experiences that week and, from that, would determine one keyword as the theme for his essay. He would write his essay on a word processor and share it with his team:

> *Whenever I had an incident that I wanted to share with my team, I first determined the theme that I wanted to express, and then I thought about*

how to share the story. I kept the goal of writing every week. It wasn't easy for me, but it was important. It inspired me to think about the things that amazed me and how I could share them with my people.

One of his staff members suggested to Yoshino that they select some of the essays and collate them into a booklet, which they titled "Post Script (P.S.) from Yoshino."

P.S. FROM MR. YOSHINO – ESSAYS FOR HIS EMPLOYEES

As Yoshino and I were preparing to write this book, Yoshino went on an expedition of sorts, searching through archives and boxes and closets. In doing so, he found the "Post Script (P.S.) from Mr. Yoshino" booklet written in Japanese. On my request, he translated a selection of the essay titles and key topics, which are included below.
Yoshino's essays hearken back to the musings of ancient Asian philosophers — at times simultaneously esoteric and profoundly insightful.

普通 *(August 5, 1991)* — **Being Normal and Ordinary**

Being an ordinary and decent person should be the first thing we try to be. It is the very basic value as a human being. Without attaining this goal first, how can we become extraordinary next?

国際人 *(August 7, 1991)* — **Internationally Minded Person**

What is the qualification of "an internationally minded person?"
A person who has lived overseas for a long time, or speaks foreign language fluently? A person who can understand and accept different viewpoints and way of thinking? A person who can look at things from many different angles?

欠点 *(August 20, 1991)* — **Everybody has Faults**

People who strongly believe they are superior and have no faults often disillusion others. A real capable person is the one who knows their faults and can face them squarely.

名前 *(August 28, 1991)* — **Names**

"Hey, you with glasses!" My big boss called me that way as he didn't remember my name. Remembering someone's name is a good way to establish good relations with people.

振り返る *(September 3, 1991)* — **Looking Back**

A marathon runner who never looks back during the race is considered to be the strongest. But, looking back is not so bad. We can learn so many things by looking back and reflecting.

優秀 *(October 14, 1991)* — **Brilliant vs. Capable**

A brilliant person is the one who is excellent, confident in oneself, and highly evaluated by others. A capable person is the one who makes sound judgment, has flexibility to cope with problems and knows how to work together with others.

肩書 *(October 28, 1991)* — **Position Title**

Business cards have a position title along with the name. It shows how high-positioned a person is. We always have to ask ourselves whether we live up to our position title.

一流 *(November 5, 1991)* — **Top-Ranked**

Toyota is one of the most excellent, top-ranked companies in the world. Does it mean that people working at Toyota are also top-ranked? It all depends on how you think and behave.

違い *(November 7, 1991)* — **Difference**

Partners are often likened to "two wheels on the car." Now, I believe it should be "both feet." If both feet try to go forward at the same time, you can't walk. Being different helps us to know something new.

To download a copy of these select "P.S. from Mr. Yoshino" essay excerpts, visit LearningToLeadLeadingToLearn.com.

Provide Experiences

Third, Yoshino challenged — and supported — his staff to try new experiences. These started with smaller challenges, such as "talk with more business colleagues" or "go to a new city and observe," and culminated with broader experiences, such as taking a trip either outside of the Nagoya area or overseas. Yoshino not only issued these challenges, he enabled them to happen by providing both the time and funding to his people. He wanted to give them the opportunity to develop — to change yourself to be a "new you" — hearkening back to the NUMMI name of becoming a "new me."

CREATING LOCAL CONNECTIONS AND LEARNING OPPORTUNITIES

Yoshino asked his staff what types of people and businesses they would like to meet locally in Nagoya. One staff member suggested an advertising company that made commercials — because creative work was so different from their work in human resources. Yoshino drew on the many connections he had in Toyota and talked with a colleague who worked in Toyota's public relations office. This colleague was, in turn, able to make an introduction at Dentsu, the largest advertising and public relations companies in Japan, which had an office in Nagoya that was walking distance from the Toyota office.

> *I went to Dentsu with Kyoko, my staff member, to talk with their General Manger. I explained the "Change Yourself" Program to him. He was so surprised, and said, "Oh, you are trying to develop your people's mentality! I've never heard of something like this."*
>
> *He liked my idea, so we decided that each month we would get together, one month in Toyota's office and the next in Dentsu's office. We would choose a guest speaker from each company to share a new topic with the group. I picked up some of the best people from my network at Toyota to come and present to my staff and Dentsu! Everyone loved it. We did that six times before I left.*

Just as he learned through his experiences in the San Francisco Liaison Office, building and leveraging relationships — creating networks and connections — helps everyone learn.

> **Building and leveraging relationships – creating networks and connections – helps everyone learn.**

INSPIRING DREAMS AND HELPING TO MAKE THEM HAPPEN

Yoshino knew that it would be difficult for these young people to have the money to travel in Japan — and even more so to go overseas. So, undaunted, he became creative about how he could help make it happen. For staff members who had a dream of going to Tokyo or another city in Japan, he told them that he would provide a budget for one day of travel. For overseas experiences, he had a grander plan.

Drawing on a self-described, now bolder "American" style of doing things, Yoshino decided to leverage his Jack-of-all-trades skills honed over four years in California. During that time, he had developed good relationships with most of the international airlines, as he managed flights for the Toyota expats and visiting executives. He boldly decided that he would ask each of the major airlines to donate free tickets for his employees!

In the "Change Yourself" booklet, Yoshino declared his plan:

> *"Airline companies that I have an association with are considering giving me free air tickets (economy) for you to fly overseas. I will try my best to make it happen. Just keep your fingers crossed."*

Yoshino laughs at this memory and recounts that his employees would say, "Yoshino, you are crazy!" Yet he persisted, and each week he would go to a different airline office in Nagoya to explain the purpose of the program to the airlines and make the request. The airline representatives not only liked Yoshino's idea, they also wanted to keep a good relationship with Toyota. Ultimately, Yoshino ended up securing 22 roundtrip tickets (from companies like JAL, ANA, Lufthansa, Qantas, and others) — enough for 11 pairs of employees to have their first experience overseas! Some companies donated multiple pairs of tickets because they liked Yoshino's idea so much.

After putting in the hard work of getting the tickets, Yoshino did not want the responsibility of determining who would get to use them — plus he saw this as an opportunity for his staff to develop negotiation and decision-making skills. He left the decisions to the staff:

> *Whenever I got a pair of free tickets, the people who wanted to go abroad would determine who would get to use them. I told them, "It's my job to get the tickets, it's your role to decide who gets to use them. That's part of this program."*

However, there was one time when Yoshino intervened in the process because he wanted to make sure that all of his staff — including his assistant managers — could experience the benefits of the program:

> *My assistant manager — who later became Mr. Cho's secretary*[8] *— was a very nice and humble guy. I knew that he would like to go overseas because he had never been outside of Japan, but he always gave the chance first to his own people.*
>
> *So, one day I said, "Why don't you go somewhere with this ticket? You always give the chance to your people. You are so modest, but you also deserve it." Even though he protested, I insisted that he take it and somewhat jokingly said, "It's my order!" Nobody complained. He went to Great Britain and enjoyed it very much! He was so excited about it, and I was so happy that I was able to encourage him to have the experience.*

---

8 While "Secretary" is the correct and direct translation of this title from Japanese to English, the English word "secretary" belies the scope and responsibility of what this role was at Toyota. This position is more akin to a "chief of staff" or "executive advisor" role (think "Secretary of State" in U.S. government), and is filled by a senior manager of high rank.

GO BEYOND A JOB DESCRIPTION TO DO NOT JUST WHAT IS REQUIRED, BUT WHAT IS MEANINGFUL

"It was not necessary, but it was meaningful to my people."

- *Isao Yoshino*

What an amazing experience for these young people, most of whom had never experienced life outside the greater Nagoya area, much less outside of Japan. And what a testament to Yoshino's greater purpose of helping develop others and having a broader worldview.

When looking back on his efforts, Yoshino says:

> *It was a bit crazy, but the program worked, and my staff liked it so much! I did all kinds of things that people had never thought of before. It was not necessary, but it was meaningful to my people.*

Word of the program spread throughout Toyota's Nagoya Office and, as a result, another division approached Yoshino's assistant manager to learn how they could develop their own similar program.

IMPACT OF A CARING LEADER WHO SETS A CHALLENGE AND PROVIDES SUPPORT

"I learned that we can change ourselves if we have an intention and some trigger."

- *Isao Yoshino*

Yoshino's people-centered leadership approach — his creativity, caring, and courage to develop the "Change Yourself" Program — had a positive and lasting impact on his people. Yoshino recounts the impact the program made on one staff member in particular:

> *I encouraged one of my staff members, who was very calm and quiet, to go to Europe on one of the free pairs of tickets. I wanted to help her*

change her perspective from being less positive to more positive. On the third or fourth time I spoke with her, she finally decided that she would go, and she flew to Germany with another staff member.

I talked to my friend in Germany and asked him, "Please take care of my people." And then he took them out to the Autobahn, going 250 kilometers per hour! She returned back to Japan very influenced by her trip to Europe, and she later decided to quit the company and go to university.

Her father sent me a special New Year's postcard the next year. He said, "Mr. Yoshino, you have changed my daughter's character in a better way. She expanded her perspective and now is starting something new. I really appreciate what you have done."

It was one of the results of the program! It's a small incident, but she changed her life path because of it.

A SHORT-TERM ROLE, A LONG-TERM IMPACT

Both Yoshino and his staff were surprised when Yoshino was reassigned to a new role less than 10 months after he started in the Nagoya Office. One of the roles of the Human Resources Department was to manage all the transfers that happened between the Nagoya Office and other Toyota sites and, because of this, they were the first to know of new assignments. Yoshino recalls the shock of learning of his reassignment:

When the reassignment list came through, one of my staff members was looking through the names and exclaimed, "Mr. Yoshino, your name is on the list!"

Yet even though his assignment in the Nagoya Office was only 10 months long, his impact was powerful. In one of our later conversations about this period, Yoshino reflected on his tenure in the Nagoya Office:

One of my staff members said to me, "Mr. Yoshino, you arrived in March like a wind, and you are leaving like a wind again!" In looking back at that time, I was just a strong wind, a typhoon named Yoshino, who came in and did something different, something extraordinary, and then departed.

> *I was so happy to have worked together with those nice people. They were not necessarily so open-minded or positive at first, but 10 months later they had changed. I learned that we can change ourselves if we have an intention and some trigger.*

Yoshino was that trigger for these people. He fully embraced his role as a leader — set a challenge, help them develop, and developed himself at the same time. Yoshino took advantage of his global perspective, the interweaving of his warp thread of international experiences with his weft threads of developing others, and helped his employees start on their own paths toward weaving their own lives of purpose. Instead of "rehabilitating" himself to a more traditional Japanese approach (as Toyota wanted him to do during his repatriation from the United States), Yoshino focused on people development and opened up a world of possibilities for young people reporting to him. Yoshino's leadership style was contagious!

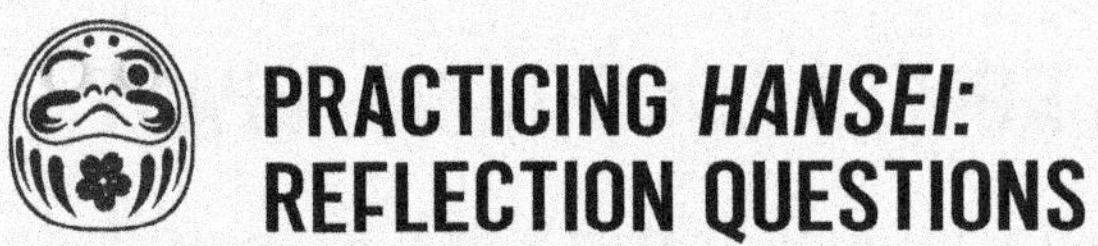

PRACTICING *HANSEI*: REFLECTION QUESTIONS

- Think back to your experiences with a leader, coach, or teacher who truly cared about your development. What was the impact on your life or career?
- What have you done to change yourself? Who has helped you?
- How can you help others broaden their perspectives and even their worldviews?
- What is your leadership credo?
- What are some actions that might not be "necessary" for your role, but could be meaningful for your people?
- Which of the "P.S. from Mr. Yoshino" essays resonate the most with you?

“Failure isn’t failure if you learn something important you could never have learned elsewhere.”

– Isao Yoshino

REFLECTING ON FAILURE: TOYOTA'S WATER-SKI BOAT BUSINESS

In the last third of his career at Toyota, on a project that spanned much of the 1990s and into the 2000s, Isao Yoshino experienced his biggest professional failure — one that cost Toyota $13 million and required Yoshino to test all that he had learned about leading and learning.

The water-ski boat saga that you will discover here comprises many stories about learning and leading. It's about innovation and entrepreneurship — about coming up with an idea, setting a goal, and pursuing it with patience and perseverance. It's also about falling down many times, but still getting back up. It's about doing one's best to lead (and learn) in the face of adversity and complexity. And, ultimately, it's about failing to succeed. Neither Yoshino nor Toyota achieved their goal of a successful water-ski boat business in the United States. But, most importantly, this is a story about learning. In reflecting on this poignant and difficult experience, Yoshino concedes that the water-ski boat business was not a *complete* failure; he was able to learn, and Toyota was able to learn, and now he shares these lessons with us.

As a leader, Yoshino has many regrets over his part in what transpired — some decisions and actions that were in his control and many outside his control. He acknowledges that he tried his best to achieve success for the business venture overall and to ensure that other people had the capabilities and support they needed for success.

However, this is not just a story of personal mistakes, failures, and learnings; it is also one of organizational mistakes, failures, and learnings. It is an account of a failed business venture that contrasts with Toyota's successful automobile expansion efforts — such as the NUMMI (California), Kentucky, and Ontario production sites — where considerable effort was made to create a unified culture and to teach the fundamentals of the Toyota Production System (TPS) and Toyota management culture. At its conclusion, when they decided to shutter the U.S. water-ski boat business, Toyota leadership acknowledged that the company needed to learn from their mistakes made along the way.

What follows is a narrative, pieced together over years of reflection, organized into four distinct phases of the water-ski boat project and Yoshino's personal growth. During the nearly 10 years that the water-ski boat venture spanned, Yoshino first set a personal challenge, and as he wove his warp and weft threads together to pursue a new business for Toyota in the United States, he was continuously leading to learn, and still learning to lead.

- **Phase 1:** A New Target for Yoshino — Toyota Marine Sports USA
- **Phase 2:** Doing His Job, But Secretly Working on a New Idea
- **Phase 3:** The American Water-Ski Boat Business Launches in Rough Waters
- **Phase 4:** Managing the Water-Ski Business in Florida

There are many rich lessons in Yoshino's reflections of this failure: what to do and what not to do as a leader, the responsibility a company has to its people, and how failure can be the source of rich learning. And, now it is time for you to discover and learn from this story. But first, a quick timeline to orient you to this vital decade in Yoshino's life, and a sidebar on the spirit of innovation at Toyota, to provide the context you'll need for what you're about to learn.

TIMELINE

January 1992	Yoshino is assigned to the Marine Business Preparation Department (Toyota City, Japan)
January 1993	Yoshino discovers the U.S. water-ski boat market is large and potentially promising for a new Toyota product
January 1994	Yoshino informally establishes a team to begin a feasibility plan for a U.S. water-ski boat business
Late 1996	Yoshino proposes the U.S. water-ski boat business plan to top management and receives approval
January 1997	Yoshino is assigned to Toyota Motor Sales (TMS) USA (Torrance, CA) and TMS establishes a U.S.-based Marine Division
Mid-1998	Toyota begins water-ski boat manufacturing in Orlando, FL
May 1999	Yoshino is promoted to Plant Manager for the water-ski boat factory and relocates to Orlando, FL
January 2000	Mr. Fujio Cho, President of Toyota Motor Corporation, visits the water-ski boat plant in Orlando, FL
August 2001	Toyota decides to officially exit the U.S. water-ski boat business and informs Yoshino
September 2001	Yoshino is called to Torrance just a few days before 9/11 to discuss the plant closure
October 2001	Yoshino temporarily returns to Toyota Motor Corporation headquarters in Japan to receive the news of his next assignment in Toyota's home-use Fuel Cell Project (where he will remain based in Torrance, CA)
November 2001	The Orlando water-ski boat plant closes and Yoshino begins his role working on the Fuel Cell Project

January 2004	Yoshino retires from Toyota Motor Corporation and joins a small consulting firm working on Toyota's home-use Fuel Cell Project
January 2007	Yoshino repatriates to Japan and starts teaching at Aichi Gakusen University (Nagoya, Japan); he later joins the faculty of Nagoya Gaguin University

TOYOTA'S SPIRIT OF INNOVATION

While known for its focus on continuous improvement, Toyota is a company grounded in innovation. Toyota was founded by innovators seeking to create new ideas for the future, and the spirit of innovation continues to be core to its ethos.

In the mid-1980s, at the same time it was starting to expand its automobile production outside of Japan, Toyota Motor Corporation formed a Business Development Department, charged with exploring diverse future business opportunities beyond car manufacturing. Based at headquarters in Toyota City, the Department represented the company's entrepreneurial spirit and commitment to looking for new and different ways to create value for customers.

Yoshino describes Toyota's spirit of innovation:

> *The concepts of innovation, new ideas, creativity, and starting something new has been passed from one generation to the next at Toyota from the very beginning of the company. Kiichiro Toyoda was advised by his father, Sakichi Toyoda, to find something different from the automatic loom machine as the core business, and he subsequently started the automobile business. Kiichiro's son, Shoichiro Toyoda, followed his family tradition and started the housing business in the 1980s.*

While the first new business idea (Toyota's housing business, which continues to thrive in Japan today) came top-down from Shoichiro Toyoda, most other ideas originated in the 1980s came through a bottom-up approach, whereby innovations and new business ventures were proposed by mid-level managers and engineers working at Toyota.

One of these early concepts became known as Toyota's "airplane project," which was introduced by Yoshino's friend Mr. Shimada while working at Toyota's Technical Center in Torrance, California. The project turned into the Airplane Business Planning Office,[1] focused on exploring ways to manufacture a small-sized business airplane that used reciprocated engines. The airplane idea ultimately did not succeed.

A second concept was focused on pleasure boats. Another engineer, who also had worked at the Toyota Technical Center for many years, had invented a new technology for manufacturing a boat hull (the lower part of the boat). His initial idea was to use Toyota's Lexus engine to manufacture small and mid-sized pleasure boats (for ocean cruising, ocean fishing, freshwater fishing, etc.) in Japan — later called the "Ponam" boats. This idea was the beginning of the Marine Business Planning Office in 1990, which Yoshino was tasked to help manage beginning in January 1992.

And a third concept (of many more[2]) was introduced by Isao Yoshino in the mid-1990s while working in the Marine Office: a water-ski boat business targeted for an American market. It is Yoshino — and Toyota's — pursuit of the idea that is the focus of this chapter.

While the U.S. water-ski boat venture was ultimately a failed business, Toyota's Marine business continues to successfully make pleasure boats for Japan and other markets at the time of this book's publication.

---

1 Yoshino explains that "Office" is a smaller group within a "Department."

2 To see a list of the diverse business enterprises Toyota has explored, visit Toyota Motor Corporation's website: https://www.toyota-global.com/company/history_of_toyota/75years/data/business/diversification/new_business/index.html.

PHASE #1

A NEW TARGET FOR YOSHINO: TOYOTA MARINE SPORTS USA

After his temporary "rehabilitation" in the Human Resources Department of the Nagoya Office, Yoshino was given his next assignment: Chief of the Marketing Planning Group in the Marine Office within the Business Development Department back at headquarters in Toyota City. Yoshino would oversee the group charged with launching Toyota's new pleasure-boat venture in the Japanese market. These 27-foot yachts would be designed for ocean cruising, deep sea fishing, and freshwater fishing, and would be manufactured with two marinized Lexus engines.

With only three weeks before leaving Nagoya, Yoshino's staff quickly organized a farewell party for him in December 1991. In the middle of the festivities, one of Yoshino's staff asked him, "What do you hope to accomplish in the Marine Office?"

It was a fair but challenging question, as Yoshino admittedly had no experience (or much interest) in boating, nor knowledge about the boating market in Japan. But during his four years of living in the United States, Yoshino had observed how much Americans like boating — particularly on small speed boats such as for water-skiing and fishing in both fresh and salt water.

Within seconds, without much contemplation, a "crazy" thought popped into his mind: wouldn't it be amazing if, somehow, he could build on Toyota's new venture in marine production — and his knowledge of the U.S. — and help Toyota expand to the American market? Maybe it would be possible to establish a boat business in the U.S. too!

Yoshino recalls speaking this spontaneous new business idea out loud to his employee:

> *"I don't know much about the marine market in Japan, but I know the U.S. boat market is huge compared to Japan. It's kind of crazy, but my new target is going to be to establish a boat business for Toyota in the U.S., not just Japan! This idea just came to me because you asked me. I don't have any details now of how to make it happen, but I just had an idea for a name — TMS! It stands for Toyota Marine Sports. How does it sound?"*

Just like with many innovations and entrepreneurial pursuits, the initial idea was a sudden spark of a possibility — one that would require great focus, experimentation, research, and falling down and getting up to try to make a reality. Reflecting on his new target, conceived at his going-away party, Yoshino exclaimed: *"I did not know that my impromptu response at the party would become a reality four years later!"*

Yoshino's unplanned idea — in part inspired by the strength of his warp threads and desire to continue his American dream — set into motion a renewed perseverance to return to the United States, to pursue what would be Yoshino's biggest project — and biggest failure — of his entire career.

PHASE #2

DOING HIS JOB, BUT SECRETLY WORKING ON A NEW IDEA

Yoshino began his assignment in the Marine Office in Toyota City in January 1992. When Yoshino joined, the Marine Department consisted of about 40 staff members: 10 non-engineers, whom Yoshino was assigned to manage, and 30 engineers managed by the same technical engineer who had developed the original marine business concept in the late 1980s.

ASSIGNED AN OFFICIAL TASK AND AN UNOFFICIAL CHALLENGE: FIX A MANAGEMENT PROBLEM

While Yoshino's official assignment was to oversee the team developing the marketing plan for Toyota's pleasure boat and marine-engine business in Japan, the top management hired him to help solve a different problem. When he found out about his transfer while still in the Nagoya office, Yoshino had done some quick research and learned about the reason behind his quick reassignment:

> *When I learned that I was to be transferred to the Marine Office in Toyota City, I was so shocked because I had only been in Nagoya for 10 months. But then I found out the reason: the Business Preparation Department had a management problem in the Marine Office and they were looking for somebody new from outside their division to help. I was not a boater and I didn't like boating or fishing so much, but I was quite interested in the reason why they were looking for somebody to handle the management problem.*

By this time, Yoshino had been learning and leading for decades, and his threads of purpose for developing people were strong. Yoshino dug a bit deeper to get the background of the challenge he was stepping into:

> *I found out that the engineering leader of the department was running the office like a dictator, being aggressive and making all the decisions himself. His subordinates were unhappy and complained about him, and top management had become concerned about the inadequate steps or process he was taking to manage the business.*
>
> *I learned through the grapevine that the general manager of the Business Development Department wanted to hire a non-engineering manager who had a broader point of view. Human Resources saw that I had experience working with engineers and working in many places, and thought that I would know how to handle this situation. My job was to fix a management issue (i.e., how to make the worksite enjoyable for all), not to step into a technical role responsible for how to make a nicely designed boat.*

Yoshino's leaders had given him an assignment — both officially and unofficially — and he accepted the challenge.

LEADING TO LEARN: USING HIS WEFT THREADS TO CREATE A NEW GROUP CULTURE

"Once again I learned so many things about what to do and not to do as a leader."

- *Isao Yoshino*

Yoshino's unofficial challenge to reshape the team's culture drew on his leadership strengths — his weft threads — the skills he had learned and led over the past three decades at Toyota. Even though Yoshino had no direct authority over the engineering department, he had been brought in to help influence team dynamics and to bring more structure to the management of the entire Marine Office. Toyota management had determined that Yoshino — who had learned to lead, and now had years of experience in leading to learn — would be the countermeasure to this management problem.

Assessing the Situation

The engineering manager was a highly skilled technical engineer, but he was not a people-centered leader nor a team player. While Yoshino acknowledges that the engineer was technically smart, Yoshino found him overly confident. Yoshino describes the situation:

> *While it is true that this engineer was the one who proposed to establish a small group to conduct a feasibility study of the marine business, he often said to other people that he was "the father of Toyota's marine business." I thought it was too early for anybody to declare that he was "the father of the marine business." He just started to work on the feasibility study, which is the very early stage of the business start-up.*

Yoshino quickly observed that the manager operated by making decisions by himself, rarely asking for input from or listening to his subordinates, and he boasted of his academic and professional accomplishments. Yoshino recalls:

> *Based on how he talked about his people — his subordinates — I had a feeling that he regarded himself as one of the smartest people at Toyota, and that he regarded his subordinates as immature and less knowledgeable. I rarely heard him say anything good about his people, but he often made bad comments about them or criticized them.*
>
> *The reason why the people in this department were unhappy is because they didn't feel they were part of the team. The dictator-type of manager started his own style first. Then, an atmosphere of "one dictator decides everything" emerged and took root as the group's culture. He lacked a people-centered mindset and, as a result, his own people showed him no signs of respect.*
>
> *It was unfortunate and disappointing that I had to work with someone like him, but it was fortunate and meaningful because, once again, I learned so many things about what to do and not to do as a leader.*

Pulling in His Weft Threads to Help Tighten the Culture

Yoshino had to work through influence, not authority, to improve team dynamics. He began by drawing on the lessons he had learned long ago about people-centered leadership — such as "go to gemba" to understand the employees' work situation and to show that you care about them as people. Yoshino describes how he approached his challenge:

> *I tried to spend time with the engineers, listening to their effort and worries, although I could not fully understand their specific technical areas. Bringing myself to their desk and talking with them closely and patiently was so welcomed by them. They told me that their boss did not come to them, but that he summoned them to come to his desk. They appreciated my style. This is a "go to gemba" example in a small office.*

Yoshino also discovered that the team did not have clarity on their goals and did not communicate with each other. The work was not visible. As a countermeasure, Yoshino proposed that the broader team set up committees for each key area, such as "technical development," "sales and marketing," and "business feasibility study." People agreed with Yoshino's idea and they decided to set up a cadence of monthly meetings where team members could update their current status, present potential problems, discuss the next steps, and talk openly. Yoshino reflects on the impact of this small but important change:

> *I knew that just setting up committees would not necessarily solve all their problems, but it helped them to more clearly see their current situation. It also helped them to look in the same direction and be aligned. Most importantly, the idea helped to create a place where people could say anything more freely. We also decided that a meeting summary report should be completed within the same week and be shared among all the members involved.*
>
> *As to "who makes the final decision," many people started to have heated discussions in the committees and people started to work together to find problems and set up new goals together. It made each member feel that everybody was part of the project. It did not happen overnight, but I saw things were changing slowly and steadily.*

> *My committee idea was nothing new or nothing spectacular, or difficult to do. I believe it brought in a new sense of a teamwork to the stagnant group. I felt so happy to see that my small idea had contributed to the changeover of their culture.*

Yoshino was embodying the key responsibilities of a leader: set the direction and provide the support for the team to effectively work toward these goals, all while he continued to develop himself.

MANAGING THE PLEASURE-BOAT VENTURE

Concurrently as he was establishing more effective management practices and a culture of teamwork across the division internally, Yoshino was also mitigating the engineering manager's impact externally.

The engineer had invented a new way of manufacturing the boat hull as three separate components and then attaching them together to make one unit. His hypothesis was that this method would save the cost of time and material. He was so excited about his invention that he started to approach U.S. pleasure boat companies to establish relationships in anticipation of a future opportunity to export Toyota's pleasure boats to the United States. The engineer's outreach to these companies took place before Yoshino joined the project. Yoshino says that when he heard about this outreach across the Pacific, he was shocked. He felt it was premature, as the pleasure boat business was just in the early conceptual idea stage for a Japanese market:

> *While I was first impressed with the engineer's broader perspective about the boat business possibilities, when I heard more details about his idea to approach well-established U.S. pleasure boat manufactures (such as Brunswick), I discovered that he did not have a clear-cut target or idea how to approach them. My concern was that we were still at a very early stage of our boat business plan. In order to seriously consider stepping into the U.S. marine market, we would first need to conduct thorough research of the market, including the key players in the U.S. marine business.*

Yoshino was especially worried when he found out that the engineer had already made plans — and gotten approval — to visit the U.S. for two weeks in April 1993:

> *Although I was new to the job (only three months or so), I thought I could help slow down what I saw was a speeding train. I proposed to our boss that I would like to accompany the engineer on the U.S. trip and we should have another engineer accompany us. My boss liked my idea and approved my request. So, the three of us — me, the technical engineer, and another level-headed engineer — traveled to the U.S. to visit several boat manufacturers.*
>
> *As I had anticipated earlier, the engineer tried to make business commitments, although Toyota was not ready to make any serious commitments at the time. The purpose of our trip was to assess the U.S. boat manufacturers who were interested in Toyota's pleasure boat concept, not enter into business arrangements. We had discussed this several times prior to our trip and I thought we had a mutual understanding on the purpose of our U.S. trip. But I was wrong.*

This trip was a challenging experience for Yoshino as he recalls his frustration with the engineer's behavior, but it was an important learning opportunity about how to manage group dynamics and about the potential future for Toyota's marine opportunities in the United States. Yoshino reflects:

> *It was a tough week, but a good learning opportunity. I succeeded in attaining our original goal, which was to deepen understanding between the Toyota Marine Office and the U.S. boat manufacturers' executives. I also succeeded in getting to know about the engineer more deeply. I learned many lessons.*

FRUSTRATION BUILDS

As his first year in the Marine Office progressed, Yoshino grew increasingly concerned with the feasibility of the Japan pleasure-boat project — that it was too "dream-like" without a realistic plan to achieve it. He was worried that the engineer was more focused on the technical aspects of boat manufacturing than he was on understanding the actual market potential of pleasure boats in Japan. Yoshino recounts that his marketing team discovered that, at that time in Japan, the *total* pleasure-boat market — across all sizes from 15-foot fishing boats to 27-foot boats — was about 10,000 units per year, while the actual market for 27-foot boats (like the proposed Toyota pleasure boats) was less than 3,000.

PUTTING POWER BEHIND HIS "AMERICAN TOYOTA MARINE SPORTS" DREAM

While Yoshino's official assignment was to help develop a plan for the new Japanese domestic boat and marine-engine business, his warp threads were taut, and his personal target remained focused on his idea for a Toyota Marine Sports product for the United States. As I shared at the beginning of this chapter, this new career target had come to Yoshino spontaneously at his farewell party in the Nagoya Office. He didn't know much about the American boating market, besides having discovered during his four years living in California that American people enjoyed boating generally. But the idea for Toyota Marine Sports USA continued to sit in Yoshino's head like a new "North Star" dream, while he continued to take care of his official responsibilities to support Toyota's pleasure boat business in Japan. One year into his tenure in the Marine Office, he had a breakthrough idea!

As part of his official role, Yoshino would often visit an automobile engine tuning company located near Toyota City. The company was run by a former Toyota engineer who was the son of a former Toyota Motor Sales Company president and was an automobile racer who liked all kinds of adventures, including ocean cruising. On one visit to discuss the marine sport segment in Japan, the discussion turned toward the U.S. marine market. Yoshino recalls how this conversation sparked the idea to make Toyota Marine Sports USA a reality:

> *At that time, I didn't know that the U.S. marine market was 30 times larger than the Japanese boat market, I just knew that Americans liked boating. He was so kind to tell me the ABCs of marine sports in the U.S. — including what water-skiing and water-ski boats were all about. I was very interested to learn that most of the water-ski boats in the United States carried older-style GM-made engines with 300 horsepower. He said*

> *that a Lexus 4-liter engine had the same 300 horsepower and suggested that it would be a good fit for water-ski boats. I was hit by lightning!*

The business case for focusing on the American market was strong! Not only was the U.S. boat market 30 times bigger than Japan's, but why not leverage Toyota's existing capabilities as one of the world's leading engine manufacturers to make and sell powerful engines suited for the large water-ski boat market in the United States? Perhaps this, more than the pleasure boat idea, could be Toyota's differentiator to succeed in the American market?

While Yoshino admits that he had no actual knowledge of the water-ski boat market (and didn't even really understand what water-skiing was all about), his warp threads were pulling on him to pursue Toyota Marine Sports USA. And now he had a clear idea to pursue, a business that he believed would benefit Toyota and could connect him again with the United States.

A SECRET MISSION IS LAUNCHED

"At the beginning, we didn't even realize how much we didn't know."

– *Isao Yoshino*

In January 1994, one year after joining the Marine Office, Yoshino formed a small, secret team with two young engineers to explore the water-ski boat engine idea. Taking time outside of their official roles, Yoshino and his informal project team pursued the idea thoroughly and developed a robust business plan for a Toyota Marine Sports business in the United States:

> *There were so many things we needed to tackle before we developed our basic concept. At that time, there was no internet and no email system widely available. We worked hard to establish our business plan, including understanding the U.S. boat market size, pricing, American boaters' preferences, technical features such as our strength (Lexus engine) over other U.S. water-ski boat engines, and so on.*

Yoshino leveraged relationships he'd built over a lifetime to help with their research, including consulting with engineers in Toyota's Engine

Development Division (where his junior high school friend was a senior leader in charge of Lexus engine development), an American friend at Toyota Motor Sales in California who was a big boater, and the head of the engine tuning company who inspired the water-ski boat idea. Plus, during his trips to the U.S. on behalf of the pleasure-boat business, Yoshino also was able to learn directly about the U.S. water-ski boat market by talking with boat manufacturers.

A FIRST IDEA IS JUST THE STARTING POINT: SELL LEXUS ENGINES

"There were so many things that we didn't know about water-ski boats and the needs of their customers when we started this project."

- Isao Yoshino

Yoshino and his team's initial concept for the water-ski boat business was for Toyota to sell Lexus marinized engines directly to U.S. water-ski boat manufacturers to install in their own boats. Yet, through his discussions during visits to the U.S., Yoshino discovered that American boat manufacturers were not interested in the high cost of the Lexus engine. Yoshino recounts:

> *We discovered that the Lexus engine price was too high, and we could not make a deal with any of the U.S. water-ski boat manufacturers. Our high-tech engine had a price tag around $9,000, when they could get engines from GM for less than $5,000. While GM-made marine engines were quite old-fashioned, boaters liked their simple structure as they could fix them on the water when something went wrong. The high-tech, computerized Lexus engines could not be fixed while the boat was still in the water.*

This "go to gemba" experience to learn about the market interest for their Lexus engine idea was disappointing, but gave important insights to Yoshino and his team about the realities of the American water-ski boat market. As he recalls:

We discussed why they would choose a low-cost and old-fashioned marine engine. After some heated discussions among ourselves and with input from marine business experts, we discovered that while the boat manufacturers didn't like the price of our Lexus high-tech engine, it didn't mean that they didn't like our Lexus engine. Actually, we found out that they were fascinated with the high performance and newest design concept of our Lexus engine. They just could not imagine the combination of their traditional boat design concept with the high-tech Lexus marine engine.

Yoshino and his team were disappointed with the responses from the U.S. water-ski boat manufacturers and thought this might be the end of their water-ski boat idea. But they remained persistent.

REFINE THE IDEA: MANUFACTURE THE BOATS WITH LEXUS ENGINES

"Our plan started as an 'engine selling business' and then it became a 'boat manufacturing and selling business.'"

– Isao Yoshino

Yoshino and his team went back to the drawing board and came up had a new idea: manufacture a "Lexus-grade" water-ski boat (a luxury boat design with a high-end engine) and sell it directly to consumers. Yoshino remembers making this pivot:

We fell down at our first approach to the U.S. boat manufacturers, but we rose up to have a different approach for the water-ski market. How about the idea that we would manufacture a water-ski boat with the most advanced design combined with the most efficient Lexus marinized engine? Just like Lexus cars are well accepted with high-end users in the U.S., we would focus on the high-end water-ski boaters.

While the price range of our water-ski boat would be higher than competitor U.S. water-ski boats, due to the higher cost of our Lexus marinized engines, it would be just like Lexus cars compared with other Toyota cars (such as the Corolla or Camry). I thought that we could take advantage

> *of the Lexus luxury image and translate it to the boat business too if we had Lexus engines in our boats.*
>
> *We decided to switch our target from Lexus engine sales to high-end water-ski boat manufacturing in the U.S.*

Yoshino and his team dug in to understand how Lexus had successfully entered the U.S. luxury automobile market:

> *When we started to renew our strategy, we took a close look at how the Lexus car had established its position in the highest grade segment, which is so different from that of Toyota brand cars. The Lexus car concept did not start as a mere extension of an existing Toyota car segment. Lexus designers started everything from scratch. It made sense to us.*
>
> *So, we had a hypothesis that American boaters who are interested in the higher-grade water-ski boat segment would want Lexus-grade water-ski boats if the boat has a Lexus engine on it. What we had planned at the beginning was to put a high-tech Lexus engine in a water-ski boat with a conventional design. We found out that we were trying to put new wine into old wineskins.*

"What we had planned at the beginning was to put a high-tech Lexus engine in a water-ski boat with a conventional design. We found out that we were trying to put new wine into old wineskins."

The new concept: Toyota would manufacture high-end water-ski boats locally in the United States and use the Lexus engines made (and converted for marine use) in Japan. The finished boats would be assembled in the United States and sold directly in the large American water-ski boat market. This luxury water-ski boat would be a completely new category for the American marine market, and as Yoshino explains, *"except for the engine, it would be a completely 'Made in the U.S.A.' product."*

YOSHINO PITCHES THE LEXUS LUXURY WATER-SKI BOAT IDEA TO MANAGEMENT

"We knew it would require a huge amount of research and hard work to get this new idea approved by top management."

– Isao Yoshino

Yoshino and the two engineers continued their research and put together their business plan for the luxury water-ski boat idea. In late 1994 or early 1995, Yoshino proposed their concept to his direct boss in charge of the Marine Office. However, Yoshino recalls his frustration that his boss did not seem to show any interest in discussing the plan's feasibility. Yoshino was convinced that the Lexus water-ski boat idea was worth exploring, and tried and tried repeatedly, but his boss continued to ignore his requests.

Undeterred, Yoshino and his team continued to work on their new business idea — patiently and diligently — falling down a few times but continuing to get up. Finally, in early 1996, after several years of working on his idea as a side project, Yoshino decided to break away from the official approval channels, which was an uncommon action at Toyota. Yoshino went around his boss to propose his water-ski boat to the senior managers who led the Business Development Department. While it wasn't the "proper" decision-making pathway, Yoshino reflects that, *"Even at Toyota, sometimes you have to work around to get things done."*

Yoshino's warp threads were strong even under tension. He had a new goal consistent with his original dream, and he stayed patient and persistent.

YOSHINO'S AMERICAN WATER-SKI BOAT EXPERIMENT IS AUTHORIZED

In mid-1996, three years after Yoshino first conceived of the possibility of Toyota Marine Sports USA and two years of ideation and research, Toyota senior management authorized an experiment to test the luxury water-ski boat business in the American market. Toyota's management team at headquarters in Japan liked Yoshino's concept for a Lexus water-ski boat that could create a new category in the market. They agreed that the Lexus motor would be manufactured in Japan and then shipped to the United States. The boat parts and final units would be assembled by American workers in Florida, which had the largest demand for water-ski boats.

Yoshino believes that Toyota's senior management was willing to take a risk on his idea because the opportunity to learn from a new business venture was worth the risk of failure. Plus, they were willing to experiment because the projected financial risk was small for a company as large as Toyota. Yoshino was excited to know of the top leaders' broader entrepreneurial perspective and willingness to take on a new challenge for the company — to try something new, and perhaps seemingly impossible to attain — and to hopefully make a success.

Yet, little did Yoshino — or Toyota — anticipate the challenges that lay ahead to turn this idea into a successful reality.

PRACTICING *HANSEI*: REFLECTION QUESTIONS

- Think of a time that you had sudden spark of inspiration about a new idea or path you wanted to pursue in your career, your company, or your personal life. What was the idea? What did you do?
- How can you encourage innovation, ideation, and experimentation among colleagues at your organization?
- How can having a new "passion project" keep you engaged and excited about your work or life?
- Think about a project or initiative in your career that required funding and approval from your superiors, and that didn't receive an instant "yes." What was your reaction? What lessons have you learned about yourself and about organizational behavior from such experiences?
- What is your experience with leaders who have had a more "dictatorial" style? What impact has their behavior or approach had on you? On the team? On the product or service the team provides?

- When is a time you have had to work through influence rather than authority? What have you found to be most effective when you have tried to influence culture change or the behavior of a colleague or boss?

PHASE #3

THE AMERICAN WATER-SKI BOAT BUSINESS LAUNCHES IN ROUGH WATERS

Success of Toyota's water-ski boat venture would require partnership with Toyota Motor Sales (TMS) USA, based in Torrance, California.

In autumn 1996, shortly after Toyota's top management approved the idea to enter into the U.S. marine market, Yoshino arranged to visit TMS USA headquarters. His task: gain agreement from TMS USA's senior management to use the sales division's automobile transport railway network to transport the Lexus marine engines from Long Beach, California — where they would come into port from Japan — to Orlando, Florida, where the other parts of the boat would be made and where the final boat would be assembled.

Yoshino flew to California to meet with Mr. Shinji Sakai, TMS USA President, at his office in Torrance. Yoshino recalls Mr. Sakai being enthusiastic about the proposal. He not only agreed with Yoshino's plan for the transportation of the Lexus marine engine, but offered to establish a new division at TMS USA — to be called TMS Marine Division — where the new American-focused water-ski boat business would be based. Yoshino would be the Japanese representative from headquarters leading the Division, and Mr. Sakai would assign an American senior manager to be Yoshino's American partner.

Yoshino was thrilled. Not only was his long-planned business concept — which began as a "crazy" spontaneous glimmer of a new idea made at a party four years earlier — authorized, but his dream to return to the United States to live was coming true.

A PARTNERSHIP IS PLANNED

In January 1997, just a few months after this agreement regarding the transport of the engines from California to Florida, Yoshino relocated from Japan to Torrance (located in Los Angeles County) to co-lead the newly created Marine Division at TMS USA.

Yoshino was given the official title of "Vice President." However, as was typical at that time for this type of partnership between Toyota's corporate headquarters in Japan and TMS USA, the American partner was given the working title of "General Manager," while Yoshino's was considered the "Coordinator." Yoshino explained to me that this type of partnership was the basic framework between Toyota's expatriates and local managers in any Toyota worksite outside of Japan. A general manager at TMS had a wide range of authority and decision-making autonomy over his division, while the coordinator's role was to represent the Japanese headquarters' view and to ensure that the general manager's decisions and management practices aligned with both that of the coordinator and TMC Japan. Yoshino elaborated on this arrangement:

> *The American general manager and Japanese coordinator were supposed to work closely together and be aligned in the management of their business. If the coordinator felt that the general manager's decision or management significantly derailed from the track agreed to by headquarters, the coordinator was supposed to discuss it with the general manager and find the best solution together.*

Although the U.S. water-ski boat experiment was an important test of a new business idea, it was a relatively small venture for Toyota and Yoshino was the only Japanese team member assigned to support the program.

ONE COMPANY, TWO COMPANY CULTURES – TMC AND TMS

When Toyota was first established in 1937, the two functions of manufacturing and sales co-existed in one company. However, in 1950, Toyota was forced to split into two different companies — Toyota

Motor Company (TMC) and Toyota Motor Sales (TMS) — a condition set by local banks in order for Toyota to receive financial support for recovery from a business slump. Until the early 1980s, TMC and TMS functioned as two separate companies and developed their own distinct corporate cultures, with TMC advancing the Toyota Production System concepts and culture that Yoshino learned, starting when he joined TMC in 1966.

Yoshino explains his observation of the different cultures between the two companies:

> *TMC is an auto manufacturing company located in a rural area of Japan's Aichi Prefecture — where diligence, humbleness, and patience have been valued since the feudal period of the 17th century. How to reduce manufacturing cost was one of the first priority items for the manufacturing company.*
>
> *TMS, on the other hand, is a car sales and marketing company located in Nagoya, with its sales network widely scattered across the country. How to sell as many cars as possible was the first priority of the sales company.*

In 1982, Toyota's top management decided to merge TMC and TMS into a single company, which is the current Toyota Motor Corporation. From that point forward, all sales and marketing functions within Japan rolled back into the main corporation. However, TMS USA remained a separate subsidiary company, based in California, responsible for sales and marketing within the United States.

Thirty-two years of functioning with different cultures and different priorities continued to impact how leaders acted — depending on which part of the broader company they worked for and in which part of the company they had begun their Toyota careers. This difference in business culture played a significant role in the process of building the water-ski boat venture, and its ultimate demise.

ROUGH WATERS AHEAD

When Yoshino arrived in Torrance, there were approximately 70 Japanese Toyota expatriates stationed at TMS USA headquarters. Most were from sales, marketing, service, and finance divisions. Yoshino was one of three Japanese expatriates from the manufacturing side of Toyota who were, as Yoshino describes it, "neck-deep" in Toyota's manufacturing culture.

This was Yoshino's first role reporting *outside* of the original TMC organizational structure, and while he was prepared for some degree of difference between Japanese and American cultures, he was not prepared for the difference in company cultures between TMC and TMS. As well as being less familiar with the technical production principles of TPS, Yoshino observed that TMS leaders — in Japan and the US — were not as grounded in the leadership principles that Yoshino had learned and taught over the prior 30 years at TMC. Yoshino was shocked at the differences between the manufacturing side and the sales side of the company.

A PARTNERSHIP IN NAME ONLY

"Everyone has their own way of doing things, so I tried to respect his style as much as possible."

– Isao Yoshino

These differences became immediately apparent in Yoshino's relationship with his Marine Division partner. Although Yoshino and the American general manager were supposed to work very closely together, Yoshino found that this was not his counterpart's intentions; he wanted to make most of the key decisions by himself. Yoshino recalls his frustration with two of their early interactions:

> *When I returned to visit TMC headquarters in Japan for a week, the general manager had already hired a finance manager without discussing it with me. We had earlier agreed that we would discuss and finalize any important decisions together. My partner did not practice what he had promised at the beginning. Because our boat business*

was a small project, adding just one staff member was a big financial burden on our budget.

At a later date, he also added one more staff member in the advertising section without my consent. Our agreement was that we would start with the smallest number of staff members and see what would happen. I did not think we needed two people working on the boat advertisements and believed that the advertising function could be handled by the sales manager whom we had already hired.

I couldn't believe it! We were supposed to be partners and he should have discussed these decisions with me first.

Yoshino acknowledges that everyone has a different way of managing, yet he was frustrated by what he perceived to be lack of partnership and trust. Yoshino predicted that this would be the beginning of what would become a series of struggles.

AGREEING ON A NAME AND LOGO: TOYOTA MARINE SPORT'S EPIC WATER-SKI BOAT

Despite their challenges, Yoshino and his American partner collaborated well on the decisions for the names and logos.

Isao Yoshino still has one of his shirts from the Toyota Marine Sports days.

First, for the water-ski boat business, they agreed to use the name that Yoshino had originally conceived at his going-away party in the Nagoya Office nearly six years earlier: Toyota Marine Sports. Together, they decided to use this name and create a logo to put on t-shirts, dress-shirts, and giveaway ballpoint pens and other novelties. Yoshino still wears the dress shirt with the Toyota Marine Sport logo.

Next up was to decide the name for the boat. After going through the English dictionary, each generating words that could represent the boat, they settled on Epic.

A DIFFERENCE IN STYLE RISES TO THE SURFACE: CHOOSING A MANUFACTURING PARTNER

"You cannot make important decisions with your own instinct or personal feeling or based on limited information."

– Isao Yoshino

One of the first significant jobs for Yoshino and his partner to do together was to find the right manufacturing partner. The American manager took the lead at first. This was another early indication for Yoshino of the difference in working styles across company and country cultures:

> *At first, my partner took an initiative to start finding the best company, but his working style was so different from what I expected. He came up with his ideas without much detailed research but instead through his own intuition, and then just called prospective companies on the phone to discuss details. I was so surprised at his approach.*

Yoshino proposed that he and his partner take a more structured approach — that they first agree on the key qualities upon which they were assessing the potential manufacturing partners and then develop a grid on which to evaluate each potential company. By having an objective framework to evaluate the potential partners, Yoshino believed this would help them not make any oversights in making an objective decision. His partner did not agree with this approach, but they agreed to compromise. As Yoshino explains:

> *My partner and I spent a lot of time discussing the process of developing our chart. He insisted in his selection style, but I did not agree. I did not mean to completely dismiss his idea, but I thought his style was too risky and it would not be approved by our headquarters back in Japan. My partner did not want to agree with my idea either.*

So, I proposed that we would send two choices — one by his style and another by my style — to the Marine Department in Japan. My partner reluctantly agreed with my idea and I sent the two ideas to our Marine Department for their final choice. My approach was chosen.

Ultimately, after Yoshino and his partner assessed different partnerships in Indiana, California, and Florida, Toyota chose to partner with Gambler, a fishing boat manufacturer in Orlando, Florida. Toyota Motor Sports would rent the vacant space in their facility to manufacture the Epic boat and would hire their own local management and employees to build the boats.

ATTEMPTS TO IMPROVE DYNAMICS

Yoshino decided to do what he could to influence his relationships at the Torrance office.

First, Yoshino focused on his relationship with his partner. Even though he was frustrated with his partner's working style, Yoshino had gotten insights into his partner's history from a Japanese colleague who had worked for many years in the Torrance office. This gave Yoshino a different perspective:

I wondered why my partner always talked so confidently and why he always had a stern face. At first, I thought his style was just because of his own strong character. But I learned that he had had some challenging experiences with his previous Japanese coordinators. Whenever we talked, I recognized that he was trying his best not to let me know any of his weak points or mistakes he had made. He just wanted to show me only the strong aspects of his character.

As someone who had grown up in the TMC culture of "bad news first" and "no problem is a problem," Yoshino was not accustomed to this attitude. Yoshino, always wanting to find the good in people, wanted to give him the benefit of the doubt:

I tried to contemplate what was behind his aggressive business style. I came to think that, to cope with his past more hard-core Japanese coordinators, my partner must have intentionally developed a strong character to protect himself. I thought that he must have a different face with a milder and more cheerful aspect — as his own real character.

Based on these insights, and drawing on some of the lessons and leadership learning threads (such as the importance of "being flexible first" when working with different cultures), Yoshino decided that he would take the first steps to create a better relationship with his partner:

> *Now that I knew my partner's character, as well as his own business style and background, I decided to try to create a good relationship with him, which no other Toyota coordinator from Japan in the past had accomplished.*
>
> *One day, I had a chance to talk with him in a very informal manner. I talked about my own career and shared how I came up with my idea for the water-ski boat business. I tried my best to open up and just be myself. After the informal get-together with him, I had a feeling that he started to like my character.*

Yoshino was hopeful that this conversation would result in greater trust and an improved relationship with his partner.

ENGAGING THE TEAM BY MAKING THEIR WORK VISIBLE

Yoshino also tried to improve the team dynamics within the Torrance Marine Division. He observed that decisions were top-down and didn't engage the thinking of others — similar to the situation he had found when he arrived at the Marine Office in Toyota City. Yoshino describes his experience of the Torrance team when he arrived:

> *Each week, we had a regular update meeting with all the members attending. The purpose of this meeting was for all the staff members, around seven at that time, to be on the same page. My partner always talked about his opinion and the plan he had created, and then told them to proceed. Interaction among members was not lively and it was just a one-way communication from him to the staff members. At that time, I was new to the U.S. and to the group and I was not very aware of the details of my partner's plan. So, I stayed quiet for a while.*
>
> *One day, when the meeting was over, one of the members came up to me and said that the general manager only talked about his plans and ideas*

> *but did not ask members' opinions. He also said the general manager always communicated only verbally without any memos or documents, which did not motivate members so much.*

Yoshino decided to show his American Marine Division teammates some of the basic concepts of Toyota's management that he had learned and taught over the previous decades at TMC, such as communication on A3-sized paper, making thinking visual, making potential "bad news" visible, and discussing a plan with the group to get alignment and buy-in:

> *When I heard his comment, I decided to do something new that was a different style than they were used to. I tried to develop an A3 document in a grid-chart style where all the key information was shown visually. I put a short comment in each space of the grid so that the reader could easily and quickly understand what it meant. There was no need for me to go into details of each note as the grid was already self-explanatory.*
>
> *The grid included all the elements of the general manager's plan that he had explained a few weeks earlier, but nobody had followed it through. I included my own opinions and also my findings on the general manager's ideas, both from positive and negative viewpoints, so that we could have a discussion.*

This simple change of making work visible and engaging in discussion with team members created a positive change in the group dynamics:

> *It was a kind of revolution for our team because my chart was so easy to read and to understand. It triggered our members to start making comments and asking questions. From this experience and experiment, my team members at the Torrance office started to recognize that this guy from Japan was always thinking deeply about what we needed to do as a team.*
>
> *I believe that this was the time they started to show me more respect and accepted me as one of their comrades to pursue common goals together.*

However, despite these small improvements in Torrance, many other challenges for the Marine Division's operations soon rose to the surface.

TWO KINDS OF DISTANCE ON THE TEAM CREATE TENSION

One of the other major differences Yoshino quickly determined between TMS managers and his TMC management approach was that the fundamental mindset of "go to gemba" was not a core part of the TMS culture. Yoshino had learned (and taught) that proximity matters for team success — that teams should work near one another, and that leaders should "go to the gemba" by visiting the actual workplaces regularly. (Remember, this was at a time before video conferencing and other technologies made remote visual communication a possibility. Today, Toyota's leadership is rethinking how to keep the spirit of "go to gemba" in new and innovative ways, even while not actually being physically present.)

As such, Yoshino was surprised to learn that the general manager had decided to distribute the workforce for the water-ski project between two locations. Yoshino — the only Japanese member of the team — would be based in Torrance, California, along with the general manager, the advertising manager, and the accounting manager. All other functions, including the sales manager and sales staff, quality control manager, engineering manager, production manager, and all production shop staff would be in Orlando, Florida. The two groups were separated by a three-hour time-zone difference and more than a five-hour flight.

Yoshino was worried that this separation would negatively impact the business and their ability to be effective as leaders:

> *From a communication point of view, I thought this work location arrangement was inappropriate. I spent a lot of time advising my partner to reconsider this arrangement that called for the four of us key managers to be separated from the rest of the team based in Orlando. I proposed that everyone based in Torrance move to Orlando, so that we could all work together as one team.*
>
> *My partner insisted that we could communicate through emails and telephone calls any time we wanted, as that's what they did in TMS's car sales and marketing divisions. He showed no interest in revising his decision.*

Yoshino further recalls how "go to gemba" was not an important management principle to his partner, who preferred to stay in his office in Torrance:

> *My partner did not visit our manufacturing plant in Orlando very often, even though he was the general manager. Instead, he advised me to fly between Los Angeles and Orlando whenever something happened and people in Florida needed help from the California office.*
>
> *I actually flew between LA and Orlando more than 40 times each year for two years, not because my partner asked me to do so, but because I believed that someone from the LA office needed to "go to gemba" in Florida, to have discussions and solve the problems together.*
>
> *It was disappointing to see no sign of the "go to gemba" concept in my Torrance office.*

Think about that level of commitment to "go to gemba" — for 40 weeks out of the year, Yoshino got on a plane to get to Orlando because he believed in the importance of management being in gemba — to show that he cared and to help solve problems! Yoshino recounts that these trips left him exhausted from jet lag and he was concerned about the cost impact for the project. Yet, the general manager still wanted the leadership team to remain based at TMS USA headquarters in California.

PRODUCTION BEGINS, AND CULTURE CLASHES CONTINUE

For the water-ski boat production in the rented space at the Orlando plant, Toyota had to create its production capabilities from the ground up: designing the manufacturing process, hiring managers and workers locally, and training them on how to produce the boats.

During his many early trips to the Orlando plant, Yoshino grew concerned about the lack of TPS knowledge among the managers and employees. He observed them working in a more traditional manufacturing style, such as checking quality at the end of the line and relying on one-way communication from the managers to their direct reports. This was a new experience for even a manager like Yoshino, who had trained American NUMMI managers in the past.

Unlike Toyota's other foreign production initiatives for automobiles, such as NUMMI, Kentucky, and Ontario, where North American managers were steeped in Toyota's culture through extensive hands-on training and coaching support to embed the Toyota way of working and managing, the U.S. water-ski boat experiment had not been given the same level of training support from Toyota. The American boat managers and frontline workers had only their prior experiences on which to draw, and had no exposure to TPS or Toyota management practices.

Once the water-ski boat production started in 1998, Yoshino quickly realized that this knowledge gap needed to be closed. He put in place two counter-measures to help bring TPS thinking to the Orlando plant, and soon realized that they were insufficient to close the gap in capability.

Issue 1: Training Does Not Equal Learning

"I learned that being patient requires a lot of patience."

- *Isao Yoshino*

First, Yoshino tried to find a way to get training and coaching for the Orlando managers and workers on the concept of TPS. Yoshino flew to Kentucky to visit the Toyota Suppliers Support Center (TSSC), a group that Toyota had organized to help train American suppliers in TPS concepts. Yoshino was not sure if they would be able to help him in Orlando, but he knew that he needed to ask:

> *I didn't think they would accept my request. I knew they were busy with coaching the Toyota parts suppliers across the United States and had no time to take care of the non-automobile business like mine. However, to my surprise, Mr. Teruyuki Minoura, the top management of TSSC, made a decision right away to send one young kaizen coach to my boat plant in Orlando for three months starting the following month.*

Yoshino was relieved when the kaizen coach came to Orlando to train the managers and workers in the gemba, but unfortunately it did not have a lasting impact:

> *It must have been an eye-opening experience for our workers to have this hands-on training in TPS. But when the young kaizen coach left Orlando, what they learned from him did not take root at the worksite. The number of defects returned to the same level as before and the thoroughness of observing the standard work started to diminish.*

Without ongoing coaching and support for each manager (as Toyota had provided at NUMMI, and which was more than Yoshino himself could give), it was just too easy for everyone to revert to their old ways.

Yoshino reflects now on why the TPS training didn't stick. First, the workers did not have enough of the foundational knowledge of TPS on which the kaizen coach could build:

> *Before the TSSC kaizen coach arrived for the practical coaching, we should have spent more time with our workers to discuss what they would learn from him. Our workers knew nothing about lean concepts and we needed more time than we anticipated for them to get an in-depth understanding of the concepts before they actually started receiving coaching in the gemba.*

Second, the follow-up coaching that Yoshino and the kaizen coach provided was not sufficient:

> *We Toyota people from Japan didn't necessarily have a thorough check-up with the workers on their new learnings as patiently as we should have. We learned an important lesson: when we provide any new training, new coaching, or new advice to people who have no knowledge of the topic, we need to be very patient and take enough time to prepare and to check whether they can proceed with the training on a step-by-step basis. We should have checked with our workers whether they had truly understood the core part of the learning.*

Yoshino realized that coaching and developing people while doing the work (i.e., while managing the pressures of the business) was difficult. He was pulled in many directions and did not feel he had the time to spend training people in the gemba every day. He had learned throughout his career that training requires time and patience, but the immediate pressures of the boat business left him feeling there were too many urgent fires.

When looking back, he recognizes that due to the sense of urgency he felt, he lost sight of the process required to change a culture, and that he was not as patient to get to the result he desired. He told me: *"I learned that being patient requires a lot of patience."*

Issue 2: Different Approaches Don't Always Work Together

The second countermeasure that Yoshino put in place was to request that TMC headquarters assign two Japanese engineers to Orlando, one for the technical development and another for boat production. His thinking: these two functions were so critical to the success of the boat business that they should be handled primarily by staff who deeply knew the technical aspects of the Toyota Production System and TMC management culture. These Japanese engineers could help coach and teach the Americans the Toyota mindset.

However, the countermeasure did not close the gap in TPS knowledge. It just highlighted the divide between cultures:

> *The engineers newly assigned to the Orlando plant were both young and smart. I was so relieved to have them at the production gemba in Orlando. I thought their joining would greatly help solve many problems we were facing. It did not take too long, however, before I found out that my relief was temporary.*

Cross-Cultural Tensions

First, a tense dynamic started to play out at the production site between the American production manager and the Japanese production engineer — similar to what Yoshino was experiencing with his American partner:

> *When we started manufacturing water-ski boats in Orlando, production was primarily managed by an American manager who had working experiences at other U.S. boat manufacturers only. He had a more typical American working and managing style. He made decisions from his past experiences, and he didn't discuss much with the Japanese engineer from Japan. As a result, the relations between them became awkward and weakened.*

Yoshino shared with me some examples of how the different approaches between the Japanese engineer and American manager resulted in strained relationships and impacted the quality of the production. For one, he recalls that:

> *We received a lot of quality reports from the customers in the market. The Japanese engineer and the American were both in charge of handling those quality-related problems. Yet, it became apparent that their methods for handing the problems were so different from each other. When they discussed the quality issues, they would each insist that their own way was right. After a series of arguments, they started to discuss quality issues together less and less.*

This was the opposite of Toyota's culture where everyone was encouraged to make "bad news" visible and openly discuss potential problems.

Reckless Behaviors and Americanized Attitudes

Second, Yoshino found that the young Japanese production engineer quickly adapted to the mindset of the American engineer in a way that Yoshino did not expect. As one example, Yoshino describes going to a local lake in the early stages of the water-ski boat development, to take the first Epic boat to the water for a test ride. The ride did not go well from Yoshino's perspective:

A Toyota Marine Sports Epic boat in Florida, photographed by Isao Yoshino.

> *When it was my turn to get in the boat, our American engineer drove the boat fast. At a very high speed, I felt that the boat was skidding and getting off course slightly, not maintaining a straight line even when the wheel was held straight. I asked him whether this type of boat performance was acceptable or not, as I felt a little scared when the boat was moving very fast.*

Yoshino describes that the American engineer tried to justify the issue as normal and didn't want to admit there was a technical problem with the Epic boat:

> *He said, "Yoshino-san, this is not an abnormal behavior. This happens to many other water-ski boats too. We call it 'ventilation.' It's nothing unusual."*
>
> *I was no expert on the boat design and engineering, but I was actually on the boat on the water and felt uneasy when the boat was not going to the right direction. I said to him, "You said this happens often to other American water-ski boats too. Yet it's not the matter of 'it happens to other boat too' or not. What matters is that our boat should behave right without making the passenger feel uneasy."*

Yoshino recounts that the American engineer stuck to his opinion, so he asked his Japanese engineer — who also had been taught to focus on the customer's perspective while at Toyota headquarters — what he thought. Yoshino was surprised with his response:

> *To my big surprise, the young Japanese engineer was on the American engineer's side. He said, "Yoshino-san, he said it's nothing unusual here in the U.S. and this ventilation behavior happens to other famous boats too. We are now in the U.S. and we need to accept the American's opinion."*
>
> *To me, I felt that this Japanese engineer, who I had brought from headquarters in Japan, believed in the engineer's comment without any legitimate analysis; he had already lost the Toyota spirit. It was really a shocking moment for me.*

Yoshino recounts that it was after this experience that his further struggles started — not only between himself and his American partners, but also with the Japanese engineers. Yoshino recalls how this dynamic played out:

> *After this on-water test, I did not try to compromise with the engineers any longer and instead insisted we go back to the basics. After a series of ugly discussions with them, the engineers decided to accept my experience on the boat and started to find the proper countermeasure to correct the "ventilation" behavior. We ended up putting a small ugly aluminum*

> *plate at the lower portion of the boat hull. With this aluminum plate in place, our boat started to behave right.*

These technical fixes impacted the "luxury" aesthetic intended for the Epic water-ski boats. Tempers flared and the cultural divides (between production and engineering, and between the Japanese and Americans) quickly became a chasm.

LEADERSHIP FUNDAMENTAL: LEADERS NEED TO BE IN THE GEMBA

Yoshino, who was onsite at the plant most weeks each month, knew that these challenges were growing more intense. His nearly weekly visits to Orlando (departing early Tuesday morning and returning late Friday) would not suffice and were costing the organization money. From the beginning, Yoshino believed that he and the other three managers in California should move to Orlando to be closer to the gemba. However, he explains that most of the staff in the Torrance office did not want to relocate to Florida for the business:

> *Many of our staff in the Torrance office were from California and had lived there for a long time. My partner himself was born and raised in Los Angeles and he did not want to leave California. It was the same for all the other staff members.*

This mindset was very different from what Yoshino was accustomed to in Japan, where it was common for staff and leaders to regularly be reassigned to positions in different locations. Even Yoshino, as you know, had relocated himself — and his family — multiple times as he took various positions in Nagoya, Tokyo, and the United States. And in this case, his family had decided to remain in Japan while he pursued the U.S. water-ski boat business. Yoshino could not understand the Americans' reticence to relocate.

Yoshino knew that something needed to change or the boat business was destined for failure. After an exhausting year of flying back and forth between Los Angeles and Orlando, and after the general manager's refusal to relocate, Yoshino determined that at least one of the Marine Division senior leaders at from TMS USA headquarters needed to be onsite. So, Yoshino moved to Orlando in 1999 and took on the role of Plant Manager.

PRACTICING HANSEI: REFLECTION QUESTIONS

- When have you encountered a situation in which you had shared authority for decision-making? How did this work? What did you learn?
- How do leaders make decisions at your organization? What is more typical: making decisions by instinct and feeling, or by facts and a structured process?
- What do you think about how Yoshino built trust with his American partner? How have you built trust with your colleagues?
- What did Yoshino do effectively to influence the culture in the Torrance office? And in the Orlando plant? What could he have done differently? What would you have tried in a similar situation?
- How does a sense of urgency — or "many fires to put out" — impact your actions and the trade-offs you make as a leader? How about for other leaders at your organization? How does a culture of urgency or crisis impact your organization's focus on people development or learning?
- What were some of the critical differences in the investment in learning and development between the Toyota Marine boat plant in Orlando and Toyota's NUMMI automobile joint venture? How does this make you think about your own organization's approach to people development?
- What is important about the "go to gemba" concept? What are ways to practice the principle of "go to gemba" while not being physically onsite with technologies available in 2020 and beyond?

PHASE #4

MANAGING THE WATER-SKI BUSINESS IN FLORIDA

YOSHINO'S FIRST PRODUCTION OPERATIONS MANAGEMENT ROLE

Yoshino's relocation to Orlando in 1999 to take on the role of Plant Manager offered him a new challenge. This was his first production management position. He was no longer a "coordinator" functioning only through influence, but a "general manager" with responsibility for directly managing — and making the final decisions for — the water-ski boat operations, including manufacturing, sales, and after-sales. Responsibility for technical design would be jointly handled by the local American boat engineer and the Japanese technical engineer who Yoshino had brought out from Japan.

Now in his mid-50s, Yoshino was — for the first time — responsible for the production of a Toyota product. It was an opportunity for him to use all the management skills and Toyota Production System concepts that he had learned (and supported through training and development programs at Toyota) and apply them directly into the management of actual operations. It would be a chance to learn to lead, and lead to learn in a new scope and level of responsibility.

Now in his mid-50s, Yoshino was — for the first time — responsible for the production of a Toyota product. It would be a chance to learn to lead, and lead to learn in a new scope and level of responsibility.

MANUFACTURING AND MANAGEMENT COOPERATION CONTINUE TO DEGRADE AND QUALITY PROBLEMS REACH THE CUSTOMER

More problems rapidly emerged.

First, as described earlier, neither managers nor workers in the plant put Toyota Production System manufacturing processes or management principles into place. Despite Yoshino's efforts to bring TPS to the plant, the manufacturing process was not "lean" at all.

Second, technical quality defects continued to come off the line — some of which made it to customers. Several boats broke down on the lakes in Florida and Texas and had to be replaced.

Third, the TMC Marine Division in Japan wanted to make day-to-day decisions for Toyota Marine Sports USA themselves, which hindered Yoshino in his ability to actually run the operations. He was given responsibility without power — a no-win situation many of us have faced in our careers. Yoshino elaborates on his challenge:

> *Although we were a boat manufacturer in Florida under TMS USA, the key area of boat design and engineering remained within the Toyota Marine Office, located in Toyota City, Japan. The Marine Office at our headquarters in Japan wanted to make the important decisions themselves, particularly regarding the boat design and technical development areas. I felt like this was a very odd arrangement as it would be difficult for me to successfully run the boat business without any authority to make decisions on the technical aspects of the boats.*
>
> *I had insisted to headquarters that, because the boat business was focused on the U.S. market and not the Japanese market, we at Orlando should make the key decisions with close communication with headquarters. But they did not agree with my idea and insisted on keeping the authority to make any changes in the technical area. The bad effect was that we were too slow in making decisions and taking countermeasures when problems occurred.*

And fourth among the problems that plagued the business was that the deterioration in communication continued — between the Japanese team members (including Yoshino) and the Americans in Orlando, as well as between Yoshino and his American "partner" in California. Despite Yoshino's best efforts, relationships across the cultures — national cultures *and* business cultures — were strained, and his two young Japanese engineers wanted to defer to the American style now that they were on American soil.

All these problems hindered Toyota Marine's effectiveness in producing — and delivering — quality products — a direct result of its failure to fully develop the people in the organization. This was not an example of Toyota's motto: "good thinking, good product" nor of its belief that "we make people while we make cars" (or, in this case, boats).

Toyota Marine Sport's Epic Water-ski Boat: Yoshino's vision created! (Photo from Toyota marketing materials in Isao Yoshino's archives.)

A DIVIDED CULTURE RESULTS IN A DIVIDED BOAT

Yoshino recalls one example of a quality defect that exemplified Toyota Marine's issues both with technical quality and with management: a customer in Texas was driving his boat on a local lake when the deck peeled off of the hull and the boat split in two! Thankfully, the boater was not injured, but this was a huge problem that Yoshino knew needed to be addressed immediately. In hearing this story, I couldn't help but think that if such a disaster had happened not in the late 1990s but a decade or more later — when photos or even video from this boater would likely have made their way immediately to the world via social media — this moment would have been the death knell for Toyota Marine Sports USA.

First, Yoshino describes the technical decision-making issues he believes impacted the boat construction in the first place:

The structure of our water-ski boat was that the deck was glued to the hull on a very narrow area that connected both portions all around the connecting portion — called the "conventional-connecting" style.

There was another way of connecting the deck and hull, which was called "shoe-box" type. Just like in a shoe box, where the top lid of the box is slightly wider than the box underneath, the deck and hull were glued with overlapping elements. Many boating design experts in the U.S. believed that the shoe-box connection was better for a water-ski boat, but our Japanese boat engineer insisted on using the conventional-connecting style.

As I did not have any technical knowledge in this area, I reluctantly agreed with what our Japanese engineer said. From the technical side of the problem, I believe our use of the "conventional-connecting" style could be one of the reasons for the peel-off problem.

Technical decision-making was not the only problem. Management dynamics with headquarters impacted Yoshino's abilities to respond to the Texas boat defect. As soon as the company learned of the split boat in Texas, Yoshino immediately wanted someone on his team to "go to gemba" to go see what had happened, but headquarters in Japan had a different response:

In the case of the Texas peel-off accident, our marine headquarters in Japan insisted that they would handle this accident case themselves and advised me to just wait until they developed a technical solution. The accident happened on a Sunday in June, but they did not advise the Japanese engineer to fly to Texas immediately to find out what exactly happened on the lake.

I kept calling headquarters in Japan, asking them to let me handle this case from the United States, and to send someone out to investigate, but they did not listen. Nothing happened on Monday, or Tuesday or Wednesday. I was so worried with the slow pace that I finally decided to send my American service manager to Texas to meet with the boat owner and find out what exactly happened.

It was on Thursday night, four days after the accident happened, that I received detailed information from my service manager. Very fortunately, the boater in Texas was not injured — only the boat was heavily damaged. And very luckily for Toyota, the boater did not pursue legal action.

Yoshino recalls feeling stuck between what he knew he should do as the leader of this problem and the decision-making protocol he was supposed to follow:

My deepest regret was that I should have sent my service manager to Texas right after I heard the accident news on Sunday evening. I did not do that because we had an agreement with our headquarters that they should take care of this "typical technical development" case and they advised me to wait. So, I reluctantly accepted their comment.

I was a bit surprised that our headquarters guy did not practice "go to gemba" in a very serious case like this, though maybe I have no right to blame our headquarters as I did not send my service manager right away either. I failed to practice what I had been coaching others on the importance of "go to gemba." It was one of my biggest mistakes to follow headquarters' insistence to handle the case from Japan, particularly under this serious case.

This was the most egregious quality example that occurred, but not an isolated case of quality issues. Yoshino believes that technical quality problems underlying the production quality, exacerbated by Toyota Marine Office's slow response from headquarters to follow up with customers or to fix the root causes, contributed to unfavorable customer reviews of Toyota's water-ski boats. This incident made it clear to Yoshino that the water-ski boat business was on a downward spiral to failure.

BE BRAVE ENOUGH TO ASK FOR HELP

"If you believe you are perfect, you won't find the answer. If you don't believe you are perfect, then you are open to finding the answer. Once you are ready to accept that mistakes can happen, then you are okay because you will learn."

– Isao Yoshino

In late 1999, just under a year after taking the role as plant manager in Orlando, Yoshino flew back to Torrance for a meeting between Mr. Cho (who by then had been promoted to Toyota's President) and the 70 native-Japanese managers working within TMS, USA. Compared to the other Japanese managers who were part of successful billion-dollar automobile ventures with hundreds of thousands of units, Yoshino's water-ski boat business was relatively small with roughly $3 million in annual sales and 100 units.

Yoshino describes that this type of meeting was regularly held whenever Toyota's top management flew into the United States. The purpose was for top management to talk to the frontline expatriates to show appreciation for their daily efforts and to get firsthand reports from them about the status of their businesses. It was a way of "going to gemba" — while not on the production floor, at getting closer to where the work happens by talking directly to the managers rather than staying in Japan and receiving only emails or phone calls.

Yoshino had already sent some private messages to Mr. Cho's secretary (i.e., his senior advisor), whom Yoshino knew from previous roles in Toyota City. Yoshino hoped that the secretary passed on some of the information, and that Mr. Cho already had some small idea of the boat business challenges. But the time had come to speak honestly and directly to Mr. Cho about the troubles in Orlando. Yoshino needed to "pull the andon" to signal that he needed help; he would ask Mr. Cho to come to Orlando and visit the failing boat business.

Yoshino did not think it was very likely that Mr. Cho would be able make it out to Florida. Compared with all the important business sites across North America, the water-ski boat business was a low priority. At that time, there were many other key places that Mr. Cho needed to visit in the U.S. and in other parts of the world. Orlando was very out of the way to easily tag onto any other site visits that Mr. Cho would make in the United States.

Finally, it was each manager's turn to speak with Mr. Cho. Each person only had two minutes to share the highlights of his business. As was usual for their regular Wednesday morning sales recap meeting for TMS USA, most of the Japanese managers only reported positive business outcomes, but Yoshino — having learned to lead in the TMC culture — knew that he had to muster the courage to tell a different story. Yoshino vividly remembers what happened when it was his turn to give a two-minute update:

> *Mr. Cho turned to me and said, "Yoshino, long time no see. How is your boat business?"*
>
> *I drew a deep breath and said, "The water-ski boat business is not doing well, sir. I cannot explain the boat business status and our problems in just two minutes, which was given to me at this meeting. I know it would be inappropriate to ask you in this meeting, but I would like you to please come to Orlando and see the gemba yourself."*
>
> *Mr. Cho paused a moment and then replied, "Let me check my schedule."*

Yoshino was pleased with this response, as these words meant that Mr. Cho was seriously considering coming to Orlando. A response such as "Let me think about it," in Japanese culture where "no" is rarely uttered, would have been Mr. Cho's way of saying no. But Mr. Cho's response meant that it might be possible. Yoshino did not think it was likely that the visit would happen anytime soon, but he was relieved that Mr. Cho had heard his request for help.

After the meeting, Yoshino recalls that Mr. Jagawa, a vice president who was traveling with Mr. Cho, came up and elbowed him in the side, and whispered "Hey, Yoshino, you did a good job." Yoshino interpreted this gesture from a senior TMC leader as a way to tell Yoshino that the senior management appreciated that he had stepped up to share the bad news and ask for help.

GO TO GEMBA, ASK FOR BAD NEWS, AND PROVIDE SUPPORT

A few months later, Yoshino received a surprising call from Mr. Cho's secretary saying that "Mr. Cho will be there in four weeks." Mr. Cho had found one day in an upcoming trip to the United States when he could fly to Florida to see Yoshino at his boat plant. What would follow was proof that the spirit of people-centered leadership existed at the highest levels of Toyota. The president was going to go to gemba to show that he cared (even about a relatively small business venture), he would ask for bad news, and he would provide support.

When Yoshino told the general manager that Mr. Cho was going to gemba in Florida in just a few weeks, his American partner was completely surprised. He not only couldn't believe that Yoshino had asked Mr. Cho to come to Orlando in the first place, but that Mr. Cho had accepted. And, based on the culture at TMS, the Marine Division general manager was worried that this would reflect badly on his own management. Yoshino saw this as evidence that sharing bad news was not rewarded at TMS; in fact, it was the opposite. The general manager worried about how a failing business would impact his own career at TMS.

But Mr. Cho, as president of all of Toyota Motor Corporation, exemplified the principles of the Toyota Way that TMC had long been cultivating. In late January 2000, just a year after Yoshino took over as plant manager, Mr. Cho arrived at the water-ski boat manufacturing plant gemba.

As soon as he arrived, Mr. Cho asked Yoshino, "Tell me the problems you are facing. What help do you need from me?" Yoshino started by highlighting all the things that were going well, but Mr. Cho stopped him and said that he didn't come to Orlando for sightseeing. He wanted to see the problems and to help.

Yoshino recalls Mr. Cho telling him, "Yoshino, that is good that you have some good news. But there is no need for you to report the good news to me. Tell me the bad news, because that is why I am here."

> **"There is no need for you to report the good news to me. Tell me the bad news, because that is why I am here."**

Yoshino's American direct subordinate, Bill, was astounded by this request for the bad news and turned to Yoshino, who had been translating the conversation from Japanese to English and back again. Bill said, "Yoshino-san, it sounds like Mr. Cho really would like to hear our bad news. Is that what he really meant?"

Yoshino replied to his direct report:

> *"Yes, Bill, you can talk about anything — any of our bad news. Tell Mr. Cho all the things you are facing right now." Bill was surprised! He did not expect that reaction from the big boss at Toyota. Mr. Cho's request for the "bad news first" really impressed him.*

After walking Mr. Cho through the plant and detailing their struggles, Mr. Cho concluded the visit by telling Bill and Yoshino, "Thank you — your direct comments are very important."

Yoshino and his team did not know what help Mr. Cho could provide at this point in the failing business, but they knew they had done their part to make their struggles visible to senior management.

LEADERSHIP RESPONSE: OWN THE CONDITIONS FOR SUCCESS

Two months after Mr. Cho's visit to Orlando, Yoshino started to notice that people in the TMC Marine Office at headquarters in Japan had changed their attitude toward the water-ski boat venture overseas. They stopped trying to make as many day-to-day decisions, and instead gave Yoshino more decision-making responsibility. Yoshino remembers this time:

> *I found out that Mr. Cho came back to Japan and discussed with Mr. Jagawa, the vice president who had also been in Torrance, how to help my boat project. Mr. Jagawa then talked to the Marine Office in the Business Development Department and advised them to provide any help that my team in Orlando needed from Japan.*

Mr. Cho's response to Yoshino's request for help — his proverbial pulling of the andon cord — had a profound impact on Yoshino. Unfortunately, despite Mr. Cho's interventions, which Yoshino says helped to prolong the boat business's ability to function for another year, it could not be turned around. Yoshino looks back:

> *It was very unfortunate that the help I received from Japan's headquarters was a little too late for us to get back on our feet, but I will never forget the consideration and compassion that Mr. Cho showed toward a smaller project like ours. What Mr. Cho showed us was "respect."*

To this day, this experience with Mr. Cho is one of the most significant memories Yoshino has of what it means to be a Toyota leader. Mr. Cho responded to a request for help, then found a way to create time in his busy schedule to fly across the United States to go see with his own eyes what was happening, to ask questions, to listen and learn how he might help, and to offer assistance to Yoshino to support this failing business.

Mr. Cho's response to Yoshino's request for help – his proverbial pulling of the andon cord – had a profound impact on Yoshino.

THE DREAM ENDS

Ultimately, Yoshino's American water-ski boat dream came to an end.

In the spring of 2001, Yoshino recalls hearing news "through the grapevine" that TMS management did not intend to keep the water-ski boat business within TMS USA. Shortly after, Yoshino flew to Torrance to provide his regular status update and recounts TMS management's intimation of their intentions:

> *When it was my turn to give my update, the TMS President replied, "Yoshino-san, I don't think we can support your project anymore." He did not use clear words such as "close your business or plant," but he used the English word "support" instead, even when speaking in Japanese to me. Of course, he meant that he would not let our boat business continue to operate in Orlando, but he avoided talking so straight.*
>
> *I thought the president intentionally used the word of "no support," with a hope that I would take "no support" as actually "close the business" without actually saying it. But I did not continue the conversation any further. I knew their true intention, but I kept my style as usual. From time to time, TMS sent somebody to Orlando to talk to me with that purpose, but they did not articulate their real intent so much.*

Only as this book was going to print did Yoshino recall this declaration of "no support" and we talked about its significance related to his belief that a leader's role is to provide direction, provide support, and develop himself. In this case, the company president's withdrawal of support went against Yoshino's beliefs in people-centered leadership. Rather than declaring a clear direction (e.g., "we need to close the business"), the TMS president instead was withdrawing support of his people. In Yoshino's mind, this was not how leaders should act.

So, water-ski boat production continued, even though Yoshino knew that, sooner or later, TMS would announce their decision to close the business. Finally, in August 2001, the TMS messenger from Torrance told Yoshino officially that the water-ski boat project was to shut down. TMS had talked with corporate headquarters in Japan, which agreed to close the plant. Yoshino recalls, *"It was not unexpected, but it was still a big shock."* The dream was over.

In early September 2001, just days before the 9/11 terror attacks, Yoshino and the two Japanese engineers based in Orlando were called back to Torrance to discuss how to handle the plant closure.[3] It was a tough time for Yoshino, both professionally and personally. His idea for Toyota Marine Sports USA, born nearly a decade earlier and finally authorized after five persistent years, was a failed experiment that cost the company $13 million. He considered this a "miserable ending" to what had started as a passion project to create a new business in the United States:

> *My boat business plan started in 1994 with a lot of excitement and a big smile on my face, and it ended in 2001 with a lot of disappointment, ugly arguments, and a frown.*

Yoshino was demoralized. He was worried that he would be blamed for the boat business failure by TMS leadership and that now, in his late 50s, he would not be granted a good role in his final professional years.

---

3 Yoshino and the two Japanese engineers were stuck in California following 9/11 with no flights or trains available to facilitate their return to Florida. Ultimately, they rented a car (a Mazda, as it was all that was available) and drove from Los Angeles to Orlando over three days and two nights (one in Albuquerque, New Mexico, and the other in Baton Rouge, Louisiana). Yoshino recounts that tensions were high and it was a miserable drive: a terrorist attack, a shattered dream, and stressful interpersonal dynamics between the engineers who had long held different opinions on the business. It was Yoshino's first — and last — American cross-country road trip.

IF THE COMPANY AUTHORIZES THE EXPERIMENT, IT OWNS THE OUTCOME

What happened next is a lesson for us all. Just as blame should not be placed on individuals for process-related problems (like when Yoshino's paint mistake in his first weeks of employment at Toyota resulted in an apology from supervisors for not labeling the cans more clearly and providing better training), individuals should not be personally blamed for a failed business experiment that the company authorized and backed. Yoshino had made mistakes, but so had the organization.

Shortly before the boat business's closure, the head of the Business Development Department called Yoshino back to Toyota corporate headquarters in Toyota City to discuss his fate at the company. Although Yoshino was nervous about his next assignment, his fears were ultimately unfounded. Toyota owned the water-ski boat failure itself rather than "blaming by firing," as is often the case in other companies. Toyota wasn't looking to assign blame or select scapegoats. It had authorized the "experiment" to enter the water-ski boat market in the United States, with full understanding that experiments involve risk and carry no guarantees. Despite the business failure, senior leaders at Toyota knew that failure was part of pursuing new ideas and that it was the source of valuable learning. They didn't solely place blame on Yoshino for the project not working, nor did they punish him by giving him a bad subsequent assignment. On the contrary, Toyota leadership gave Yoshino a role in another important new business venture, in which he could leverage his personal and organizational learnings.

Isao Yoshino "testing" a jet-pack flying device at the Hiller Museum in San Carlos, California (early 2000s).

Yoshino recounts arriving at his meeting with the general manager of Toyota's New Business Development Department in Toyota City, and his relief to hear, "Yoshino-san, a new job is waiting for you in another new product." Toyota had learned the value of retaining knowledge learned from failure — and from success. This reassignment from headquarters gave Yoshino renewed confidence in himself — and the company. At a company where loyalty and commitment are valued on the part of the employee, the company demonstrated loyalty in return.

Yoshino would take on another position based at TMS USA headquarters in Torrance to conduct market research for Toyota's newest business venture — a Fuel Cell Project focused on a new market for household use. Yoshino was excited to be part of this new cutting-edge research — and for the opportunity to remain in the United States. Yoshino returned to the U.S. with a new job and a renewed enthusiasm for the future. His boat-business days were behind him and an exciting future awaited.

In November 2001, the Marine Division at TMS USA (i.e., Toyota Marine Sports USA) was officially disbanded. Yet Yoshino's American dream lived on.

MR. CHO REFLECTS ON FAILURE

"Celebrate the attempt, not the failure. Failure is the source of so much learning."

– Isao Yoshino

Just over two years later, in January 2004, Yoshino reached Toyota's retirement age of 60, and was again called back to Japan — this time for a small ceremony and celebration. Mr. Cho and many of Toyota's senior management team were there. Yoshino recalls an important and powerful comment that Mr. Cho made to him that day:

> *After the ceremony, I had a chance to talk with Mr. Cho and other top executives over a soft drink. I started talking to Mr. Cho and sought to acknowledge his thoughtful decision to come all the way to Orlando to visit our boat plant two years earlier.*

> *I said, "Despite your great support, Mr. Cho, I failed to make the boat business recover. I am very sorry for that. There were so many factors for the failure, but the biggest factor is my poor management ability. I made a lot of mistakes in my boat business operation."*
>
> *Mr. Cho responded to me saying, "You were new to the boat business, and so were we at our headquarters. We all make mistakes, particularly when you try something totally new. We know you took on a challenge and worked so hard to make it happen. The lessons you have learned from the failure is the most important. Don't blame yourself for the failure. I heard that you have been working hard again on our new Fuel Cell Project. Good luck in this new assignment."*
>
> *Again, I felt "a sense of respect" from Mr. Cho. This was really a moving moment for me.*

In this simple exchange, Mr. Cho made an indelible and positive impression on Yoshino, shaping his experience of "failing." Mr. Cho, the most senior leader at Toyota, acknowledged that the company had also made many mistakes that contributed to the failure of the boat business. And he honored and supported Yoshino for his actions — his attempts to succeed, even if he made mistakes and fell down — even if they, too, contributed to the failure.

IT'S ONLY A FAILURE IF YOU DON'T LEARN

"Failure is not important. It is the process and what we learn from the failure that is more important."

– Isao Yoshino

Of all the things Yoshino and I discussed across hundreds of hours as we prepared the content for this book, our conversations about what he learned in the wake of the Marine Sports failure were perhaps the most profound moments for me — as a leader and a coach — and were the most challenging for him to revisit. However, he said to me, *"While it was a horrible experience to lead a failed business, it was a great experience because I learned so much."*

Before Yoshino stepped into his next role in the Fuel Cell Project, Toyota leaders modeled the company's own commitment to learning from failure by asking him to formally reflect — to conduct *hansei* — on what he learned from the Epic water-ski boat business failure. As part of his *hansei*, he was to prepare a document that the company could use as a case study (for training purposes) regarding what not to do when running a new business — from both an organizational perspective and a personal one.

While he does not have a copy of his original *hansei* document, we share his *hansei* — of what he learned then and what he has discovered through the lens of time — here for you too to learn.

ORGANIZATIONAL LEADERSHIP LESSONS

From an organizational perspective, Yoshino and his colleagues involved in the water-ski boat venture experienced system-level challenges that, at the outset, may have doomed the business to failure. At the very least, as Yoshino reflects below, suboptimal organizational conditions didn't set the business up for success. These organizational lessons are instructive to any of us who own or lead inside organizations seeking to build a new business venture across cultures or company divisions.

Organizational Lesson #1 – Provide Training and Coaching to Develop New Habits

Companies must provide thorough training and coaching support to ensure people understand company culture and values and are able to ingrain these cultural behaviors and shared values as habits. In this case, more training support — over a sustained period of time — was needed to teach TPS technical production principles and Toyota Way management capabilities, such as "go to gemba" and respect for people. Without the level of intentional support, as was provided to NUMMI and other sites, operations in Orlando just continued as they always had.

Organizational Lesson #2 – Delegate Authority While Maintaining Visibility

When leaders are not located directly at the local production site, the company should delegate authority to the local site, while maintaining communication channels and visibility to the decisions. Yoshino reflects upon the degree to which micromanaging from afar can result in slow decisions — often based upon assumptions rather than facts:

> *The company, or headquarters division, needs to make sure that specific authority can be delegated to the person who runs the project at the site.*
>
> *In my boat project case, our headquarters did not want to delegate any authority on the technical decision-making to those of us in Orlando. The bad effect was that we were incredibly slow in making decisions and taking countermeasures when problems occurred. Leaders need to know that you cannot judge something based on the assumption. You need to see things by your own eyes before you make an important decision.*

Organizational Lesson #3 – Be Patient and Understand Differences

Leaders need to be patient to understand differences across cultures, regardless of whether those culture differences include local cultures, company cultures, or country cultures. As Yoshino reflects now:

> *When you do business with foreign people on foreign soil, you have to spend more time to listen to them and more time to discuss with them. People have different views, opinions, and preferences. Everyone is different from each other.*

He further reflects that cultures can collide in unexpected ways. You might think you have enough in common with your colleagues because you all work for the same company, but dissonance emerges because of variations in attitudes or practices across different locations in the same country or across different divisions of the same company:

> *People have different values in life and work as well. What makes people happy differs depending on the culture people work in.*

> *If you face something that initially feels odd or different (or wrong or abnormal) from your standard, it is recommended that you should not judge things right away, but look at it from different angles and take more time to draw any conclusions. And, to understand people's mindsets, opinions, or characters, you need to listen to them more carefully until you have something for certain.*

When looking back on these cultural differences, the gap in understanding of TPS, and his own contributions, Yoshino reflects that:

> *I now believe that this situation came primarily from a lack of communication and a lack of patience between the people involved, including myself, to understand each other. I know that good communication could not necessarily solve all the problems, but I believe good communication and the attitude to show respect to others could have greatly helped us to handle problems with a more coolheaded mindset.*

PERSONAL LEADERSHIP LESSON: FOLLOW THE PROCESS – KNOWING DOES NOT EQUAL DOING

"I didn't follow the process. I had a passion for the boat business, but the process I took to lead it was wrong."

– *Isao Yoshino*

In practicing *hansei* after the water-ski boat experience and before starting his new job on the Fuel Cell Project, Yoshino also realized that he learned a key personal lesson in addition to all the organizational lessons. After much reflection, he considers his top personal management mistake, which contributed to the water-ski boat business failure, something we've discussed at length in this book: he didn't practice *hoshin kanri*! When faced with leading his own operation, Yoshino succumbed to the same management challenges that many of us do: he had the knowledge and skills, but under pressures and challenges, it felt easier to take shortcuts.

> **When faced with leading his own operation, Yoshino succumbed to the same management challenges that many of us do: he had the knowledge and skills, but under pressures and challenges, it felt easier to take shortcuts.**

For example, Yoshino recalls that when headquarters in Toyota City asked him for a *hoshin* document for the boat business so that they would know what he was up to, he "checked the box" by delivering a document that he created alone. He intentionally skipped the critical element of *hoshin* — engaging his people in conversation and input:

> *I agreed that developing a* hoshin *was a good idea, but I was busy, so I made just a simplified* hoshin *A3. I set the target and created a plan on my own, but I didn't consult others as much as I should on how we could attain it. I realize now that I was rushing and skipped the process.*
>
> *I knew that* hoshin *was just a tool, and that we had to spend time to discuss the targets, but I didn't do all of those things I had coached others to do! While I set monthly targets — for sales, production, and defect rate — we didn't set more granular process measures to know if we were on track to hit our monthly targets. There were so many urgent problems that we needed to tackle on the production site that we had little time to discuss the details of how we would achieve the monthly targets.*

Yoshino experienced what many managers and leaders do: with quality issues and fires to put out, it felt like there was never time to have the conversations needed to clearly communicate strategic priorities or engage others in problem solving. The urgent took priority over the necessary:

> *I didn't take the time to make sure that everyone understood what we needed to achieve. We were so desperate to tackle the defects on the production site and also in the market and we were so focused on handling the immediate problems at hand.*

Yoshino felt the immense time constraints of daily operations and didn't spend the time to teach his American managers, who had never been exposed to a process like *hoshin kanri,* what its purpose was:

I forgot to discuss thoroughly with my managers what the target and action plans meant to us. What was most important was for us all to be on the same page, and I skipped that critical step. I did not spend much time or talk to the people working directly for me to help them understand the purpose of the hoshin *process, so they didn't really believe that they were part of it. Their basic understanding wasn't there.*

Looking back, I learned that before we can discuss the details of a plan, we have to share an understanding of the big picture. Only once we have agreement on where we need to go can we discuss the details of how we will get there. If you go into details too much at the beginning, then we don't know why we are getting into these details.

"Only once we have agreement on where we need to go can we discuss the details of how we will get there."

Only afterwards, did Yoshino realize that by developing the plan by himself and jumping in for day-to-day problem solving, he had taken away a crucial opportunity to develop his people. Yoshino elaborates:

I forgot to recognize that what I was doing to tackle all our problems was actually the responsibility of my managers at each section. My key role, as a general manager, was not to handle day-to-day problems myself, but to make sure that each manager was pursuing the target at each site, and I would provide any help if I saw something was missing and they needed my help. My role was to make every manager to be on the same page on our target and what we needed to do to make it happen.

I should have had a mindset of "macromanagement" instead of "micromanagement." I was not fulfilling my role as a general manager, although I had witnessed and learned how important it is for higher bosses to show directions to the target and help the team to reach those targets.

In retrospect, Yoshino recognizes that the Americans did not fully understand the purpose of *hoshin* and that he needed to take more time to explain the process:

I should have spent more time and discussed thoroughly until they understand what hoshin kanri *meant to us. I sensed that they didn't fully*

> *understand the basic purpose of the* hoshin, *but I still hoped that they would understand.*
>
> *In the end, I wanted to blame my subordinates, but it was my problem to assume that they would agree with my idea and that they would understand the* hoshin *process. I tried, but I did not do enough.*

Ultimately, there was not cross-functional alignment on what the various groups needed to do to ensure success of the water-ski boat business. Coupled with the cross-cultural and structural challenges, this lack of alignment and understanding across departments of the challenges facing the business ultimately contributed to the downfall of the business. Yoshino took the insights he had gained from this experience, determined to put them to good use in his new role.

A FINAL REFLECTION ON PURSUING A CHALLENGE AND FAILING

Looking back while we prepared for this book, nearly 20 years after this experience, Yoshino had a new perspective on the outcome of the water-ski boat business — a career journey that started as a dream to return to the United States and to create a new business for Toyota, and turned into the most significant management challenge and failure of his career. He commented to me:

> *Even though the water-ski boat business was unsuccessful, I feel happy to have had a chance to start with a concept and then bring it up to the top management for approval and make it happen. We challenged our minds and energy. We worked so hard to try to make it happen. That fact means a lot to me, although it ended up with a failure or exit.*

He took on a challenge, pursued an idea, and did his best despite falling down many times. And ultimately, it was *not* really a failure, as both he and the company were able to learn and grow.

INTO THE TWILIGHT OF HIS CAREER

After the conclusion of the water-ski boat business, Yoshino worked on Toyota's Fuel Cell Project out of California for four years — first while employed at Toyota and then as an external consultant. Yoshino worked on Toyota's vision for a home-based stationary fuel cell that would produce electricity with hydrogen extracted from city-provided gas and oxygen from the air.

While this household Fuel Cell Project has not yet (at the time of this book's publication) resulted in a product going to market for Toyota, Yoshino played an influential role at the genesis of what has become a signature element of Toyota's plans for the next generation. Central to Toyota president Akio Toyoda's vision of the future into the 21st century is a focus on hydrogen fuel cells. The Toyota Mirai is an example of Toyota leading the edge in technology for a fully operational automatic-use fuel cell car.

Yoshino finally concluded his Toyota career in 2006 and repatriated to Japan in January 2007, where he shares his lessons from a lifetime of learning to lead, and leading to learn with the next generation of Japanese and foreign university students — and with us.

PRACTICING *HANSEI*: REFLECTION QUESTIONS

- How have you handled differences in work culture? Company culture? Country culture? What impact did these differences have in your success or failure?
- What is the impact of senior leaders micromanaging instead of "macromanaging," as Yoshino commented?
- When is a time that you knew you sacrificed people development or problem-solving in exchange for expediency or other time pressures? What happened as a result in the short term? What was the impact on the long-term culture of your organization?

- How does your organization react to failure? How does this impact innovation and continuous improvement?
- What do you think about Yoshino's perspective about failure as a source of learning?
- How does your company practice *hansei* (i.e., reflect)? How does it learn?
- How much time do you take to reflect each day? How do you learn?

THE TOYOTA WAY – LOST IN TRANSLATION?

The Toyota Way 2001 was published as an internal company document just before Yoshino's retirement from the company. It details the leadership mindset and philosophy that Yoshino experienced over 40 years of learning to lead and leading to learn at Toyota.

When I asked Yoshino why Mr. Cho had asked for Toyota to codify its leadership principles into one document, he replied:

> *TPS prevails around the world with a different naming of "lean." Many people have some knowledge about the key elements of TPS/lean. There are so many books now about lean, and the word "kaizen" is commonly used as an English word in the manufacturing community.*
>
> *I believe that Mr. Cho was concerned that just understanding key technical elements of TPS, such as "standardized work," "just-in-time," and "mistakeproofing," was not enough to manufacture good quality cars. All these key concepts and processes are important tools to make TPS/lean take root in the production site.*
>
> *However, such key elements as "leaders' role," "show your respect," "no problem is a problem," and "make people before making cars" are not necessarily treated as equally as "kaizen" and other practical tools to make good cars. These elements of our culture were somewhat unique to Toyota.*
>
> *By 2001, Mr. Cho probably had a similar thought or concern as Mr. Nemoto had in the 1970s when he introduced Kan-Pro. Mr. Cho must have thought that it would be essential for autoworkers in foreign countries to deeply understand the key concept of Toyota's business principles, including TPS or lean.*

Out of this concern from Toyota's most senior leader came *The Toyota Way 2001*. Written in both Japanese and English, it was distributed to Toyota's sites around the world.

Lost in Translation

As you learned in this book's Introduction on page 21, the two pillars of *The Toyota Way 2001* are translated into English as "Continuous Improvement" and "Respect for People." Yet, in looking back at what he knows about Toyota's culture of leading and learning, Yoshino believes that this translation has lost some of the richness of meaning of Toyota's fundamental values.

So, what is the essence of these original concepts that we have missed?

What does "Respect for People" really mean?

Yoshino believes that the pillar "Respect for People" — as intended in the Japanese version of *The Toyota Way 2001* — has a broader and deeper meaning than these words represent in English. Yoshino says:

> *People often ask me, "Does respect mean that leaders should go to gemba just to say hi to the workers? Do leaders need to be superficially nice to everyone?" I am afraid something is missing in their understanding of respect.*

First, Yoshino explains that in the Japanese version of *The Toyota Way 2001*, the object of the verb "respect" is not "human being" or "person" (written in Japanese as 人間), but rather represents the broader concept of "humanity" or "humanness" (人間性).

Second, he elaborates that there are two Japanese words with different interpretations for the English word "respect," depending upon the context.

The first word is *"Sonkei"* (尊敬), usually used in reference to a specific person or people. Yoshino explains this type of respect:

> "Son" *(尊) means "valued" and the* "kei" *(敬) means "worship." So,* "Sonkei" *(尊敬) means that "one has a high regard for somebody" or "one admires somebody for the tremendous efforts to achieve the high goal." It is an expression to recognize or admit somebody else's outstanding ability or excellent accomplishment. In most cases, this expression is used when somebody is far superior to the person himself or in relation to average people.*

> *When the word* "Sonkei" *(尊敬) is expressed, it implicitly means that the person puts himself at a lower position than the person who is rated highly.*

The other word is *"Soncho"* (尊重), which is used to more broadly represent the concept of humanity or our humanness. Yoshino explains this broader concept of respect, which he believes is the intention in *The Toyota Way 2001*:

> *As mentioned earlier,* "Son" *(尊) means "valued." And* "cho" *(重) means "main" or "important." So,* "Soncho" *(尊重) means "holding precious what it is to be human." You can also say "value humanity" or "respect humanity." In this meaning, people are positioned on the same level, not higher or lower than the other. The expression of respect* ("Soncho") *can be used not only on "people" but also on "things" as well.*
>
> "Soncho" *reflects that each person has a different way of thinking, different values, different beliefs, different tastes, different customs, different lifestyles, different religions. Each person's uniqueness needs to be recognized and considered important.*

It is this broader concept of respect for humanity and for the greater diversity of perspective that is the essence of respect at Toyota.

> **The broader concept of respect for humanity, and for the greater diversity of perspective, is the essence of respect at Toyota.**

What Does "Continuous Improvement" Really Mean?

In *The Toyota Way 2001*, the second pillar is translated into English as "Continuous Improvement." However, the Japanese version is written with the words *"Chie"* and *"Kaizen"* (知恵 + 改善), which directly translates to "Wisdom and Improvement." The direct translation of *"Kaizen"* alone just means "Improvement."

Yoshino's interpretation is that the addition of the English word "continuous" was intended to imply that we are not perfect and, therefore, we need to get better on a step-by-step basis:

> *This is based on the concept that we are not perfect, and we need to try to always make something better, and there is no end for this approach. This expression has been shared among all the employees for years.*

However, the English words "Continuous Improvement" — instead of the direct translation of "Wisdom and Improvement" — do not bring forward the richness of the meaning of the word "wisdom." Wisdom is much deeper than just being continuous and ongoing. Wisdom reflects the deeper process of learning and reflection that happens over time.

Wisdom reflects the deeper process of learning and reflection that happens over time.

Wisdom is about knowledge, reflection, learning, and understanding that comes with experience — and is passed down through generations. Wisdom is the "Check-Adjust" — the *hansei* and learning — part of the PDCA cycle of continuous improvement. Wisdom is how we take knowledge and use it to make solid and good decisions now and in the future.

This nuance of wisdom as a force for learning over time is lost in translation.

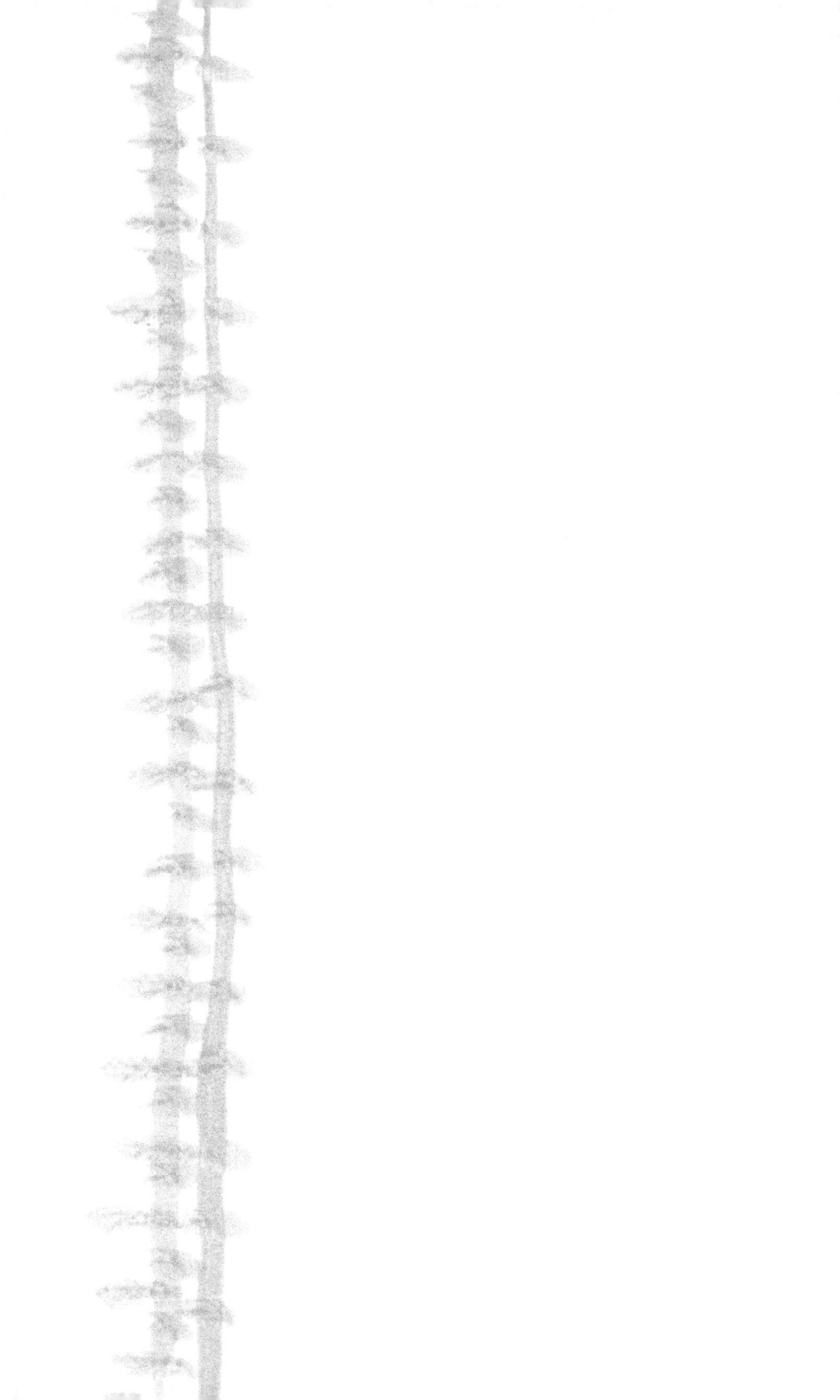

CONCLUSION: LOOKING BACK AND LOOKING FORWARD

"Everything is my learning journey."

– Isao Yoshino

Isao Yoshino's lifetime of continuous learning exemplifies how one person's leadership learning journey can inspire generations of leaders — aspiring or established, male or female, in any industry, and anywhere on the globe. Through reading his personal stories of learning and leading, we also discover stories of how Toyota evolved, grew, and learned to become one of the most successful auto manufacturers — and companies — in the world.

The stories in this book represent the wisdom that comes from a process of purposeful reflection and learning. Throughout this book, you have followed Yoshino along the warp and weft threads of his life as he created a fabric uniquely his own — strong and beautiful, with some broken and tattered threads, colorful and well-worn. Through these stories about leading and being led, we too can learn and reflect about the importance of successes and mentorship, of challenges and failure, and ultimately of reflection and learning. What does it mean for each of us, personally, to have a dream and set a goal, and to help others discover their own purpose, set goals, and develop themselves?

The stories in this book represent the wisdom that comes from a process of purposeful reflection and learning.

Yoshino's first words that I heard him speak reveal what he learned about leadership over the course of his life and career at Toyota and beyond, and are the themes of learning and leading presented throughout this book. In short, the role of a leader is to:

1. **Set the direction:** Issue a clear challenge, goal, or target to your people.
2. **Provide support:** Help your people develop themselves as learners and leaders, and create systems that enable their success.
3. **Develop yourself:** Constantly improve yourself as a leader and a learner.

Set the Direction

Yoshino personally discovered the power of having a personal challenge to pursue, of having a dream, and of setting goals and targets to achieve in that direction. His clear vision and inner determination to achieve that dream — his warp threads — helped him stay focused. Just like the proverb "Fall down seven times, get up eight," this clear inner direction and sense of purpose gave him the strength to rise when circumstances pushed him down.

And through his decades at Toyota, Yoshino learned the importance of a leader's role in defining a purpose, providing a challenge, setting a direction with clear goals and targets, and of communicating to ensure that everyone understands these goals and are aligned. And importantly, he discovered that a leader can help people identify their own personal purpose — identify their own warp threads — on which to build and create their own life fabric.

Provide Support

Throughout his interactions with mentors, teachers, colleagues, and students — first at school, then through his career at Toyota, and now in retirement — Yoshino learned about (and from) helping others to develop their own capabilities — in problem solving, in people development, and in life. These are the many weft threads that he picked up and incorporated in the life he was weaving.

Develop Yourself

In the end, Yoshino has never lost sight of developing himself. He was always seeking to improve as a leader and as a learner. While creating this book, he remarked that — through our working together — he learned how to ask even better and more effective questions to help others think more deeply about their lives. It is through the process of reflection, of remembering and examining the pattern of his life fabric, that he has learned and re-learned more deeply than he originally thought he would.

As Yoshino discovered, developing others is a path to helping you develop yourself and to creating a purposeful, fulfilling life.

LOOKING BACK, WE CAN SEE THE PATTERN – THE THEMES OF PEOPLE-CENTERED LEADERSHIP

Yoshino wove an intricate pattern of purpose, shaped over a lifetime. His experiences highlight the importance of so many leadership principles that embody the Toyota Way themes of what is means to be a people-centered leader who develops people, of continuous learning, and of reflection. These include:

- Know — or discover — your purpose
- Set a direction and clear goals
- Be persistent
- Always seek to learn and remain curious — and encourage others do the same
- View things from many angles or perspectives
- Make the invisible visible
- Find the good — in people and in situations
- Pursue excellence, yet embrace imperfection
- Create the conditions for people to learn and be successful

- Be patient — it takes time to develop people and accomplish challenges
- Make the extra effort — go beyond your job description to help others
- Go see — "go to gemba" — to learn and to show you care
- Create culture change by developing people one at a time
- Focus on the process, not just the outcome
- Ask questions, listen openly, adjust your style, and be flexible
- Delegate authority, trust your people, and provide help when needed
- Share (and ask for) "bad news first" and speak up, even if it's difficult
- Recognize that failure is the ultimate source of learning
- Never forget that learning comes from reflection
- Start with yourself.

Through Yoshino's personal stories and experiences at Toyota — both the successes and the failures — we too can learn about what it takes to be a people-centered leader, to continuously learn, and to develop an organizational culture that embodies these principles.

> **Through Yoshino's personal stories and experiences at Toyota – both the successes and the failures – we too can learn about what it takes to be a people-centered leader, to continuously learn, and to develop an organizational culture that embodies these principles.**

THE SECRET IS TO LEARN MORE DEEPLY – FROM FAILURE AND SUCCESS

"Failure is not necessarily bad as long as you learn something."

- *Isao Yoshino*

This book started with Yoshino's statement that, "The only secret to Toyota is its attitude toward learning." Toyota's people-centered culture of learning was created by the consistent mindset that its leaders embody, taught (and re-taught), and passed down through generations. They believe that each person has the responsibility to make the most out of his or her own role, and to always help others grow and learn. The attitude of "bad news first" and "no problem is a problem," where experimentation is encouraged and individuals are not blamed, creates the space for learning.

Yoshino's career at Toyota was bookended by two "mistakes" — one relatively small and the other much more significant. The way in which organizational leaders responded to these mistakes shaped Yoshino's experience and speaks to the consistency of the culture.

In his first months at Toyota, after causing hundreds of cars in the Motomachi plant to have to be repainted, Yoshino was approached by the Paint Shop manager, who apologized to Yoshino and told him:

> ***Don't worry, mistakes can happen. You are just a beginner and you did your best.***

And at the conclusion of his Toyota career, after leading a $13 million failed business experiment, Yoshino was told by the President of Toyota, Mr. Cho:

> ***You were new to the boat business, and so were we at our headquarters. We all make mistakes, particularly when we try something totally new. We know you took on a challenge and worked so hard to make it happen.***

In both of these failures, the response of the leaders was similar: You were new to the situation, you tried your best, and we too have responsibility for the outcome. Neither placed blame, and instead took ownership from the organization's perspective for the ultimate outcome. It is this attitude that gives Toyota its competitive edge — its attitude toward learning from both failure and success.

REFLECTION – *HANSEI* – IS WHERE LEARNING HAPPENS, WHERE WISDOM IS CREATED

"It is an important learning journey to work together. To be asked questions, and to think about what I have learned, I learn even more."

- *Isao Yoshino*

As we concluded the final interviews for this book, Yoshino and I reflected on the journey of *hansei* that we have undertaken together. We spent some time talking about the process of reflection and how crucial it is for learning. We can learn in the moment, when we are close to an event, but then later we can learn more deeply when we can step back and see the bigger picture.

We also talked about how reflection and learning happen more effectively when people who are working together ask questions from a place of caring, helping the other person examine their experiences from different perspectives. Reflection, of course, can happen as a solo endeavor (which is why I included the "Practicing *Hansei*" reflection questions for you throughout this book), but partnership and collaboration can create a deeper level of understanding.

Collaboration and shared learning is the major theme of my relationship with Mr. Yoshino and the undercurrent of this book: the richness of learning we have both received from our conversations — of sharing our perspectives across generations, geography, and different backgrounds. I encourage you to think about how you can use this book to foster collective learning in your own relationships and organizations.

REFLECTION IS NOT ALWAYS EASY

Over the two years we spent creating this book, our conversations continued to go deeper, to uncover nuances and new perspectives on memories. We have laughed heartily as Yoshino remembered some long-forgotten stories, like the paint mistake, and the elaborate — and sometimes wacky

— experiences in the San Francisco Liaison Office as a glorified gofer, cat wrangler, and travel advisor.

Collaborating on this book was not all laughter, though. There were many times that I asked Yoshino to tell me more about situations and experiences he found difficult to revisit — especially when reflecting on the period of the water-ski boat business. While he had often referenced "the water-ski boat failure" with me and in presentations to other audiences, Yoshino had not previously shared the details we have written about here. It was a large patch of densely woven black threads interspersed with knots from broken ends in his life fabric. He personally felt the weight of much of the failure on his shoulders. Yet as I continued to ask questions and as we talked, a more complex story emerged — one with so many interrelated and interdependent factors that coalesced and contributed to the boat business's ultimate failure.

One night, after many video calls and sharing drafts and emails back and forth over several months about the water-ski boat decade, something shifted for Yoshino. Instead of a somber face, as he had worn in many of our earlier conversations about this time, he said with a big smile:

> *This has been a really amazing experience for me!*
>
> *While this has been a tough topic for me, and I didn't want to remember some of those challenging times, at the same time I don't want to forget it. Sometimes if you have a terrible experience, you have to think about the benefit. Instead of only looking at the bad side, you have to look at the good side of the facts. And now, I am balancing the good and the bad things. Your questions triggered it, and it's great! I am thinking about my experience in a different way.*
>
> *This is the power of asking questions. You did not force me to answer. You just kept asking me questions in a different way that helped me face the facts of what we have done, what I have done, and what I haven't done. I appreciate that you kept asking me, as this is the first time that I have really been asked to think more about this time.*

In the end, Yoshino shared his thoughts on the importance of reflection as a source of learning — for both failure and success — and the foundation of the PDCA cycle. As he learned and taught over the course of his career at Toyota, the process is more important than the result. It is through the process of (and understanding through) reflection that we can learn and adjust in the future. Yoshino elaborates:

> *Everybody wants to make a success. Nobody wants to fail or make mistakes. However, we need to know that we all make mistakes or fail, although we really want to do things right. We are human, we make mistakes, and we have to accept this. The most important thing is how much we can learn from our experiences.*
>
> *If we make a big success and we also learn a lot of things from the success, it is great. But sometimes it often happens that we tend to skip the review to understand the real factor that brought us the success. It means that we don't learn from our success. Then our success is just a one-time good luck and we don't grow.*
>
> *In the case of failure, we usually try to look back at what has brought a failure, what was wrong in our decisions, what action was wrong, what timing we should have taken the action, etc. We want to learn some important lessons from the failure we have made. If we learn enough lessons from the failure, then the failure is no more a failure.*

"If we learn enough lessons from the failure, then the failure is no more a failure."

A FABRIC OF PURPOSE WOVEN TOGETHER FROM THE KNOWN AND THE DISCOVERED

Today, Yoshino's warp and weft threads are tightly woven into a complete fabric. It is difficult to see which is the warp and which is the weft. It is the relationship between the threads that we see.

Having international experiences — Yoshino's warp threads — continue to remain the foundation of his life's fabric. His desire and commitment to living an international life are as strong as ever. As well, Yoshino remains passionate about teaching and developing people — his weft threads — and passing down the lessons that he learned from a lifetime of success, failure, reflection, and learning.

Since his retirement from Toyota, Yoshino serves as a lecturer on American cultural studies and language at Nagoya Gakuin University, and travels internationally to teach and share his leadership insights with business leaders around the world. Yoshino says that he wants to pass down the tradition of learning and people development that was passed down to him — first by his *juku* teacher and then by his bosses and colleagues at Toyota.

Yoshino reflects on how his warp and weft threads have become integrated, and how these shaped his purpose in coaching his students and sharing his insights with leaders around the world. His warp and weft are inseparable:

> *Now my warp threads have expanded to a strong desire to become more involved in different cultures. It started as a small boy with a dream to go to the United States. It has now expanded to Europe and beyond. I like to travel and meet new people. I'm not so much interested in the scenery or sightseeing. That could be a reason why I come to the university every day. I am interested in people — and helping them grow. These are my weft threads. It's never ending.*

Yoshino coaches his university students as if he were developing someone who reported to him at Toyota. He wants his students to learn critical thinking skills to solve their own problems. While it is not required as part of his role, he gets joy from spending extra time coaching them outside of class — teaching them how to think more deeply about how to get clear on their purpose or goal, how to solve problems, how to make a plan to take action, and — most importantly — how to reflect and learn. And just like he created opportunities for his staff in the Nagoya Office to have international experiences, in recent years, Yoshino has invited several pairs of students to join him on his overseas business trips.

Yoshino is helping these young people to identify their warp and weft threads, and then begin to weave them together. This brings him great satisfaction:

> *I now just want to pass the tradition, which I enjoyed at Toyota, to my students as long as our talks can help them to find the right direction. Each student has their own belief or determination or target in life*

— their own "warp threads." Very often, students are too young to think more deeply about how to make their dreams happen. They have no idea how to set action plans to attain their goals. They don't know what kind of steps they need to go through to reach the goal. They don't know how to solve a problem when they run into it. They don't know who they need to talk to for help and advice. I believe all of these items are so important to make their "warp threads" happen.

It is always a great pleasure for me to see my students learn something new from working together with me. When they have a big smile on their face with a sense of accomplishment, I can feel that they become more confident in their ability to tackle the problems. At the same time, I also enjoy a sense of satisfaction with a feeling that I have made a small contribution to help my students to develop themselves.

More importantly, I believe I keep learning these important lessons once again: Ask more questions. Listen more. Be patient. You can learn from anything and from anybody.

"I believe I keep learning these important lessons once again: Ask more questions. Listen more. Be patient. You can learn from anything and from anybody."

And, of course, this book is yet another way for Yoshino to help share his rich experiences and stories to help people around the world learn. He has taught me, and he is generous enough to teach you too.

YOSHINO LOOKS BACK AT THE PATTERN HE HAS WOVEN

"Bad news comes after good news. Good news comes after bad news. Don't worry about it. Neither good or bad will last long. That is life."

– Isao Yoshino

When we look back on something that was a hardship or failure, it may seem like there are more dark colors than light in our fabric, and that can be overwhelming. But when we look back and reflect in a broader context, we can see how those challenging times helped us in unexpected ways. Perhaps we learned about how to move differently in our life — choosing different colors and patterns. It is the contrast with the darker patches that highlight the lightness.

As the writing for this book came to a conclusion, after several years of purposeful conversations and *hansei*, Yoshino reflected on what his fabric of life looks like:

> *The fabric that we weave reflects our life. Now in looking back, I'm enjoying the different colors, different patterns, different strengths. I see the combination of the strong threads and the weak threads.*
>
> *My life is made up of so many good and bad parts, thick threads and thin ones. Thick threads, thin threads, you have to combine them together. That is life. You can't enjoy every week, every month. Sometimes you have bad times.*
>
> *If the major value in your life — your top priority item — is solid, the warp thread is thick and strong — you will have passion and energy, and a will. Even though you may have some thin or broken threads — something that was not successful or a difficult time — the strong warp threads will help keep the weaker threads in condition or in place in your life.*
>
> *My fabric is made up of many different colors, with different designs. It is not a solid color, and it is not striped. Stripes are always the same, nicely arranged in a consistent order.*
>
> *When you look at just a part of my fabric, it's hard to see that it looks very different from other parts. But when you look at it from a bit further away, with a wider view where you can see more parts together, then it has some meaning. I hope this book has provided that wide-angle view.*
>
> *There are so many pieces of memories that when you look at just one memory very close to your eyes, you can get somewhat distracted and wonder, "What is this one? What is the value?" When you get back further, then you can see a more heartwarming pattern — some of the*

darker colors, black, blue, gray — but also some of the brighter colors like pink, yellow, white. It's a mixture. It's not so clear-cut or organized. But it is nice.

YOUR REFLECTION – *HANSEI* – LOOKING BACK AND LOOKING AHEAD

At the start of this book, I challenged you to practice your own *hansei.* And I posed various reflection questions to you throughout the book to encourage that practice. Yoshino and I envisioned this book as an opportunity to share the lessons he has learned about learning and leading, in hopes that it could help *you* learn to lead and lead to learn. We can learn from personal and organizational history, by looking back, and then we can apply this knowledge to create an even better future.

As you look back (and look ahead), take time to process what you have learned by reading Yoshino's experiences — hearing his words and witnessing his growth as a leader and a student of the world. My intention is that, after having learned so much from Yoshino, you will walk away— as I have — with fresh insights and excitement about leadership, about organizations, and about yourself. I encourage you to reflect on how you can move forward — in crafting your career, honing your skills, and supporting your people, customers, or clients — with an eye toward personal adjustments you can make to ensure your own life fabric is strong and vibrant. Take time to pause and reflect at every turn, knowing that reflection is the beginning, not the end.

Never stop learning. Never stop leading. Never stop weaving a life of purpose.

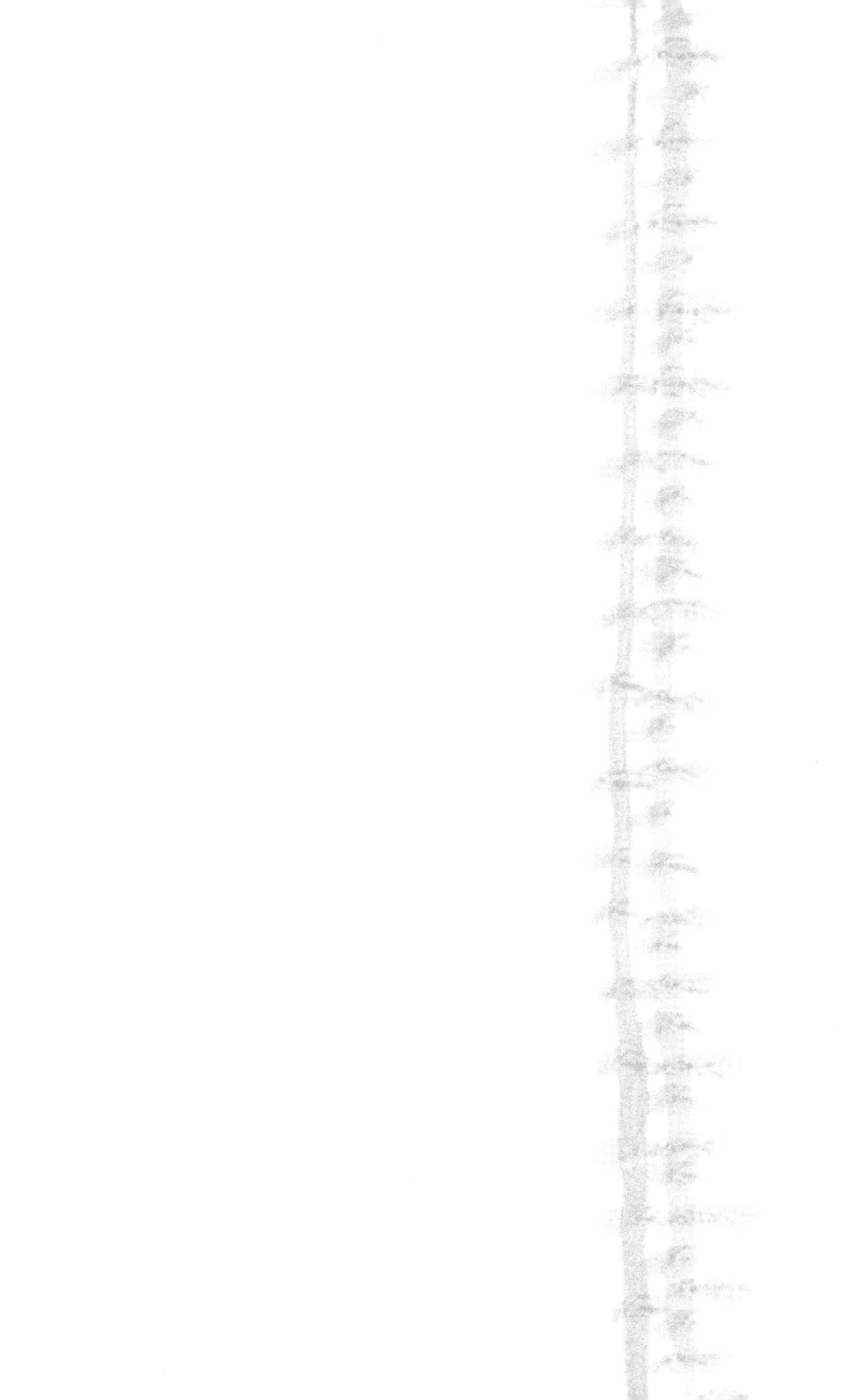

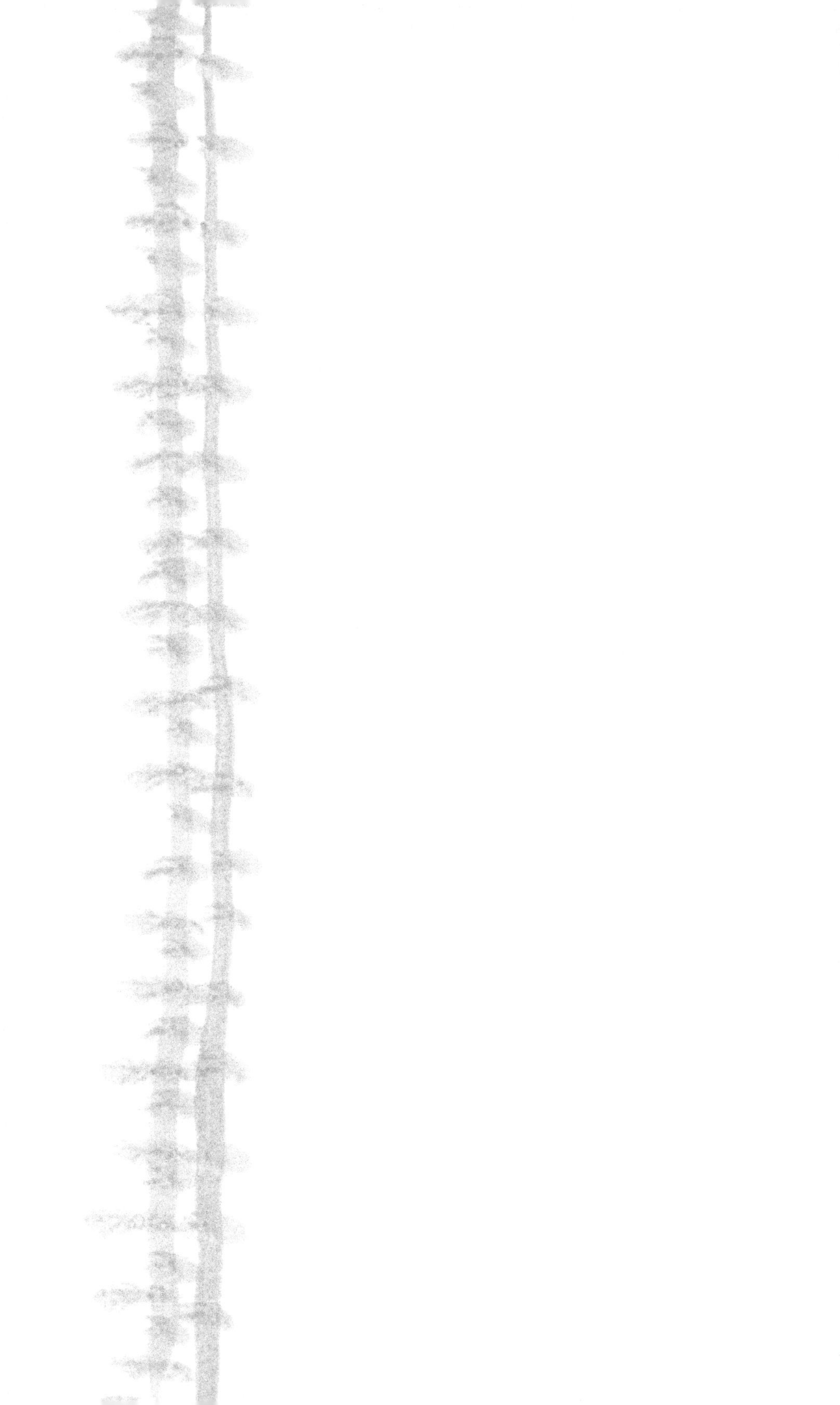

ACKNOWLEDGMENTS

1 + 1 = MUCH MORE THAN 2

Isao Yoshino once remarked to me — in one of our many conversations leading up to the release of this book — that when it comes to people, "1 + 1 = much more than 2." The results generated when people work together and help one another, he meant, are exponentially greater than when we work alone. I wholeheartedly agree, and this has become one of my own mottos.

My life — and this book — are proof of that motto. This book is the result of an incredible learning experience in Japan, and a years-long collaboration with Mr. Yoshino and others. It is the fabric of "1 + 1 = much more than 2" — not possible without the support of more people than I can possibly thank here — starting with those who have been an important part of my journey of "learning to lead and leading to learn" and ending with those who helped make this book a reality.

MY CHAIN-OF-LEARNING CONNECTION TO ISAO YOSHINO

My gratitude for this book starts with my original chain-of-learning connections with Isao Yoshino.

First and foremost, I want to thank **Mr. Yoshino** for his friendship, mentorship, partnership, generosity, and openness in sharing his lessons of learning and leading so that we can all learn from his experiences, insights, and spirit. It has been my honor and privilege to help him reflect on his life and career.

My appreciation continues to the next link in the chain — **John Shook** — for inviting his mentor Isao Yoshino to join him on stage at the Lean Coaching Summit in 2014. John's advice about moving to and living in Japan was reassuring, and people he connected me with opened the doors to some incredible learning experiences in Japan. For this book, John provided insightful comments about nuances in Toyota's culture and of his friendship with Mr. Yoshino, which helped me frame many of the stories. Mr. Yoshino and I are both honored by his heartfelt personal foreword. And special thanks to John for filling the void in Mr. Yoshino's photo history and generously allowing us to share these visual moments in time here.

To **Margie Hagene** — first my coach and then my friend — who was my original direct connection to Mr. Yoshino through her relationship with John Shook (who was her coach many years ago). Margie helped me ask better questions and listen more patiently, encouraged me to leap into the unknown when I started my consulting practice, and supported me as I established my business. Margie invited me to co-present with her at the Lean Coaching Summit, to share our story as coach and learner. This set into place an unanticipated and amazing trajectory that has resulted in this book.

MY BOOK TEAM

To **Karyn Ross** — for her friendship, partnership, and chosen sisterhood — and her invaluable developmental editing. Karyn helped me get unstuck in the drafting process when I realized that I needed to pivot the book's structure. She read early versions of each part of this book, helped me tighten and refine the narrative, and encouraged (and helped) me to find my voice along the way. Karyn and I met in 2017 at a conference in Europe where Mr. Yoshino and I were presenting, and she and I have been tightly linked since then. Through our "K2C2" (Katie and Karyn's Coaching Communities), we continue our chain of learning by developing communities connected around the world. 1+1 = WAY more than 2!

To the amazing **Silver Tree Publishing** team, which partnered with me to get this book in your hands. Thank you to **Kate Colbert**, my wise editor and publishing advisor, for helping me hone the structure and find the right words while providing reassuring support and guidance throughout the publishing process. To **Stephanie Feger**, whose energy and focus helped me reframe and amplify the book's (and my own) messages. And to **Courtney Hudson**, for crafting a visually appealing cover and interior layout.

To **Cathy Fyock**, my book coach, who helped me stay on track and navigate the world of writing and publishing. To **Rob Worth** for his sharp editing eye and quick turnaround — which improved the final typeset manuscript.

To **Laura Hunter Drago** for helping behind the scenes to further bring my "author brand" to life by shaping the book's website and supporting many additional projects with creativity and impeccable execution.

To **Ilana Dashe** for creating beautiful original cover art and custom brush strokes that have become the signature visuals for this book. A first encounter on the street outside my Tokyo apartment blossomed into friendship when our sons became pre-k buddies in Japan. When I had a vision for the cover — an artistic representation of weaving warp and weft with a Japanese *wabi-sabi* aesthetic — I immediately thought of Ilana's woodblock and graphic prints. Ilana saw my vision, improved on it, and brought it to life — all during the early days of a global pandemic during which we were both attempting to scaffold our children's new "distance learning" routines!

To everyone who read early drafts of the manuscript and whose input helped me improve the book. A special thank-you **to my editorial board: Elisabeth Swan**, **Jane Bryan-Jones**, **Cathy Fyock**, **Jannes Slomp**, and **Margie Hagene**. And thank you **to all my endorsers**, whose comments appear on the Praise section of this book and/or on marketing and promotional materials for *Learning to Lead, Leading to Learn*.

Also special thanks to **Mark Graban** for his support and advice along my writing journey, from getting started with my blog when I moved to Japan in 2015 to creating and publishing this book. To **Dan Markovitz** for our lunches around the San Francisco Bay Area and for reacting to early concepts of the book. And to **Jannes Slomp** for friendship and sponsorship of both Isao Yoshino and me in the Netherlands, plus **Silvia Witter-Vliege**,

Peter Kabel, **Jeroen de Groot**, **Arnout Orelio**, and all the other Dutch friends we have made in the past three years. Thank you!

To others who have shared writing and publishing advice (and encouragement) along the way: **Kara Levy**, **Ben Lincoln**, **Zoë Barton Slocum**, **Tom Ehrenfeld**, **Michael Ballé**, **Tracey Richardson**, **Karen Martin**, **Michel Baudin**, **Richard Sheridan**, **Jeff Hunter**, **Camille Childs**, **Janel Dyan**, **Rochelle Kopp**, **Mike Rother**, and many more!

To all the followers of my blog — particularly in the early days. Your interest and support of what I was writing encouraged me to continue to share my learning experiences and perspectives, and provided the catalyst to write this book!

To my book launch team and supporters — and of course, **to all of my friends and family around the world** — thank you for your support and interest in the learning partnership that Mr. Yoshino and I share. Moving forward to publish an almost-finished book during a pandemic was not an immediately obvious choice. Your encouragement helped me get up and persevere to the finish. My hope is that offering these stories of the past can help us all think about how we can create a better, more people-centered future.

MY CHAIN OF LEARNING TO LEARN AND TO LEAD

Like Mr. Yoshino, my solid warp threads, established in my early teen years, have been a strong desire to visit and live in many countries and gain a wide worldview. This known purpose led me to the Dominican Republic while in high school, to Spain while in college, to the United Kingdom following college graduation, to Australia with a Fulbright Scholarship, and to Japan with my young family. I am grateful to every person and organization that made those journeys possible.

Looking back, like Mr. Yoshino, I have recognized that my weft threads are all about learning and helping people. While my career has been represented by fluid weft threads traversing an often-unpredictable path, it has been filled with purpose of learning and connection.

In many ways, this book is the culmination and intertwining of all aspects of my international life and my career of academic research, consulting, process improvement, and leadership coaching.

I owe a debt of gratitude to my "superiors" along my own chain of learning: the academic advisers and bosses who guided me as a learner and as a leader.

To my undergraduate and graduate advisors Robert Siegel, **Maria Ekstrand**, **Donald Barr**, and **Simon Chapman**, for encouraging my curiosity and helping me hone my research and writing skills. Who knew these qualitative interview techniques would come around full circle when creating this book?!

To my first boss, Lisa Bero, who, like Isao Yoshino's first boss, demonstrated the type of leader I wanted to develop into. During my two and a half years at the University of California San Francisco (UCSF), Lisa went out of her way to give me opportunities to author papers and present at conferences, she supported my dreams of becoming a Fulbright Scholar, and she inspired me to be a people-centered leader. **To Brad Toussaint** for being the epitome of a leader who goes beyond his role to "give a little bit extra" every day to support the people around him. And **to James Hereford** for demonstrating what it means to lead the way and lead to learn.

And, of course, **to other colleagues, clients, Japan Study Trip participants, and friends in my chain of learning**. The greatest joy for me professionally is to hear how I have helped pass on these traditions of learning and leading to others.

MY JAPAN TEAM

To the countless individuals and organizations essential to my learning in Japan who have invited me into their gembas, made introductions, and shared their knowledge to help me learn — all with the spirit of *omotenashi*. To the following individuals, in particular (but no particular order): **Toshiko Kawanami**, **Noriko Ogura**, **Mami Takeda**, **Tim Wolput**, **Toru Takagi**, **Miwa Kudo**, **Shimpei Hashimoto**, **Brad Schmidt**, **DJ Duarte**, **Susan Piatek**, **Sandy Isaka**, **Kimio Inagaki**, **Toshiko Narusawa**, **Hiroshi and Ryo**

Tsukakoshi, **Sakashi Umemura**, and **Teruo Yabe.** I am grateful for all the leaders who have welcomed (and continue to welcome) me and my Japan Study Trip participants to their organizations to pass on their own chain of learning.

To Ali Kops Buford, my best friend in Tokyo, for sharing our lives together while living in Japan and beyond. For supporting my early Japan-related business endeavors by attending the first study trip I led in Japan in 2016, the beginning of things to come. And for humoring (enabling?!) my daruma obsession, including accompanying me to the daruma temple on one of my visits back to Japan in 2017 and being the "depository" for all my daruma orders each trip I make back to Japan.

To Mana Morita, for helping me decode the Japanese language, challenging me to pass the N5 level of the Japanese Language Proficiency Test, and supporting me along the way (including daruma doll research and procurement). *Ganbatte*!

MY FAMILY AND FRIENDS

To my mother, Jane Bryan-Jones, who has helped me hone my voice and writing since well before my high school years. She taught me about the art of human dynamics, speaking the truth, and introspection. She inspires me to be my best self. Mom, I love you more than words can convey.

To my father, Hardy Jones, who passed away in December 2016. He was always my biggest fan and cheerleader, and my most influential teacher of perseverance, positive mindsets, and generosity of heart. His love, encouragement, and spirit were always strong, and I know that he would be proud of my accomplishments in writing and publishing this book. He inspires me to make each and every day a great one.

To my brother, Bryan Jones, my first and always best friend, for sharing ideas and business tips, and for being by my side on the steep mountains when I wasn't sure I was going to be able to make it down. He always made sure that I did.

To my extended family. I am so lucky to have you all in my life. Thank you for your love, support, and encouragement. And **to my friends throughout the world** who make the globe feel small.

And most importantly, now and always, thank you **to my husband, John, and our children, Jones and Jack**, with whom I shared this incredible Japan adventure and continue to share a daily life. Japan is forever woven into our entire family's fabric. The wedding vows John and I exchanged incorporated parts of Walt Whitman's poem "Song of the Open Road." I couldn't imagine a better partner to "come travel with me." Thank you for your endless support and being the kite to my string. Let's continue to explore the world together. You three are my present and my future.

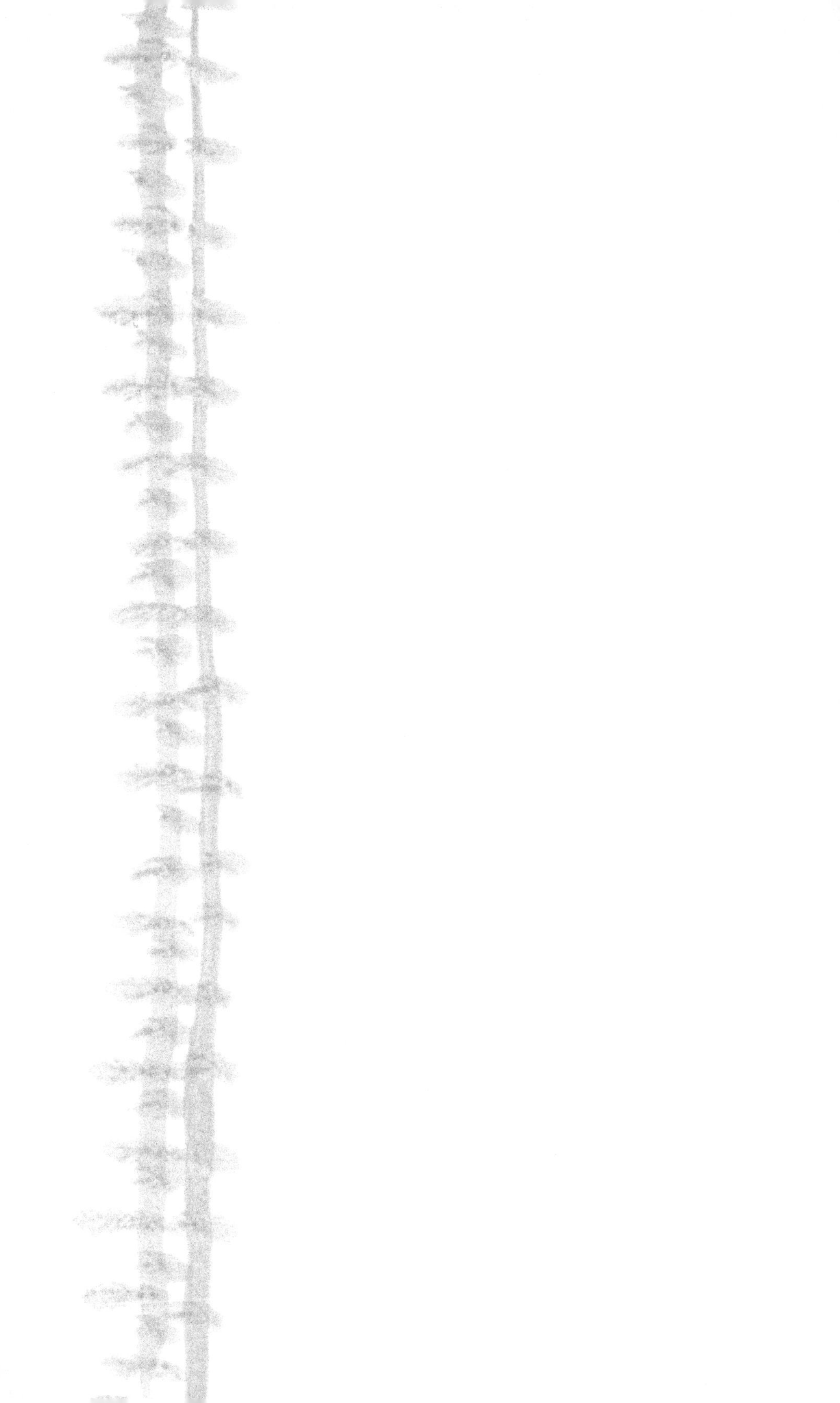

NEVER STOP LEARNING

The stories and lessons that Katie Anderson and Isao Yoshino would like to offer you (and your organization) don't end with the publication of this book. Let the reading of *Learning to Lead, Leading to Learn* be the beginning of a continuous learning journey! Continue to follow Katie and Mr. Yoshino's shared learning and access supplemental resources — developed just for you — by visiting **LearningToLeadLeadingToLearn.com.**

BONUS MATERIAL AND RESOURCES

Throughout the book were references to downloadable bonus material and additional resources to augment your learning experience. These include documents, resources, frameworks, and additional insights that Mr. Yoshino has generously shared with Katie — and now you, too! Visit **LearningToLeadLeadingToLearn.com** for these materials and links to other recommended resources.

As Katie and Mr. Yoshino continue to partner together, more moments of learning will be unlocked for you as they provide updated insights, resources, and more. To ensure you don't miss any of these ongoing opportunities, be sure to sign up — today! — for Katie's newsletter, which will help you stay informed about new posts and resources, as well as other leadership reflections and learning experiences. Use the QR code here to register for Katie's newsletter.

PRACTICING *HANSEI*

The "Practicing *Hansei*" reflection questions included at the end of each key chapter of this book are intended as prompts for you to think about your own experiences and how you can apply these lessons in your own life. Mark your calendar with a reminder to re-read these sections periodically to trigger meaningful reflection in your career and life. And think about how you can use the messages within this book to foster collective learning in your own relationships and organizations.

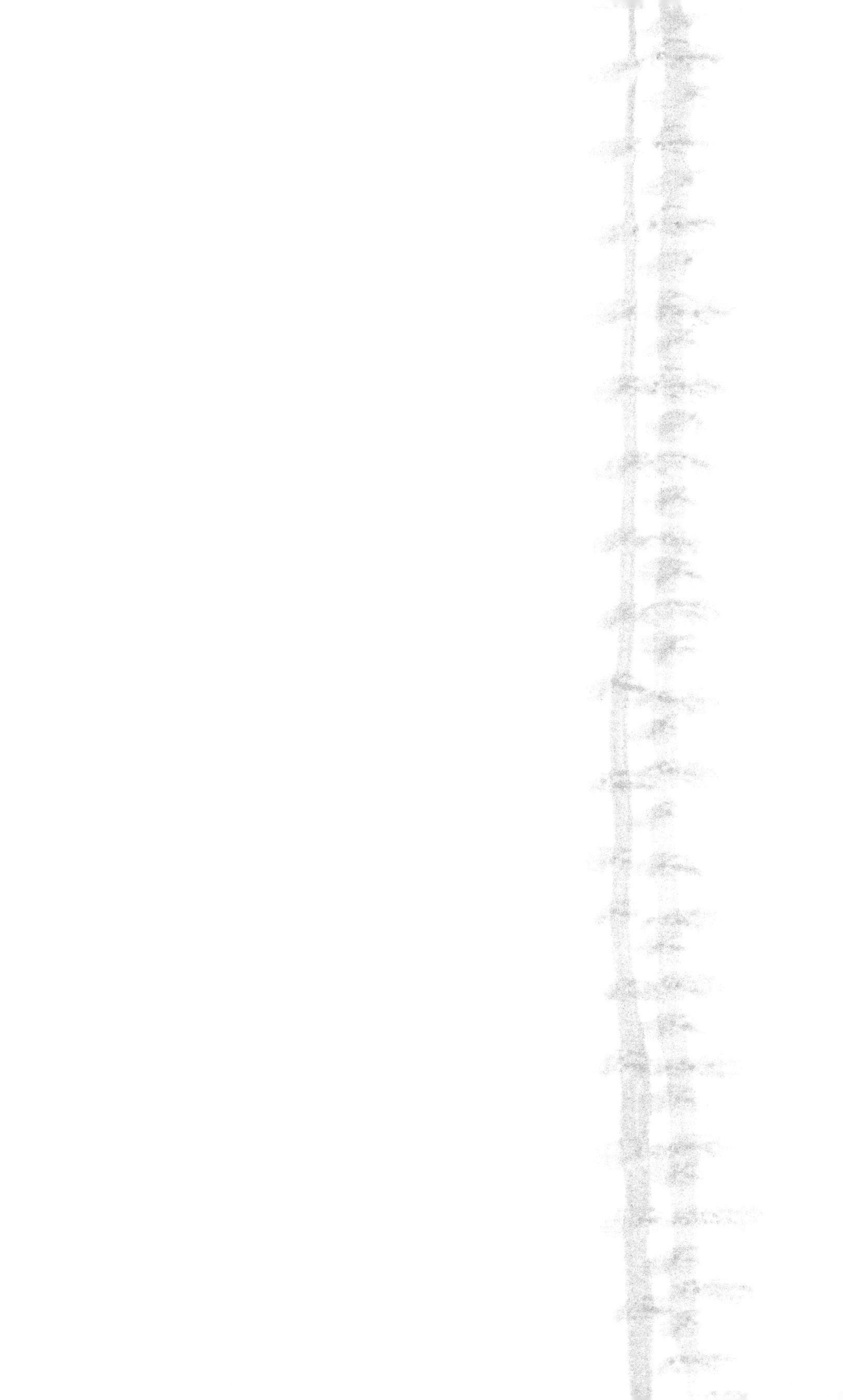

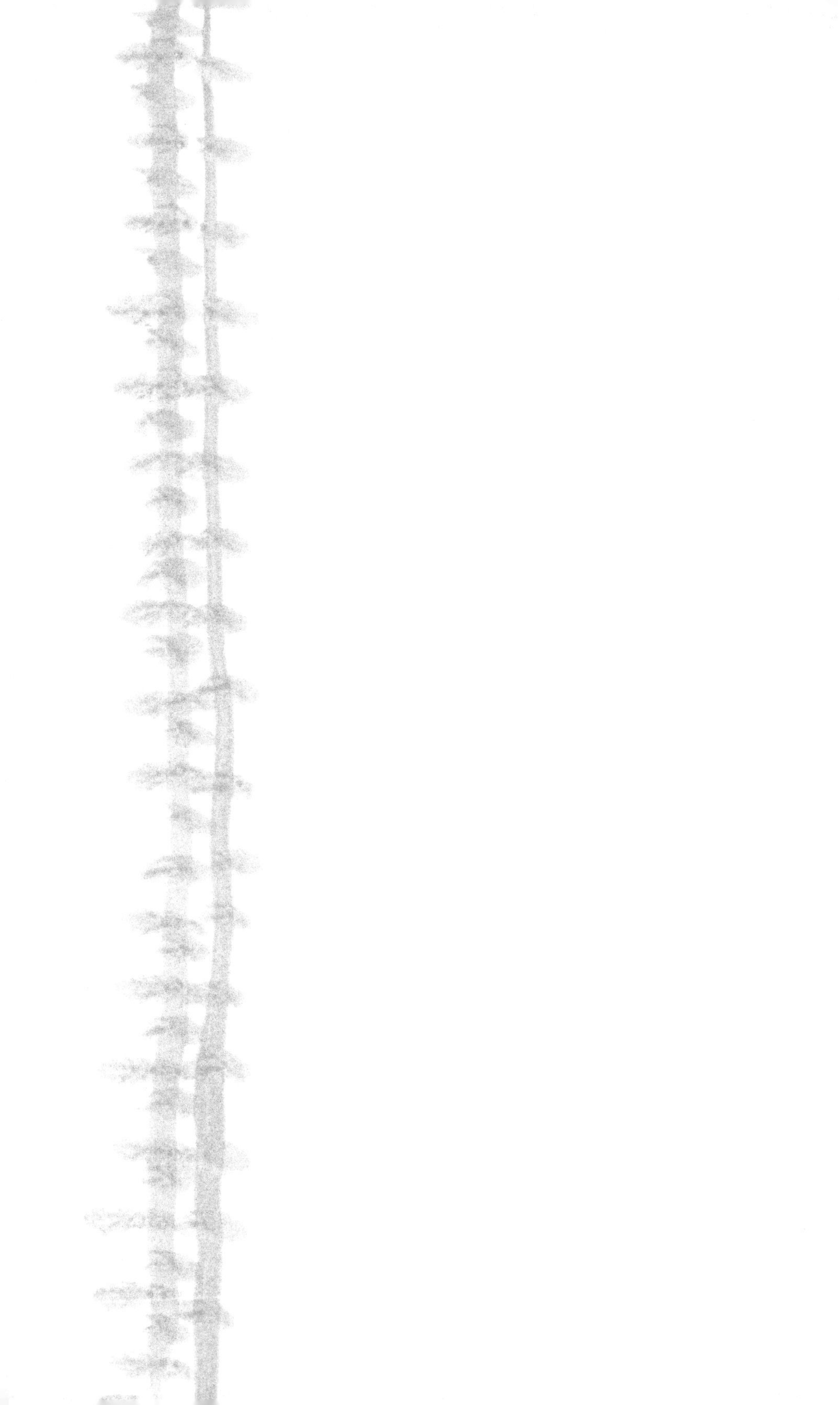

GO BEYOND THE BOOK

Are you inspired by the messages and key learnings found within *Learning to Lead, Leading to Learn*? Go beyond the book and engage Katie Anderson to meet the needs of your organization and your team. From delivering custom learning experiences such as keynote addresses to interactive workshops to empowering your leaders with companion learning tools and an expanded study guide, count on Katie to help you live and lead with intention.

SPEAKING ENGAGEMENTS AND CUSTOMIZED LEARNING EXPERIENCES

Empower yourself and your team with the principles and practices needed to be effective people-centered leaders. Katie's customized interactive learning experiences are engaging virtual or in-person events that inspire participants to lead with heart, lead with intention, and lead to learn. Collaborate with Katie in these ways and more:

- Customized keynotes and leadership presentations on topics such as:
  - Leading with Intention – Defining Your Purpose and Aligning Your Actions
  - People-Centered Leadership
  - Learning to Lead, Leading to Learn
  - Coaching – Moving from Expert to Coach
- Engaging, practical, and actionable webinars, podcasts, and media appearances

- Personalized deep-dive intensives and learning series
- Facilitated leadership events
- Individual and team/group coaching
- Read-along book clubs and book discussions
- Partnered learning sessions with Isao Yoshino.

PARTICIPATE IN AN IMMERSIVE LEARNING EXPERIENCE IN JAPAN

Learn more about Katie's popular Japan Study Trips at KBJAnderson.com/JapanTrip.

BULK BOOK ORDERS

Provide each member of your team with a unique professional development opportunity by gifting them a copy of the mass-market paperback book, *Learning to Lead, Leading to Learn.* Bulk discounts are available to support your team's learning.

Or create something truly special! Show your team how important leading with intention is by providing them a customized branded edition of the book. A custom edition of the book can be created for your team that could include your organization's logo and a special letter from your chief executive or leader.

✉ Contact Katie at Katie@KBJAnderson.com.

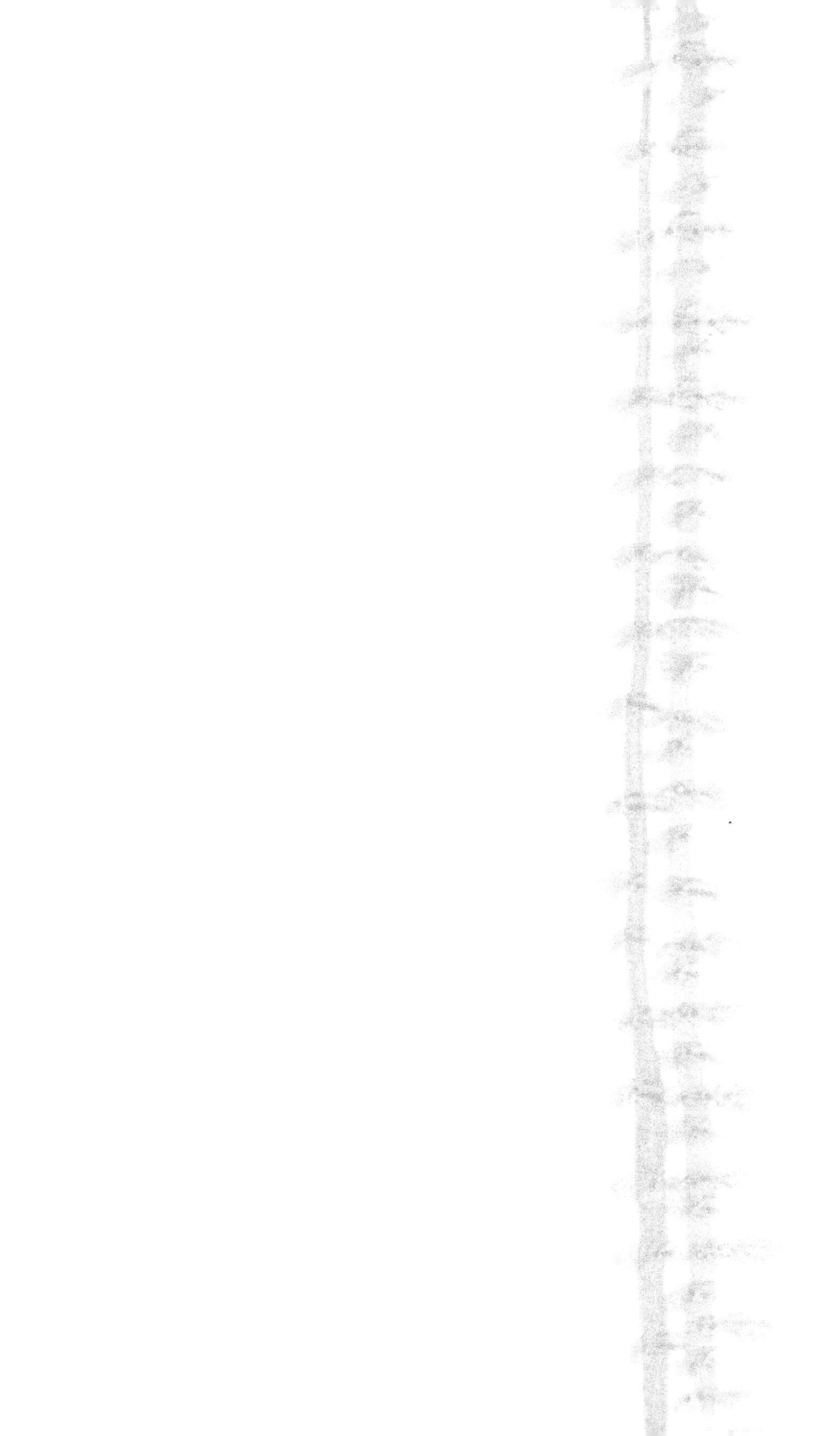

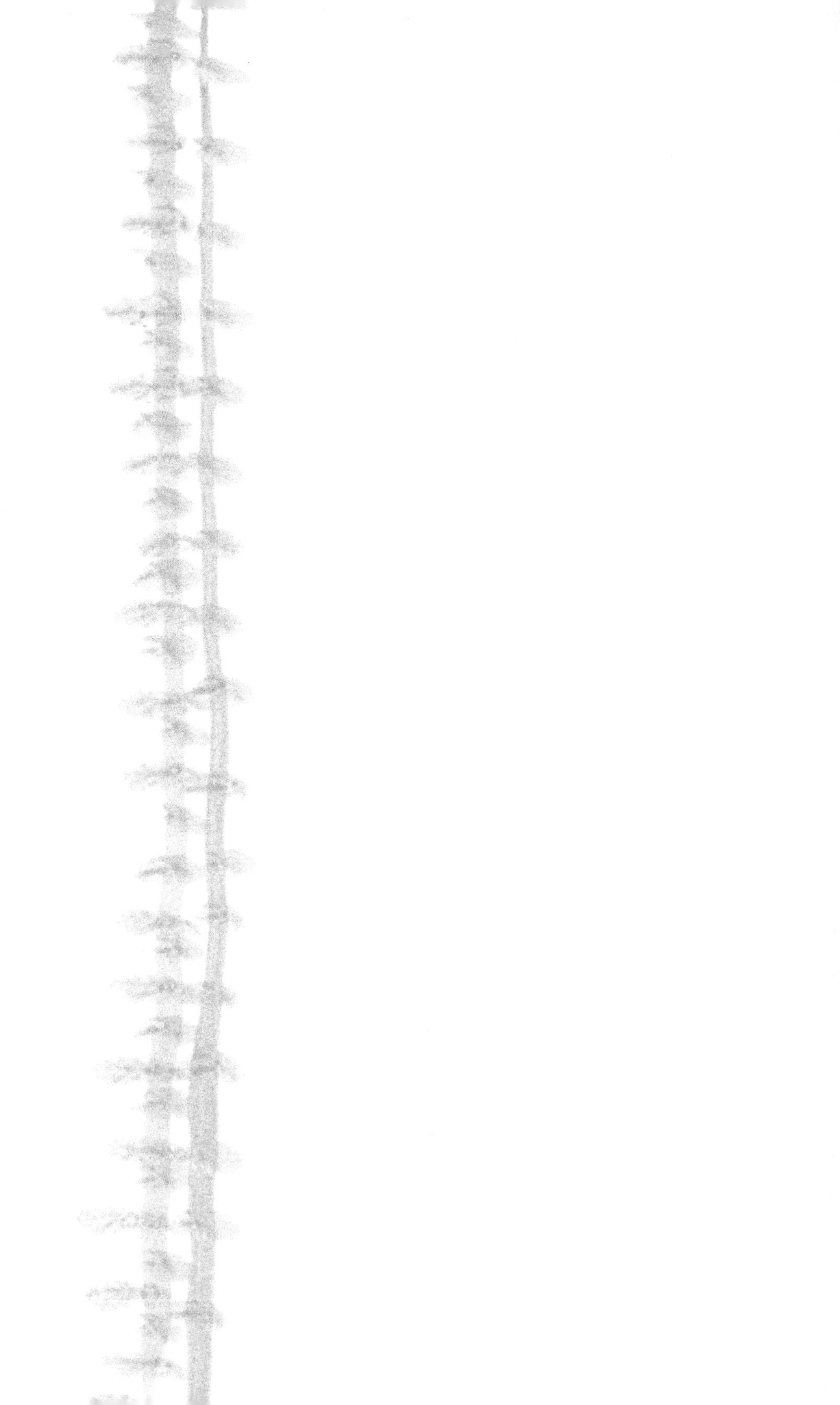

KEEP IN TOUCH

Count on Katie Anderson to help you live and lead with intention. Start a relationship today to see how she can help you:

- Identify your personal or organization's purpose
- Set the direction for yourself, your teams, your organization
- Align your actions to move towards your purpose
- Support your people (through developing coaching, problem-solving, and leadership skills)
- Develop yourself as a learner and a leader.

LEARN MORE AND GET IN CONTACT

Katie@KBJAnderson.com

KBJAnderson.com | LearningToLeadLeadingToLearn.com

FIND, FOLLOW, AND SHARE ON SOCIAL MEDIA

LinkedIn.com/KBJAanderson

Twitter.com/KBJAanderson

Amazon.com/Author/KBJAnderson

Join the global conversation about *Learning to Lead, Leading to Learn* by using these hashtags on social media:

#L2LBook

#LearningToLead

#LeadingToLearn

#KatieAnderson

#IsaoYoshino

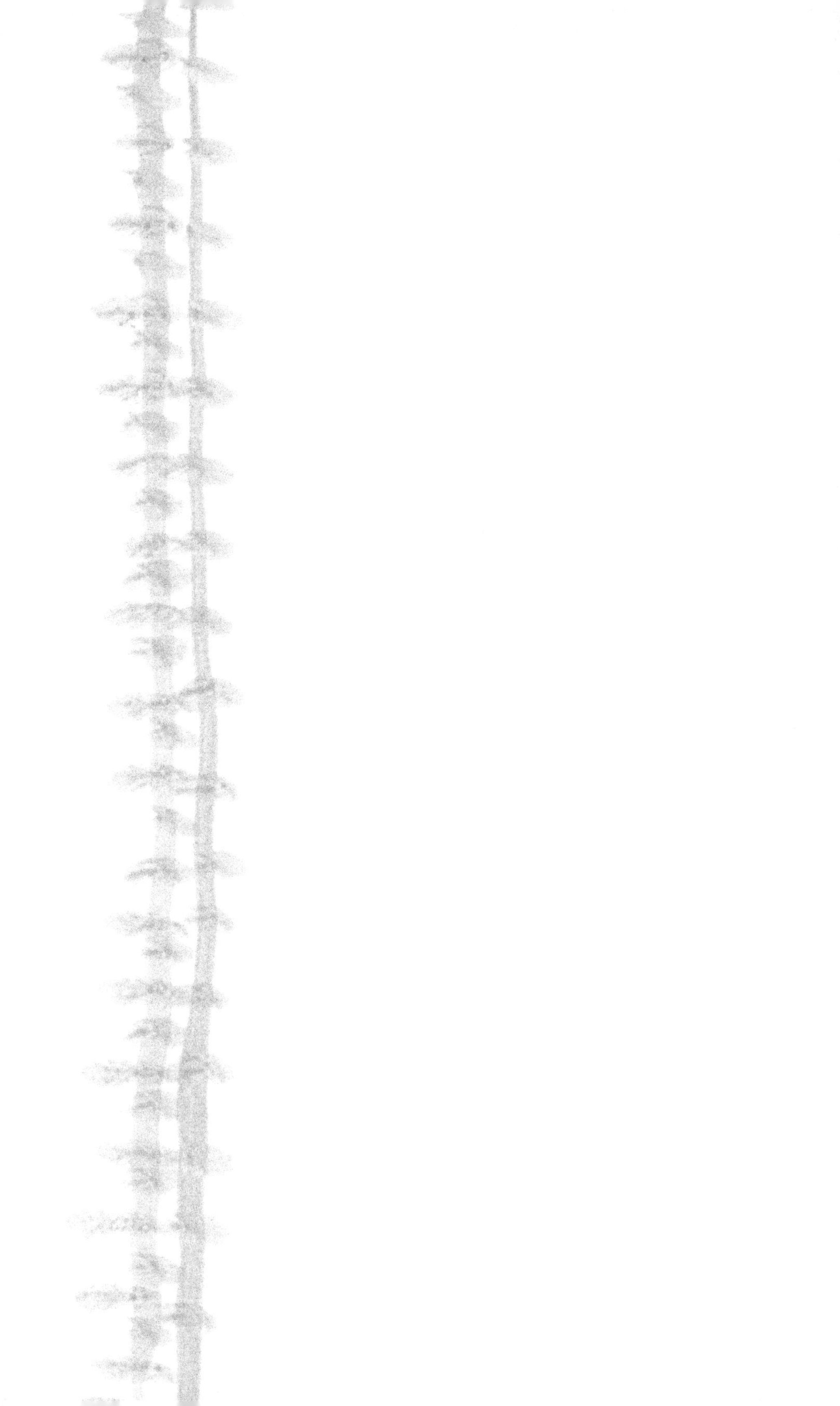

ABOUT THE AUTHOR

Katie Anderson is an internationally recognized leadership coach, consultant, and professional speaker, best known for inspiring individuals and organizations to lead with intention. She founded her consulting practice in 2013 to work with leaders at all levels and organizations of all sizes to achieve higher levels of performance. She helps leaders to develop clarity of purpose and align their processes and behaviors in service of that purpose.

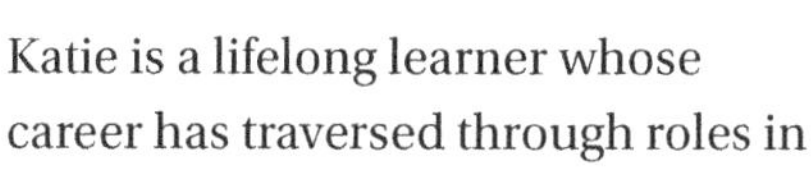

Katie is a lifelong learner whose career has traversed through roles in academia, consulting, and healthcare operations and process improvement. Prior to establishing her consulting practice, Katie held leadership roles at two prominent California-based healthcare systems, was a consultant for PwC Australia, and held academic research positions at the University of California San Francisco and the University of Sydney. She has deep expertise and experience leading and coaching change in a variety of industries, including healthcare, biotech, manufacturing, education, government, and information technology, and is highly regarded among experts in the lean leadership space.

A California native, Katie has lived in five countries outside the United States — including the UK, Australia, and Japan. In 2015, she and her husband moved with their children to Tokyo for an 18-month experience in Japan, where Katie developed a professional relationship with 40-year Toyota leader Isao Yoshino. What began as a connection filled with deep conversations evolved into a one-of-a-kind leadership book entitled *Learning to Lead, Leading to Learn: Lessons from Toyota Leader Isao Yoshino on a Lifetime of Continuous Learning*. Now back in the San Francisco Bay Area, Katie retains a strong connection to Japan and leads frequent study trips to Japan for leaders looking to deepen their knowledge of lean leadership, the Toyota Way, and Japanese culture.

Katie holds a BA with honors from Stanford University and was a Fulbright Scholar in Australia, where she received her Master's degree in public health from Sydney University. Katie lives in the San Francisco Bay Area with her husband, two sons, nearly a dozen chickens and hundreds of daruma dolls. When she is not traveling around the world, you can find her in her backyard with her family, on a bike traversing the hills of Northern California, or trying out new recipes in the kitchen.

Katie remains passionate about helping people around the world learn to lead and lead to learn. *Learning to Lead, Leading to Learn* is Katie's first nonfiction business book.

Learn more at KBJAnderson.com.

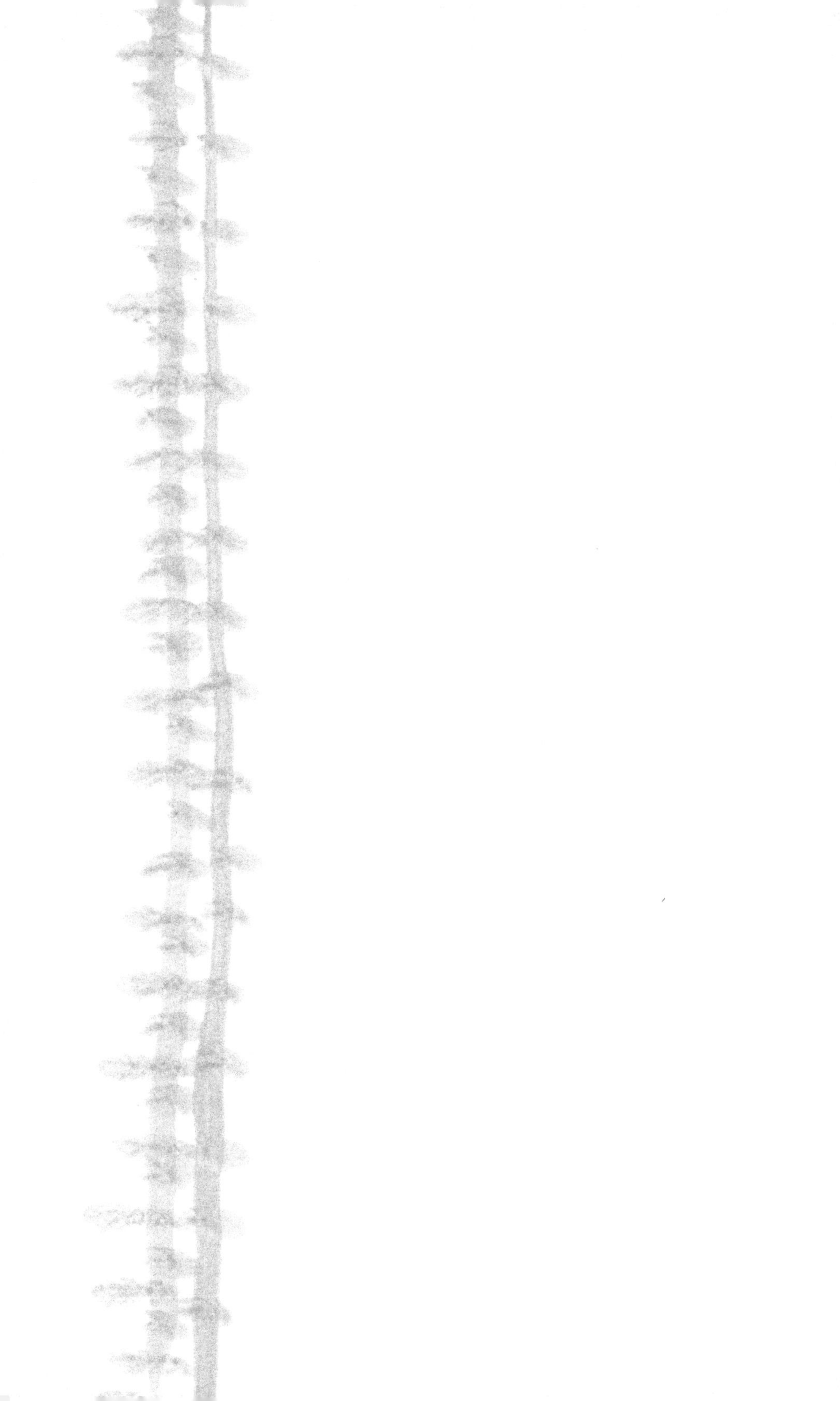

Made in the USA
Las Vegas, NV
20 August 2021

28533183R00193